DIC
THE DEVIL'S
BAIRNS

Breaking the Border Mafia

Jon Tait

For Christopher Young

With thanks to Adrian Newman, Wayne Charlton, my wife Sally, son Jack, and Stewart Bonney at *The Northumbrian* magazine, where a version of the introduction first appeared.

FYREBRAND
Border Literature Development Agency

Copyright © 2018 Jon Tait

Cover design by Adrian Newman

First Edition: 2018

ISBN: 978-3-7439-9566-6 (Paperback)

ISBN: 978-3-7439-9567-3 (eBook)

Published by

tredition GmbH

Halenreie 40-44

22359 Hamburg

Germany.

CONTENTS

INTRODUCTION: A FRIEND OF OURS

THE OUTLAW Gawen Redhead slept like a badger curled in the hollowed, decaying trunk of an old oak tree surrounded by nocturnal noises in the dark; the steady lapping run of the Coquet shimmered in moonlight, the yelp of a vixen. The swish of long grass in a meadow greyed to a negative and swayed to dance by winds, the rustle of leaves in the canopy of the forest. The bleat of disturbed sheep, wiry wool white under stars, yet safe in that belly bleached as driftwood, of rings and rough bark, the hollow knock. There is no silence in the night.

The rim of Gawen's steel helmet shading his eyes in blackness, his beard now wild as a bramble bush tangled in thorn, as if he himself was growing within the tree. The peaty smell of mulch and mushrooms and the wet squelch of a bog, the lightness of bracken in soft rain, the scent of a man on the run missed by the wet nostrils of a deer twitched in air before bowing down to drink at a burn in the broken golden light of the woods dappled by spores at dawn.

Yet these were once Gawen's hills and his gang rode high and handsome by the grey outcrops of limestone, weathered and cracked in an ice age long gone, past deposits of receding caps scratched over the valleys and gouged to scree slopes, through purple heather and bilberry. They are also the hills I call home.

Gawen Redhead was a raider of some notoriety from Rothbury Forest during the mid-1500s. The remains of old fortified bastle houses are scattered throughout what was once the Forest including Redhead's home at the Crook, near Simonside, between Forestburn Gate and The Lee. Gawen became a fugitive in 'the tenth year of Queen Elizabeth,' giving a date of around 1568, and took to hiding out in the trunk of a hollow tree close by Brinkburn Priory. The land around about was known long after as 'Gawen's Field.'

Redhead was almost certainly part of a crew of Redesdale riders, primarily led by the Halls, who attempted to break some of their friends out of jail at Harbottle Castle in 1565. The March Warden Sir John Forster also suspected them of setting an ambush to do him over when he made his way there. When Forster held a Warden Court at Morpeth on the 27th January 1566, 13 of the Redesdale men were tried for various offences and six beheaded. Two years later the Warden took some of the Redesdale riders prisoner after they'd been raiding farms around about. The most notorious were put in irons at Harbottle before being transferred to Newcastle and hanged. It's reasonable to assume that these were the men that Gawen Redhead was riding with, and the reason that he had to flee from his farm. The Halls were long in the bastle at nearby Fallowlees and in 1615 Edward Hall, of that place, was pardoned for the manslaughter of William Hall with Arthur Radcliffe of Thropton. Radcliffe had smashed his sword into the back of Hall of Hepple's head, leaving a gash four inches long and half an inch wide that pierced his brain. He died from his injuries later. John Radcliffe of Rothbury and Robert Pott of Morrelhirst were named as accessories.

It's not recorded whether the Law eventually caught up with Gawen or not, but the practice of organised crime figures hiding out to evade capture continues to this day. In 2011 an alleged boss of the Italian 'Ndrangheta, Francesco Maisano, was discovered by the authorities in a secret bunker, the entrance to which was covered by a wooden panel within his own home. And the Redheads were certainly players within the Redesdale branch of the Border Mafia; John Redhead of Rothbury Forest was raided by a West Teviotdale gang who not only took 54 sheep and 48 cattle, but also took him prisoner for ransoming in 1586; a not uncommon event. Robert Redhead of Holling Crook, possibly Gawen's grandson, also continued in the family reiving tradition. He first appears in the records in January 1598, breaking into and burgling the house of Geoffrey Story at Whitehall around midnight with Robert 'The Laird of the Moor' Ellesden of Elsdon. They stole 18 cows, 12 oxen, two horses, three bullocks and furniture from his house. Robert Redhead was indicted again in 1605, during the time of the Border pacification, as he broke into Robert Barber's at Whitton and stole nine ewes and nine pigs. Two years later his brother Edward Redhead lifted two ewes from John Oliver at Rothbury, and the following year Robert robbed his neighbour Gilbert Brown at the Crook of two cows. In 1609 he was charged again for stealing a black ox from Michael Ogle of Twywell.

The complex nature of Border crime saw Thomas Redhead of Rothbury Forest and his friend Anthony Pott of Little Tosson attacked and robbed near Callaly six years later. George Armorer, John Brocket, William Todd and John Chator, all from Callaly, with Daniel Pringle of Davysheil Hope and James Aynsley, of Alwinton, hit them in a highway robbery around ten o'clock at night. Both had their horses stolen while Pott also lost a wool hood and a sword.

The woods of Rothbury forest are long gone. There is a stillness to the fields today and a silence only broken by passing cars, curlews or the winds. While the riders of Tynedale and Liddesdale are more celebrated at places such as Hexham Old Gaol and Tullie House museum in Carlisle, the Redhead's riding tradition is all but forgotten, felled with the trees that were once their home. But there was a time when men such as Gawen were among the most feared and dangerous people in Britain and their organised criminal empire pre-dated the more famous Sicilian gangs by a couple of hundred years.

We've all seen the movies where wise guys in leather jackets, suits and dark glasses sit around smoky social clubs talking business; where they're going to rob, who is getting whacked out, when an illegal shipment is coming in. In the 1970s American Mafia lexicon popularised by these slick and moodily-shot films, when a mobster introduces a fellow member to a 'made' acquaintance, he refers to him as a 'friend of ours,' while someone that isn't connected would be 'a friend of mine.'

Between the 13th and 17th centuries the Anglo-Scottish Border had its own set of 'Goodfellas' in leather jacks and steel helmets, armed with swords and hagbutts rather than revolvers and machine guns, but the power that they held over the local population was non-the-less potent than that of the gangs of Little Italy and Mulberry Street. And it was their 'friends' that kept them out of the reach of the Law. Nationality didn't matter when it came to crime on the Border; the reivers on either side of the line regularly looked after each other when they were fleeing from justice. It was common practice to avoid the rope or the axe by joining with men from the opposite nation and leading them on incursions and raids upon their neighbours. They weren't strictly enemies – they were 'friends of ours.'

An East Teviotdale rider, 1603, by Jon Tait.

The Border Mafia were ruthless when it came to matters of retribution, so it was advisable for officials and the local populace to keep both the clans and the gangs of 'broken' men – notorious outlaws such as *Dick the Devil's Bairns* and *Sandy's Bairns* or even solitary and now obscure desperados like Gawen Redhead – maintained in at least some level of friendship.

Take, for example, Andrew Smith and Thomas Tweedy, who had the misfortune of bumping into Ninian Armstrong of Twedden, the Laird of Mangerton's man Andrew Henderson, Archibald 'Fair Archie' Armstrong and Gavin Elliot of Fiddleton one night in March 1606 in Dumfries. Smith was killed and Tweedy 'dismembered of his nose.' Robert Scott of Haining, Sir James Johnstone and Sir Gideon Murray, with others, stood the bond money for them at court.

Such was the power of a surname on the Anglo-Scottish border.

1. JAILBREAK

IT IS much less celebrated and not half as well-known as Sir Walter Scott of Buccleuch's famous breakout of the noted reiver Kinmont Willie Armstrong from Carlisle Castle, but Sir Robert Kerr of Cessford's assault on Swinburne Castle in Northumberland might just be equally important in terms of Border history.

On the night of Friday 27 August 1596, just four months after his brother-in-law Buccleuch had caused a sensation by springing Kinmont, Kerr rode on Swinburne with two hundred armed men and released the prisoner James Young of the Cove from his cell.

Cessford and his men had to cover around 42 miles, deep into the lair of the Tynedale and Redesdale clans, down to near Colwell, north of Chollerford, in the heart of hostile Robson country. He did it without spilling any blood, though he did take hostages to ransom. Like the most notorious of modern crime bosses, he was always looking to capitalise whenever the opportunity presented itself and by kidnapping Roger, the brother of Henry Widdrington, the English Middle March warden Ralph Eure's deputy, he probably hoped to cash in handsomely. The Widdringtons were the owners of Swinburne.

James Young had been taken by the Selbys and when Kerr's attempts to have him released diplomatically failed, he felt that he had to 'loose his man' to save face, if nothing else. Kerr even had the nerve to write a letter two days later to his opposite warden, Eure, explaining why he had done it. Pre-empting the gossip of any malicious informers, he claimed, but the tone of the note had swagger and more than a bit of the Devil-may-care about it, reflecting the personality of the man himself.

Cessford seemed involved in a dangerous game of one-upmanship with his brother-in-law; as the Middle March Warden, he was the ranking officer as Scott's Keeper of Liddesdale post did not carry the same prestige or power. Terse exchanges in letters between the pair give some idea of the somewhat frosty relationship that they had.

1

Scott signed one 'your brother in law, Buccleuch,' and Kerr replied with 'your brother in your own terms,' which stung Buccleuch to reply, 'your brother in no terms.' The simmering undercurrent of feud between the two powerful factions saw them described by Queen Elizabeth I as a 'brace of wolves.'

Eure claimed that Kerr was 'ambitious, proud, bloody in revenge, poor and easily framed to any purpose in court and country' with Scott 'a secret Papist...a secret enemy to England, mighty proud, publishing his descent to be from the house of Angus and labouring to be created an Earl, and claiming his blood to be part Royal.'

The English Middle March warden accepted no responsibility for the jailbreak and blamed Widdrington for detaining Young without his knowledge as 'part of a private quarrel between him and Kerr.' Sir Robert Carey despised Kerr and complained himself that 'no justice will be done while this wicked man bares office' and demanded that he be removed from his wardenry or 'compelled to keep days of truce which he has not done for three or four years.' Sir Henry Widdrington quit his deputy warden post in a huff when Eure had forbidden him to pursue the matter further, but when Eure himself gave up and resigned the Middle March Wardenry it opened the door for Robert Carey to take on the important role and bring back Widdrington as his deputy.

In the three months after the jailbreak Cessford was still hunting down Selbys to murder and his crew spent five hours attacking Weetwood tower. When they could not take it they drove off cattle, sheep and household goods and 'turned a woman newly brought to bed out of the clothes she lay in.' Eight days later they took axes to the gates at Downham but were fought off so went on to Branxton and lifted 16 cattle and 40 sheep. The people of Mindrum were paying Cessford 'blackmail' – protection money – so avoided the terror that continued through nightly raids on the Selbys. William Selby warned his nephew that they intended to burn his own property or that of his mother, his brothers and his friends, saying that although Cessford pretended the raids were for the murder of 'his cousin' John Dalgliesh, they were in fact for the killing of Ralph 'Shortneck' Burn and the hanging of Geordie Burn, who had been taken by the Selbys in a hot trod – the legal action of taking back stolen stock immediately after a raid. Going to retrieve stock after an event was also legal and known as a cold trod, so either could be used as an excuse for undertaking a raid or revenge murder.

Vendetta was very much part of Robert Kerr's psychological makeup. Sir William Bowes noted in 1596 that Kerr, Sir Walter Scott and the West March Warden the laird of Johnstone, were all still under 30 yet each were personally guilty of no less than twenty murders of both English and Scottish men.

Kerr had a long-standing personal feud with the Storeys after his crew had lifted all the sheep from Wooler belonging to 'the laird Baggott,' who rode a trod to retrieve them. The East Teviotdale mob brutally murdered two men at Wooler and laird Baggott in response, cutting them in pieces, so two of his brothers-in-law, named Storey, murdered Cessford's shepherd and Kerr swore that he would have their lives as retribution. Buccleuch was engaged in a similarly bloody feud with the Tynedale Charltons who refused to hand back his murdered grandfather's sword.

The similarities to the Sicilian *Cosa Nostra*, Neapolitan *System* and Calabrian *'Ndrangheta* are more than a little striking; the clans on the Mediterranean island originated out of the gangs of the landowner's enforcers that prevented rustling on their cattle, protected their lemon groves, collected taxes from the small tenant farmers, intimidated local officials and lived by a code of honour and respect in the mid-to-late 1800s. Remove the sunshine and replace the yellow soil with dark mud and green trees and it could be almost the same story a few hundred years removed from the British countryside.

The Camorra in Naples is the older of the Italian mobs and an urban rather than rural organized crime syndicate, but even their history is reputed to have only started around the turn of the beginning of the Nineteenth century, while the 'Ndrangheta is based more on blood ties and is probably the most similar to the Anglo-Scottish crews.

The business of the Border mafia was large-scale organised crime in family-based gangs centred on cattle rustling, kidnap and ransom, collecting protection money, counterfeiting, murder, burglary, theft, witness intimidation and corrupting officials. If someone couldn't be bought off, they could be killed off. The raids led to counter-raids and the killings to revenge attacks and feuds that could last generations. And this had been going on in the area since the late Thirteenth century.

The rural crime of reiving was a profitable business; in 1596 the take from the three English Marches alone over a nine-year period was almost £93,000. Those figures broke down into £10,458 in the East, £28,098 in the Middle and £54,422 in the West with Buccleuch's Liddesdale and Cessford's East and West Teviotdale riders accounting for 'near three parts' of that. Driving off and selling cattle and taking sheep for the wool, textile and butchery trades as well as cashing in on sales at markets had been well established over a couple of hundred years, as was the illegal cross-border horse trade. If you could take prisoners on a raid and ransom them back to their families then it was a bonus, as were any cash and goods that could be lifted and carried off. Add in the fact that the powers of both England and Scotland had their own reasons for keeping the people of the Borders active – and providing them with cash to maintain the disruption – then an enterprising Border mobster could line his pockets from many sources. It obviously took a degree of violence and menace to forcibly take the livelihood from other farmers, and that's what the reivers, in the main, were; yeomen and small landowners, lairds and barons with larger estates and even the landed gentry with titles and payments from official positions in the local organisation such as bailiffs and provosts, or jobs in the legal systems for assisting the March Wardens in their duties that the crime families jostled and vied for.

The gangsterism prevalent on the Borders obviously had an effect on the people living there and the men involved in the crews were variously described as idle, disordered and unruly by frustrated officials. Eure wrote that Kerr's mob were 'loose persons rooted in wickedness with nothing done to make them laboursome or industrious but idle and villainous' while Rowland Myners complained that the Northumbrians in his charge were 'mutinous and insubordinate to their constables, who are little above their own rank. Being of great clans and surnames, this encourages their obstinacy.'

They didn't want someone that wasn't of a surname themselves telling them what to do and obviously considered people that weren't from a riding family inferior, weak-willed and not belonging there; outsiders at best, meddlesome in affairs that had nothing to do with them at worst. Northumberland long had a saying: 'No prince but a Percy' which means that the only power that matters is that of the local headsmen and barons, not decisions being made far off in Edinburgh or London.

The Border mafia were violent, proud, fiercely self-reliant, independent and governed by a set of laws known as The March Laws of the Border which were unique and separate from those in the rest of the British Isles. Truce Days were held for the hearing of bills (claims from people for the goods that had been stolen from them), to try and reclaim the goods or take cash payments in compensation, and to dole out justice. 12 'reputed' borderers from each country formed the jury. The form and order of a day of Truce from a 1551 document stated that complainers should pass their bills on to their Warden in reasonable time for him to copy those complaints on to his opposite Warden and arrest the offenders contained in them to produce at the day. The assurances of the Truce Day were supposed to be upheld until sunrise the following day, the breaking of which was punishable by death.

If a man from either realm was bound to another for ransom and the other didn't pay up, then the man that had ransomed him was entitled to carry a glove or a picture of the offender on his spear and blow his horn to show the assembled crews that the person was 'untrue and unfaithful' and could fight him in single combat, if he wanted.

The English warden or officers appointed the six men of the Scottish assize and vice versa – murder was punishable by execution 'according to the laws of that realm so offended' and violent robbery, the whole business of reiving, was settled by a compensation system with set prices for cows, sheep, hogs and horses while household goods were assessed in value by the jury of the opposite country. The taking of timber or wood from the opposite country was an offence, not appearing to hear charges made you guilty by default, and anyone that had goods stolen was allowed to pursue them with a sleuth hound in a trod. If they came to a house, they could ask the person there to join them, basically as a witness. Anyone hindering a trod could be held responsible for the bill, while if anyone having goods stolen in revenge were to go to 'the parties that spoiled them' they would forfeit the cause or action but would be still held accountable for the goods in a special clause.

There was no compensation for houses that were burnt out, just the goods that were destroyed inside, and anyone being wrongfully taken prisoner during peacetime could demand that his taker's men or the taker himself were delivered as pledges.

The taking of pledges – hostages – was common practice and was used to ensure good behaviour of gangs or to ensure a debt or bill was settled and it didn't come without hazards – a warden could lawfully hang a pledge after 40 days if no offer of satisfaction was made. Truce Days weren't perfect and the officials themselves were wary of the 'thieves and disordered men that lie in wait to perceive if they can by any word displease of make grief between the wardens, their deputies or chief borderers' and they complained that 'justice can never have been had for lack of the obedience of the subjects and in other cases because of the maintenance that gentlemen give miss-doers and the riders of the borderers.'

The six Marches had been created in 1249 by Henry III of England and Alexander III of Scotland and comprised the East, Middle and West Marches of England and of Scotland, each with its own Warden.

The English East March stretched from Berwick down to the countryside north of Alnwick, taking in towns such as Wooler, Belford and Bamburgh. The English Middle March was huge, stretching from Coquetdale to the area around Haltwhistle and taking in the troublesome valleys of the Rede, around Otterburn, and the North Tyne, stretching above Hexham to the Border north of Kielder. The English West March was dominated by Carlisle and included the trouble spots at Gilsland and Bewcastle.

Between the English West March and the Scottish West lay a strip of land known as the Debatable Ground which was a no-man's land used for pasturing cattle where building homes was long prohibited, until families started spilling into the fertile farmland by the rivers leading to the Solway Firth and creating a major problem as the officials tried to uphold the rule by burning and destroying the towers that were constructed. The Scottish West March contained towns such as Annan, Dumfries, Canonbie and Langholm while the Middle stretched from Castleton to Yetholm, taking in the likes of Hawick, Jedburgh and Kelso and the great riders from Liddesdale and Teviotdale. The Scottish East March went from around Coldstream to the coast, containing Duns and a number of smaller villages.

Truce days were held at various points along the Border such as Hadden Stank, Redden Burn, and the Lochmaben stone; Cocklaw near Roxburgh and the Redeswire, the Sands at Carlisle, Rockcliffe and Kershopefoot. Norham, Coldstream, Wark-on-Tweed, Ebchester and Berwick-upon-Tweed were all used as meeting spots for days of truce.

The English March Wardens were often brought in from southern England with powerful local families such as the Percys, Forsters, Fenwicks, Dacres and Lowthers all retaining a large influence while the Scots Wardens were selected on a more hereditary line with the East March generally under the jurisdiction of a Hume, the Middle March under either the Cessford or Ferniehurst Kerrs or the Scotts and the West March under either the Maxwells or Johnstones. Liddesdale, Annandale, Redesdale and Tynedale had their own keepers. Often the Wardens, the men who were supposed to maintain order and keep the peace, were as heavily involved in reiving as the wild men that they were meant to keep in check.

There were also deputy wardens, captains, bailiffs and other officials known as water keepers, one for each Warden, who were able to enter the marches without licence and carry messages between them. They also acted as border control to stop men without licence entering the other realm.

One of the troubles in dealing with first-hand contemporary accounts of the Border Reivers is that the notes and details were penned by people with an axe to grind and a need to justify their actions and roles within all the villainy that was taking place, so they are littered with lies and embellishments. Take Ralph Eure's extraordinary claims in July 1597 when he wrote to Thomas Burghley that a Scottish gentleman called John Wedderburn had alighted from a Scottish ship that had docked on the Tyne at Newcastle disguised as a modest mariner. Eure claimed that Wedderburn said he was a follower of Lord Bothwell and he was on his way to Scotland under orders to 'use by all means possible to take away the life of Sir Robert Kerr.' The mysterious Wedderburn's assassination plot was simple enough; he planned to either use powder to blow Kerr up in his house at Haliden or 'intercept him on his way to or in some other house.' Wedderburn spoke good French and claimed to have been employed in the French secret service in Spain, where he avoided being hanged alongside two Frenchmen as he was Scots. He had two scars on his forehead, a yellow beard and was square bodied of reasonable stature, as Eure described him in painful detail. Someone, somewhere, was clearly spinning lines and Wedderburn was either a liar, blagging his way out of trouble or just telling the English Middle March Warden what he wanted to hear; on the other hand, he may have been real or even a fabrication of Eure's imagination to justify his own desire to have a go at killing Kerr as he ended his letter by begging Burghley to allow him to 'do one honourable day's service in adventuring the gaining of Buccleuch's head, and if your Lordship like, Sir Robert Kerr's likewise.' He felt that the job could be done by the joint forces of the three English wardens with some help out of the Berwick garrison. Four days later Eure was cranking up his black propaganda a notch or two by claiming that a Scotsman called Robert Anderson had met with Wedderburn in Newcastle and told him that King James VI had told his leaders – especially those in the Borders – to 'have all persons between 16 and 60 in readiness of twenty days warning...telling them that the Queen of England intends Royal revenge for late indignities and he intends nothing but War' and was threatening to join forces with the King of Denmark to attack England. Eure presented them to Burghley 'true or not' –his own words – and wanted the Queen to draw up a muster of the Middle March as 'little by little (the Scots) have murdered and taken away the worthiest gentlemen leaders of our country.'

Another problem is presented by the fact that the published records of the time contain just extracts from the documents so many hundreds, if not thousands, of bills of complaint remain hidden away in a dusty archive away from the public domain, while the English records are more thorough than the Scots and a somewhat skewed perception can be received. The English reivers were hitting the

Scots, as well as their fellow countrymen, just as hard but the actual documentary evidence is harder to come by and many Scottish records were also burned or destroyed by invasion forces.

It has to be noted that Eure was pressing for the destruction of Sir Robert Kerr and Sir Walter Scott in the aftermath of the jailbreaks from Carlisle and Swinburne which were events so controversial and momentous that infuriated English officials were demanding action to bring them to heel. The event at Carlisle was the more scandalous as it struck right into the heart of English power on the Border and the attempt was assisted in both the masterminding and execution by the English Grahams, which was considered a heinous betrayal.

Kinmont Willie had been captured by the English while leaving a Truce Day and was therefore supposedly still protected by the terms of the meetings. Sir Walter Scott gathered a crew together at Langholm horse races to plan springing Kinmont from his detention at the castle and it was carried out by himself with the likes of Walter Scott of Goldielands, Watt Scott of Harden, Scott of Todriggs, Will Elliot of Gorrenberry, John Elliot of the Riggs and Armstrong's kinsmen the laird of Mangerton and young Whitehaugh with his son, three Calfhills Armstrongs, Sandy Armstrong, Kinmont's sons Jock, Francie, Geordie and Sandy, three of the Twedden Armstrongs, John of the Hollows and a brother, Christie of Barngliesh, Robbie of Langholm and the Gingles Armstrongs, with Will 'Redcloak' Bell and two brothers, Walter Bell of Godsby and Willie 'Kang' Irving along with accomplices numbering around eighty. On the wet Sunday night of April 13th, 1596, they rode to Carlisle armed with crowbars, axes and scaling ladders and broke in through the postern gate, killed a couple of the watch, injured one of Kinmont's keepers and spirited him back home over the border.

Many of the main players were related to the Grahams through inter-marriage and it should be pointed out that Kinmont Will's father, Alexander Armstrong, had been a pensioner of King Henry VIII along with eight of his other sons. They were awarded lands in Cumberland known as 'Guilcrookes' for 'good service done' in the Wars with Scotland. That English land was still in the possession of one of his grandsons at the time of the escape. A William Armstrong held some 2s land at 'Ulvisby' in Cumberland by service during the rule of King Edward I before 1307. His son Adam extended that land 'by service of homage and fealty' to Edward II, with Richard Armstrong also holding land at Melmoreby, so the Armstrongs had long been on both sides of the line.

Lord Thomas Scrope, the English West March Warden, was infuriated by the escape and named Buccleuch the 'chief enemy to the quiet of the border' while also blaming the Grahams, claiming that one of them had taken Kinmont's ring to Scott as a token before the attempt, while at least one had been seen in the castle court with him during the action, so he was determined to cause as much trouble for both as he could and threatened to resign his office if the Grahams weren't punished severely.

He retaliated by ordering Captain Carvell of Carlisle garrison to burn and raid Liddesdale, driving off 1000 cattle, 2000 sheep and 120 horses, while taking prisoners and binding them together with ropes, naked, to march two-by-two back to Carlisle in one notable attack.

With tit-for-tat murders and reprisal raids occurring, it was clear that another approach would have to be taken for dealing with the troublesome Border mafia if quiet was ever to happen in the countryside.

2. WAR

THE BORDER between England and Scotland is a wild and barren land of scree slopes and moors, purple heather and dead, brown bracken. Winds whistle in down river valleys, the rain falls heavily, and snow often tops the rolling, rounded Cheviot hills. It can be a cold and desolate place at times. Herds of wild goats and horses patrol hillsides and the woodland homes of red squirrels, pine martens, badgers, foxes and deer. The border is a sanctuary for rare native wildlife and a lonely place of curlew cries and birds of prey hovering in skies grey as slate. The engine of a shepherd's quad bike can cut through the silence, with distant shouting as he calls the sheep down from the tops for feeding.

The hardy hill farmers of the Borders have been on their land for generations, with many of the old peels and bastle houses now incorporated into their buildings and out sheds. Heavy artillery guns can often be heard pounding the landscape in the Ministry of Defence Ranges that now take up much of the Redesdale wilderness and a chunk of North Tynedale was flooded to create the huge Kielder water reservoir in the late 1960s. Much of the Northumberland landscape to the Border is now National Park land and Hadrian's Wall is a World Heritage site that runs 73 miles from Wallsend to the Cumbrian coast. Most of the wall is gone now, robbed out by enterprising borderers to build their defensive structures, while some of the stone is even incorporated in Carlisle Cathedral, the grey blocks standing out against the red sandstone that is prevalent among the old buildings in the Great Border City.

It is, however, the number of castles that marks out the bloody history of the area and they stand, beaten by the weather and roofless like the skeletons of dead trees on the landscape, a testament to the violent relations between the Rose and the Thistle that existed for hundreds of years.

Carlisle's red, squat and brooding walls; Hermitage, an unusual tall and square grey stone monument to the troubled times in Liddesdale;

the great sandstone buildings of Northumberland at Alnwick and Warkworth; Bamburgh, stunning on top of an igneous outcrop by the sea; Dunstanburgh, Norham, Hexham's Old Gaol (the first purpose-built prison in England); Threave, Caerlaverock, the ruins at Berwick where the East Coast main line cuts straight through. Berwick, that changed hands between the countries thirteen times and has been English since 1482, to name just a few. As well as the great fortresses of power, the countryside is littered with the ruined remains of the great clans and crime families that built their own seats with walls metres thick. Weeds and trees now grow from fallen gables, the stone sodden and crumbling and black in a bog, the empty and neglected shells of homes once warmed by fires and laughter. Some have been restored and are now bed and breakfast or holiday accommodation, others remain great country houses and estates and many are still on working farms.

The fractious relationship between England and Scotland had been going, on and off, for around five centuries and it was the people of the borderlands that bore the brunt of the battles. Malcolm's Cross, just north of Alnwick, marks the spot where the Scottish King Malcolm Canmore was killed in 1093 by an English army led by Robert de Mowbray of Bamburgh castle. Malcolm's son Edward also fell on the battlefield and put a stop to their ambitions of adding Cumberland and Northumberland to Scotland following the Norman conquest of England and their besiegement of Durham two years earlier.

There was another battle at Alnwick in 1174 when William the Lion of Scotland was taken prisoner and detained at Falaise in Normandy after a spell in Newcastle castle. William was also attempting to reclaim lands for Scotland and had inherited the title of Earl of Northumberland in 1152. He had attacked Newcastle and Prudhoe a year previously and hit Prudhoe again before retreating back to besiege Alnwick. His army was divided into three columns and one, under Duncan, Earl of Fife, committed an atrocity when they burned the church of St. Lawrence in Warkworth with frightened people gathered inside. A small English retaliation force led by Ranulf de Glanville rode north from Newcastle and stumbled across William's camp in a heavy early morning mist. They charged and cut William down from his horse, capturing him and killing anyone that refused to surrender. Henry II then occupied the Scottish castles at Roxburgh, Jedburgh, Berwick, Edinburgh and Stirling, virtually bringing Scotland under English control, and forced William to sign the treaty of Falaise which guaranteed his allegiance to England. On his return from France, he was said to have been attacked by a mob in Newcastle who were pig sick of Scottish invasions.

The First Scottish Wars of Independence ran from 1296 to 1327 and the Second from 1332 to 1355 with the border people again facing slaughter and burnings by the armies of either side as their land became a battlefield.

The English, led by King Edward Longshanks, 'the Hammer of the Scots,' took Berwick in 1296 in response to an attack on Carlisle castle. Berwick was an important trading port for the transport of Scottish wool overseas and the bloody carnage that then followed was devastating. Over two days the English under Robert de Clifford massacred anywhere between 4,000 and 17,000 people in the town before William 'the Hardy' Lord Douglas surrendered the castle.

In 1314, just before Bannockburn, Sir James Douglas retook Roxburgh castle for the Scots by disguising his men as cows then scaling the walls to surprise the English garrison inside and butchering them before pulling the castle walls down so that the English could not occupy it again. A year later Robert the Bruce attacked and besieged Carlisle Castle, but the old fortress held firm, beating off his scaling ladders and siege towers and causing heavy losses to his invasion force.

The Bruce had also attempted to retake Berwick that year and the Scots were more successful in 1318 as they bribed an English sergeant to allow a party to scale the walls. After an unsuccessful skirmish, again led by James Douglas, Bruce and his army arrived shortly after and they starved the English out with an 11-week siege. The devastation caused by the Wars and failures of both crop and cattle meant that in 1317 in Newcastle-upon-Tyne desperate measures saw 'some eat the flesh of their own children; and thieves in prison devoured those that were newly brought in, and greedily eat them half alive.'

Northumberland was being fired and plundered again by a Scottish army that had come in by the West March in 1327. An English army was sent out from York in response when they met a second invasion force that had entered by the East March around Durham. The English army went beyond the Scots to Haydon Bridge and crossed the Tyne to cut off their home passage. When the Scots did not arrive after a fortnight, they had to go out and seek them. The wily James Douglas had taken a strong position near Stanhope in Weardale and refused to move from it to meet the advancing troops. With both armies camped up, Douglas led a night attack on the English forces and almost captured King Edward III from his tent, killing several hundred of his men who were sleeping and unprepared. When Douglas withdrew, the English did not follow, and the action led to negotiations and treaties that recognised the Bruce's claim to the Scottish throne. The Black Douglas, who was educated in Paris, died battling Moors in Spain during a crusade in 1330 with the dead Bruce's heart in a silver casket hung around his neck.

In December 1332 forces loyal to Bruce and King David II of Scotland led by Sir Archibald 'Tyneman' Douglas kicked Edward Balliol and his supporters out of Scotland after surprising them in their beds at Annan but in July 1333 Douglas fell to a crushing defeat by the English at Halidon Hill while attempting to retake Berwick.

The day began badly for the Scots when their champion, a borderer called Turnbull, and his faithful companion, a large black dog, were both sliced apart and left in a mangled, bloody pile during single combat by the sword of an English knight from Norfolk called Robert Benhale with the gathered armies watching on from the hillsides. When the Scottish spearmen charged they got bogged down in the marshy ground at the foot of the hill and were met by a sky black with arrows from the English ranks that caused carnage. The barrage was so intense that they were said to be turning away their faces 'as if walking into sleet.' As those that weren't blinded or felled by the arrows stumbled over the bodies of their fallen comrades and finally attempted an assault on the English forces, they were bedraggled, exhausted and going uphill, which made them easy meat for the English to pick off. Their army of 13,000 was decimated by an English force of 9,000 that had used their archers to devastating effect and would continue to do so in battle after battle. Douglas himself and a number of other Scottish nobles were among the thousands killed with the number of English casualties as low as 14.

The Borders were under attack again in 1346 when the Scots took Liddesdale but left Carlisle alone after being paid off with protection money as a force of 12,000 men invaded by the West and then attacked and burned Hexham priory on their way to assault Durham. With the English fighting in France, David II was encouraged to assault northern England by his friends in the 'Auld Alliance' expecting to meet little resistance. But the English had prior warning and managed to gather together around 3,000 men from Northumberland, Cumberland and Lancashire that met with around the same number of Yorkshiremen en route to what became known as the Battle of Neville's Cross. Lord Henry Percy led the Northumbrian men in the right wing of three formations that attacked the Scottish defensive position with longbowmen after a long stand-off, the hail of arrows forcing them to attack and lose up to 3,000 men in the ensuing battle, with King David himself being taken prisoner.

The King was still being held captive in 1355 when negotiations for his release broke down and the English attacked and burned the lands of Patrick Dunbar. William, Lord Douglas led a retaliatory raid on Norham castle and the surrounding countryside, either using the tactics or influencing the methods of the border crime families by burning and driving off cattle in an attempt to tempt Sir Thomas Grey out to fight. He pursued the stolen cattle and goods and rode straight into an ambush south of Duns where many of his men were killed and others taken prisoner. Interestingly, a French knight that was fighting for the Scots bought a number of common prisoners and slaughtered them in revenge for his father who had been killed by the English.

A London Commission in 1371 was looking into the fact that many merchants in Northumberland and the liberties of Tynedale and Teviotdale (at the time classed as a part of Northumberland), were defrauding the English King of custom charges on 'wool, hides and woolfells' by selling them through the port at Berwick-upon-Tweed and 'other parts of Scotland,' in an early example of the borderers using the conflict line to their advantage.

Duns was the site of another Scottish victory in 1372 when Henry Percy, the first Earl of Northumberland and Warden of the Marches, led an army of 7,000 over the border in retaliation for a number of Scottish raids and set up camp in the town. The local farmers used the skin rattles that they scared animals off their crops with to upkittle the English horses and put the English in disarray; in a farcical retreat they left their baggage behind and turned for home.

Percy's son Harry Hotspur was a main player in the infinitely more bloody and violent Battle of Otterburn in 1388. The borderers were honing their skills in cattle theft and robbery around this time as a large number of skirmishes were occurring on their farmland.

The Scottish forces of around 3,000 men were led by James, 2nd Earl of Douglas, and were in the main a large raiding party that robbed and pillaged around Durham and Newcastle before destroying Ponteland castle and moving north to besiege Otterburn. Hotspur rushed his men from Newcastle to Otterburn to meet with the enemy ahead of an army of 10,000 men led by the Bishop of Durham, who declined to attack. Percy charged headlong into the Scots and the battle raged into the night. Douglas was killed in the confusion on the field, but his army were triumphant, with almost 2,000 English slaughtered and over 1,000 taken prisoner. The Scottish losses were 100 killed and 200 captured.

A period of Truce followed but ten years later the son of the Earl of Douglas and Sir William Stewart attacked Roxburgh and broke the bridge, burnt the town, destroyed the wells and fired the hay. Stewart admitted he was there but considered that the attack was lawful and 'for all that was and is Scotsmen's heritage' and felt that it hadn't broken the Truce. In 1399 the Scottish destroyed Wark castle, which led the newly crowned Henry IV to gather an army of 13,000 men that marched into Scotland in August 1400. Unusually, the army did not devastate the countryside around them, camped at Leith and returned home after a couple of weeks without any bloodshed.

That would all change in 1402 though as the Scots launched co-ordinated attacks over the Border with 12,000 crossing in the West march to raid the countryside around Carlisle. Meanwhile a raiding party of 400 Scots riders were attacked and decimated at Nesbit Moor by a bitter and vengeful exile, George Dunbar, 10th Earl of March, who had been one of the Scottish leaders at Otterburn but had crossed over to the English after an affront to his honour by Archibald 'the Grim' Douglas. Dunbar's daughter was supposed to marry David Stewart, the Duke of Rothesay, but Douglas intervened and married her himself.

Dunbar got another chance to have a go at his former comrades just three months later when Douglas led a huge raiding party believed to be around 12,000 strong into Northumberland and they plundered, burned and robbed as far south as Newcastle.

Dunbar and Harry Hotspur were waiting for the Scots to return laden down with booty at Wooler and the Scots took up a defensive position on the slopes of Humbleton Hill. But the English archers were again deployed to devastating effect from the slopes of a smaller hill nearby, forcing the Scots to charge, and they were cut down in the Red Riggs below, suffering massive losses. Others were said to have drowned in the River Till on escaping the battlefield and many, including Douglas, were taken prisoner. The English bowmen won another conflict against a party of 4,000 raiding Scots at the nearby Iron Age hillfort of Yeavering Bell in 1415 with their arrows loosed to great effect.

The locals were certainly undertaking raids of their own around this time as in 1407 Thomas Gray of Heaton, near Wark, was unable to repair his castle nor enlarge its chapel because of the danger of raids and invasions. It's fair to say that the reiving families were almost certainly involved in the battles as a number of Scottish pledges were being held hostage in the Tower of London and requested safe passage for their men to come south in 1424. William Douglas wanted conduct for Alexander Brown, Adam Tait and John Gibson. Sir Patrick Dunbar requested Reynold Hodgson, Gilbert Dalrymple and Alexander Dodds while James Hamilton sent for John Glassford, Thomas Hamilton, Thomas Kerr, and a servant called John Syndale. William wasn't the first Douglas to be held in the Tower as William 'the Hardy' had been imprisoned and murdered there in 1298 and Archibald Douglas, Third Earl of Douglas – the man that William was pledge for – had also been detained within the walls in 1419.

Dunbar was again involved, along with Hotspur's son Henry Percy, as they attempted to take his stronghold of Dunbar castle back from the Douglases in 1436. The Scots had word of the attempt and quickly marched a couple of thousand men to Piperdean to meet them. The 4,000 strong English invaders were routed near the Breamish in the Cheviots, with around 1,500 killed.

Percy was defeated by Douglas again in the Battle of Sark fought near the Lochmaben stone just outside Gretna in 1448. The English army of 6,000 men camped up near the Solway Firth and it proved a fatal error as many of his men were drowned as the Scottish attacked. Percy had eventually succeeded in destroying Dunbar castle prior to the invasion, with Hugh Douglas responding by annihilating the Percy seats of Alnwick and Warkworth, so the hatred and rivalry between the two great border families was at its peak. The English bowmen that had won so many successes for them didn't have the benefit of higher ground to rain down their arrows and after a couple of volleys, the Scots charged full on into the English ranks with axes, spears and halberts cutting a swathe through their formations and backing them up against the rising tide of water behind. Around half of the English forces were butchered or drowned during the battle, with the Scottish dead put at around 600.

On 3 May 1453 another Truce was negotiated and declared between England and Scotland and the surnames of the signatories on the Latin document are all too familiar, with Thomas Dacre, Henry Fenwick, Robert Ogle, Richard Musgrave and John Heron among the English names and a number of Douglases, Herbert Maxwell, Walter Scott, Alexander and David Hume, Andrew Kerr, Nicholas Rutherford, William Carlyle and Adam Johnstone appearing on the Scottish side.

In 1460 their King, James II, led the Scots as they attempted to take back their castles in the Borders which were under English control, and he was killed while assaulting Roxburgh as a cannon blew up and took him with it. A fragile Truce again settled on the troubled lands but it all sparked up in 1480 with the Earl of Angus launched an assault on Bamburgh castle and the Percys responded by harrying and raiding in Scotland. There were more Scottish raids the following year so in 1482 Percy attacked and burned East Teviotdale, taking out farmsteads at Yetholm, Morebattle, Roxburgh, Jedburgh and Ednam as an army of 20,000 men split into two formations to take Berwick after a two-week siege. It was the borderers that were suffering again as the Scottish army of just 500 from the Royal garrison under James III didn't even make it to Berwick, which has been an English town ever since. The other section, under Alexander Stewart, Duke of Albany and Richard, then Duke of Gloucester, advanced on Edinburgh to try and depose Albany's brother from the throne.

Scotland was in chaos but Albany's ambitions on becoming King with English support were dampened two years later when he and the rebel James Douglas rode to Lochmaben fair with 500 English horsemen hoping to stir up the locals in rebellion against James III. They weren't impressed and, backed up by the Crichtons, Murrays and Johnstones, sent them packing. Richard, Duke of Gloucester, was now King Richard III and he gave his blessing on the attempt. Richard knew the border and borderers well; he was the West March Warden in 1470 and 1471 and was the Sheriff of Cumberland for five years at Penrith castle.

The borderers were used to warfare, devastation, raiding and having to arm themselves to protect their stocks and livelihood so it was not surprising that they should form themselves into gangs under the protection and guidance of the local barons. Perhaps it was first done as a defensive measure, but in time it had become a business and a way of life for the people on both sides of the divide. There are no records of initiation ceremonies in the Sicilian style, but young men were blooded on raids and taken along to become signatories on documents with their fathers, which certainly displayed their intentions of becoming chief men themselves. Families rode with each other over decades, forming strong bonds and ties that enhanced their reputations for violence and theft and built a notoriety that had to be upheld. In a society based on values of honour and respect, men were easily drawn into blood feuds to defend their family name and standing in the countryside because the name and the notoriety behind it were all important, above country or King.

So it is important to know that the Border mafia weren't strictly interested in fighting for any cause but that of their own mob and alliances were forged between crews of both countries as they ruthlessly exploited the geographical positioning of the border to their own ends, escaping justice by crossing the line in either direction and playing off the authorities and law upholders of both lands against each other. When you add the fact that the March Wardens and Keepers were often connected by family and crew bonds and as involved in the action as the men they were supposed to be policing, then it proved a breeding ground for corruption, bribery, crime and ruthless revenge.

The reiver families were putting on their battle gear and marching to fight in Northumberland again at the infamous Battle of Flodden Field near Branxton in 1513 where King James IV, a huge chunk of his nobility and clergy and up to 17,000 men were butchered by the English billhooks in a bog.

The battle didn't dampen the Scots reivers' appetite for raiding. In 1514 Thomas Lord Dacre was complaining of the 'annoyances' done in the East and Middle Marches by raiders and ten years later they burnt Ford, Branxton and Cornhill. Sir John Bulmer noted that they were 'growing in courage' and pleaded for 300 men to help with defence.

An old ballad from around the time tells the tale of Adam Kerr of the Moat, the Black Rider of Cheviot, who descended on a wedding at Wooperton with his gang, robbed the guests and raped and murdered the bride-to-be. The notorious outlaw Black Adam was chased back to his hide-out at the Hen Hole by the enraged groom, 'Wight' Fletcher, and the two wrestled on a rocky ravine before falling to their deaths in the College Burn. Whether the story recorded by Frederick Sheldon in his *Minstrelsy of the English Border* is based on fact or fiction is up for debate. However, the Cessford Kerrs had been granted 'the knoll or moat commonly known as Lowslaw' near Yetholm by King James IV in 1491, so there could be an element of truth to it.

Reiving was reaching a zenith.

3. THE WILD, WILD WEST

IT PROBABLY wouldn't appear in one of Tony Robinson's 'Worst Jobs in History' programmes on the TV but in terms of mediaeval employment Robert Parker's role wasn't the best.

Parker was jailer for the high sheriff of Carlisle, Sir Edward Musgrave; in March 1528 he took charge of the reiver Richie Graham of Esk, who was described as the principal person and headsman of all the West Border and incarcerated him in shackles in the high tower at Carlisle Castle after he'd been captured with 21 others by the English West March Warden William, Lord Dacre. Musgrave executed eight, including two of the infamous Armstrongs, while the rest were to be held until after the next Quarter Sessions.

Dacre planned to destroy towers in the Debatable Land below Liddesdale that John Armstrong, alias John the laird, Simon Armstrong the laird, Ninian Armstrong and others had constructed illegally, but was ambushed during the attempt. He suspected Richie Graham of using his family connections (he was married to Armstrong of Mangerton's daughter) to warn them of the impending raid.

Dacre reckoned that Graham had met with the Scotsman Sandy Armstrong at his home to warn him of the imminent danger and although Graham was deep in trouble, his reputation provided him influence within the castle walls; the jailer James Porter refused to hand Parker the keys when he brought the prisoners from Naworth then Christopher Lowther, the castle constable, ordered the shackles removed and when Graham's mother came to visit, took the keys from Parker and refused to give them back. When the jailer later recovered them, Lowther hit him with his dagger and threatened to stab him.

Parker complained, and Graham was handed back over to be held in the castle's Sheriff prison ironed to another man until under-sheriff Sir William Musgrave ordered the chains removed. On the Sunday Graham was allowed to hear mass in the chapel and dine in the hall while his brother, John, 'The Braid,' had spent an hour with Lowther in the castle earlier that day.

Parker was taking Graham back to his cell when a man named Thomas Wright distracted him. Graham said he wanted to go the privy postern gate and while Parker searched for his keys, he speared it shut. But Graham clambered over and an accomplice was waiting with a horse in the fields below to make their escape.

Parker called on several people to help him, including one Robert Storey, but was ignored. Although he went after Graham on horseback, no-one joined the pursuit.

The whole episode stinks of a set-up. Sir Edward Musgrave was implicated with Sir William Musgrave, Christopher Lowther, Parker and Robert Robson, keeper of the postern gate keys – who'd been forbidden to lock up by Lowther on the day - as accomplices, though only Parker was accused by the Cumberland gentry on the inquest panel.

It was in fact the Storeys who had betrayed Dacre's raid, not Richie Graham, and they fled their land on Esk and set up at Kilham in north Northumberland to escape retribution from both Dacre and the Grahams. That severely implicates the Robert Storey in Carlisle Castle. Richie's father Lang Will, his seven brothers and 30 followers crossed the border under the protection of the Scottish West March Warden Lord Maxwell until things settled down then returned to divide up the Storey's land.

Richie Graham and his clan – a surname that had no land on the Esk 'within the memory of man yet being' by 1583 – moved in with Rich taking Netherby, with his brothers Fergus, Tom, Hutcheon, John 'The Braid,' Will and Will of the Fauld eventually settling around about.

The following month the Earl of Angus (Douglas) was planning to raid the Armstrongs but as the Teviotdale Kerrs were under a 'band of assurance' with them, they refused to join in. Angus decided to take the official route and declare the Armstrongs rebels and 'blow out upon them, as is the custom here.' He was frustrated again, however, as Lord Maxwell refused to endorse his proclamation. Maxwell had his own reasons for doing so; he was using the Armstrongs to hit his own nephew, the Laird of Johnstone, who he was at feud with over the killing of 'Muckle Sim' Armstrong but it landed him in such trouble that he didn't dare appear before the Scottish King.

Dacre went back to the Debatable Land and burned all of the remaining houses, including a pele tower belonging to 'Ill Will' Armstrong that was so strongly built from timbers that it had to be cut down with axes first. The only houses remaining in the troubled area were at Canonbie. He was back again soon after and burnt the houses of Black Jock Armstrong's sons on the Mere burn adjoining Liddesdale. At the same time the Armstrongs themselves, with some of the Irvings of Hoddom, were burning the empty houses of the Grahams and those of the Storeys on the advice of Long Will Graham and his sons in an attempt to provoke a reaction.

William and Peter Moffatt, Andrew Little, George Scott and John Armstrong had led an earlier raid to burn Netherby and Dacre refused to meet Maxwell or offer redress for burning out John Armstrong of Stablegate's 'Hole House' (Hollows) tower near Canonbie as he stated it wasn't in Scotland, but 'in the Debatable Ground.'

A couple of months later Dacre was giving safe passage to the Scots rebels Christopher and Andrew Graham, a couple of Irvings and others that had 'committed many robberies and March treasons' since joining him at Rockcliffe castle, as he consolidated his power by adding outlawed gangsters to his crew.

By 1529 Christopher Dacre had taken the role of high sheriff of Carlisle from Edward Musgrave. Cardinal Thomas Wolsey ordered Thomas Musgrave to hand over Bewcastle castle to Dacre, but found that he'd stripped the lead, smashed the windows and left it uninhabitable. Richie Graham was an outlaw and probably one of the Grahams of Esk that were taking purses from people coming away from a Cumbrian market.

With both the Grahams and the Armstrongs heavily involved in violent organised crime and being used as mob enforcers to destructive ends by both Dumfries and Carlisle as well as imposing their own brand of gang rule on the area, the heat was turned up several notches in 1530 when King James V attempted a crackdown and hanged Johnny Armstrong 'Black Jock' of Gilnockie and 48 of his men.

Johnny is reputed to have collected protection money in England – as far away as Newcastle-upon-Tyne - and Scotland and was feared by Lord Maxwell who 'sought all means possible for his destruction.'

The King brought an army of 8,000 men south and Armstrong was on his way to meet him but hadn't been granted safe conduct. 50 of the King's horsemen intercepted the Armstrong party and took him to the monarch 'as if he had been apprehended against his will.' It was a ploy to draw him out and Black Jock was charged with 'theft, reiving, slaughter and treason' and strung up with his followers from trees at Carlenrig.

Six of his men were taken as hostages and after they'd been imprisoned for a few months, they were executed too but his brother George was pardoned so that he could tell the rest of the Liddesdale gangs what had happened but was 'in time, apprehended by the King and punished accordingly.'

The Liddesdale crime families upped sticks and moved into England where they were 'riding daily incursions.' A few days later the King received pledges from the West Border nobles and Walter Scott killed Robert Johnstone to please James, which led to a deadly feud between the two families that 'continued long after to the great harm of both clans.'

The tough justice continued and by 1534 the Elliots, Turnbulls, Armstrongs and other border thieves were appearing so regularly on the charge sheets that they merited little more than a line or two, such as John Turnbull, alias 'Black fow', who was hanged for common theft.

The following year Johnny Armstrong's brother Thomas of Mangerton, the chief of the clan, with Simon 'Sym the Laird,' Christopher and his son Archibald, Ingram, Railton, Robert and Archibald Armstrong, Mangerton's men John 'Lewis John' Elliot and Robert Carruthers, Thomas and Ninian Gray, John 'Shake Buckler' Forrester and Thomas 'Long penman' Armstrong were all denounced rebels for riding 'under silence of night' on John Cockburn of Ormiston and taking 70 oxen and 30 cows, taking three men hostage and stripping them of their clothes, purses and money, thus breaking bonds made to the King.

Sim the Laird came off worst and was sentenced to be hanged from the gallows and, significantly, all his goods and lands were handed to the crown. It was a land and profit-grab by Edinburgh as much as an enforcement of law. As well as hitting Cockburn, Sim was charged with bringing in the sworn Englishman Evil-Willed Sandy, and other Englishmen of the Armstrongs, Nixons and Crosiers to burn and rob Robert Scott of Howpaslot among other raids.

John 'Johnny in Gutterholes' Armstrong and Christopher Henderson were also hanged around the same time as traitors for common theft in England and Scotland with their lands and goods also going to Edinburgh, while Fergus the Graham, Hob Blackburn, Ronald Tait and Willie 'Auld Will' Graham drove off 22 horses belonging to Michael Murray, James Lindsay and Matthew Wilson from Preston Merse in Galloway and Maxwell wanted redress.

London had its own reasons for keeping the Border gangs busy. King Henry wanted his nephew James V to renounce the Catholic faith and his Protestant Reformist Bishop Sir William Barlow was up in Edinburgh trying to influence the Scottish Court. Barlow didn't like the Borderers much; in a letter to Thomas Cromwell, Henry's chief secretary, he wrote that the Scottish monarch had tolerated Scottish invasions into England and was just pretending to impose rule on them which were done for other reasons than a 'zeal for justice.' Barlow said that the main motive for James' hangings were as they had been accused of 'favouring Englishmen in War season' and thought that Mark Kerr, and others, would suffer before he headed south again.

His resolution was that 'No such should inhabit the Marches on their (Scottish) side that same suspected to bare any favour towards us (England)' and urged due execution 'upon thieves and robbers whose abominable absurd fashion so far out of frame a Christian heart abhors to behold. They show themselves in all points to be the Pope's pestilent creatures, very limbs of the Devil, whose Popish power violently to maintain.' I'm not sure what the Vatican would have made of that, but the Borderers seemed unperturbed by the description and one outlaw gang of Grahams and Armstrongs, denounced as Englishmen and common thieves and traitors, named themselves Dick the Devil's Bairns. Finlay Johnstone had been hanged on a gallows for bringing them into Scotland around the same time to commit murders, slaughters, fire-raisings and join in his reiving activities.

It's a distinct possibility that Richie Graham was Dick the Devil; he certainly lived up to the stereotype in 1541 when he and his gang murdered a Scotsman named George Bell then Richie and seven other Grahams – five of his brothers and a number of 'Englishmen' – forayed Kirkpatrick and murdered David Armstrong's sons Thomas, Roland and Will then showed up at a day of truce with the blood from the slaughter splattered and smeared on their faces, hands, jackets and weapons. No doubt with devilish grins, too.

The Grahams were riding with both English and Scottish felons under the pay of the English and Sir Thomas Wharton the following year as the South of Scotland went up in flames.

Lord Maxwell banished 40 men from the Scottish West March and they were implicated in reiving done on the Musgraves, burning John Musgrave's house and committing seven murders in the English Middle march; interestingly, Maxwell then called two each of the Armstrongs, Elliots and Crosiers to his house at Langholm and told them that: "You are the men I can trust: I will have some notable act done to the Englishmen to requite the great displeasures we have lately suffered by them."

He was very wrong in his assessment. By the October of 1542 Sandy Armstrong, Andrew Bell and 24 English and Scottish men, under the protection and 'assurance' of the English official Sir Thomas Wharton, hit the Johnstones in Annandale and took 20 horses, five Johnstones prisoner and killed a horse.

The following evening Wharton's cousin Thomas Dacre was with the rebel Scotsmen Sandy Armstrong, Andrew Bell and Will the Flagon, the English Grahams and 30 others, including six boys, that broke into a house on Kirk Street in Dumfries and set it alight, burning around thirty houses and 'much corn.' They murdered five men that tried to stop them, 'leaving broken spears' in their bodies, and took away horses. The 'Rough Wooing' by King Henry was well underway.

Dacre planned for 400 of his Scottish riders and their confederates in the West March to burn Hawick and ambush any that followed with the English to 'take their wallets, so that if the enterprise fails, they may do another one on the morrow.' He trusted that Liddesdale 'would do good service in Scotland' and they didn't let him down.

Sir Thomas Wharton noted that in the following month the Nixons burned houses in Jedbugh, and with the Nobles they burned houses in Hawick that same night; Bowstead in Teviotdale was burned by Gavin Nixon and other Scots while the English were burning in Galloway. The Littles set Branxholme alight and thirteen Grahams had the smoke in their nostrils from houses in Annandale on a job that the Grahams of Esk assembled for but refused to go on, so they must have had ties to the people that were burned out. The Fosters and Routledges fired two places in West Teviotdale and Robert Hetherington and others sparked up Rinion Jardine's peel tower. Wharton stated that many goods had been lifted in Scotland, but he did not write about them as 'they did not burn.'

He was plotting to gather 1,000 men to meet 1,000 of the Scottish West March at Castleton church at the next full moon to burn out Liddesdale as he had tried to bring them into the carnage without much effect and many of them had delivered their children to Lord Maxwell for safe keeping.

'Now they may be wasted in their buildings and corn, but the handling of the matter must be kept secret from any Borderers,' he wrote from Carlisle. He was also requesting that 100 light horsemen, 'evil-doers, Scots and others', should burn in Scotland twice a week and set fire in any town within 30 miles of them as the Scottish West March was left blackened and smouldering. 'The Scots have not been so wasted and the English so little hurt in any such troubled times within the memory of man,' said the Governor of the Marches.

The Scottish prepared to hit back and by the 22nd of November Sir William Eure was warning Etal, Ford and Glendale in the East March and Coquetdale in the Middle March to expect an invasion with Robert Collingwood and John Horsley to get Coquetdale ready and George Heron to prepare Tynedale and Redesdale to get to Harbottle quickly with the beacons on Simonside and other places to be lit if necessary.

John Carr doubted that the Scots would hit the East March or Coquetdale and, although Hertford had warned his men not to speak with the Scots, took advice from Mr. Utryd and Robert Raymond and sent for a Scotsman that came to his house at Wark-on-Tweed at ten at night to tell him that the King of Scots had gone from Peebles to Hawick 'intending to send 9,000 men to invade the Grahams in the West Marches, and not now meddle with these East parts.'

On the 24th of November a Scottish army of 18,000 men entered the West March and 'burnt the Graham's houses upon Esk and the Debatable Ground' but what was to become known as the Battle of Solway Moss near Arthuret was a major embarrassment for Scotland.

Sir William Musgrave, Thomas Dacre, Jack Musgrave and around 3,000 Englishmen at most, with 'border spears to prick at them,' advanced on the huge invasion force while the others tied up their horses and fired arrows. While the 'noblemen and gentlemen' of Scotland got off their horses to fight, most of the Scots army saddled up and rode away.

The Grahams were picking men off with their spears from horseback as they were withdrawing from the field when the English footmen advanced, with Lord Maxwell 'fighting valiantly at the waterside' but taken prisoner. Many others were drowned, and the English horsemen took between two and five prisoners each for ransoming; Musgrave reckoned that the Grahams would take many more before the night was out as the Scots 'were past resisting, and, having left their wallets behind are like to famish unless they come home.' Only two Englishmen were killed in the skirmish: a man called Dodgson and a pensioner named Robert Briscow. Always looking to score, Musgrave requested that his pension now go to his brother Simon or cousin Richard Musgrave. The Scottish losses were only around 120 killed during the fighting but hundreds more drowned and 1,200 were taken prisoner. It was a complete disaster and King James V died just a fortnight later aged 30. Within four months 100 Liddesdale riders burned two houses near Hexham, killed two Englishmen and took eight prisoners; they were surprised by Jack Musgrave on their way home and his thirty men rescued six of the prisoners and took twelve prisoners of their own – including seven of the chiefs of Liddesdale from the Armstrong crew. It should be noted that Patrick Hepburn, a near kinsman of Earl Bothwell, was with them and the English had intelligence that he was going to get the

Keeper of Hermitage Castle position.

The Armstrongs were imprisoned in Carlisle but in the August of 1543, they were to be set free if they would deliver Forster and three others that they held prisoner and become the servants of King Henry VIII.

The following month, in the castle garden at Carlisle, Thomas Armstrong the laird of Mangerton, Christopher Armstrong called 'Braid Crystal,' Paton Armstrong, Archibald Armstrong, Sym Armstrong called 'Red Sym,' Hector Armstrong, Rinion Armstrong, Will Armstrong of the Gingles, Davy 'the Lady' Armstrong, Sim Armstrong, Ingram Armstrong, Jock Routledge, Christie Armstrong, Archie Armstrong, George Forster of Greenow and Christie Armstrong all appeared before Sir Thomas Wharton, the deputy warden of the West Marches, and 'took solemn oath that they, their sons, kin, friends and clans whose names are expressed in a schedule unto this present bond annexed, and all other their kin, friends, and clans will henceforth serve the King and his officers of the Marches; and appointed sixteen persons to lie in pledge for this.' The Liddesdale Armstrongs were now English; the Douglases were to be similarly signed up in the December, but Sir George of that family said it was impossible for him to get any of his or his brother's friends to stand as hostages for their assurance as they were not like 'the Armstrongs, Crosiers and Nixons (who were in danger of the laws of Scotland and lived upon reiving) but gentlemen living upon their own in no fear of the laws.'

Not that it bothered the Armstrongs and they soon set to work for the English running forays on their Scottish neighbours hitting the Lairds of Greenstone, Cardoney and the Scotts of Howpaslot, then burning the laird of Applegarth's towns of Over and Nether Hawhill. The Beatties, Thomsons and Littles were also burning while the Armstrongs fired Langhope tower, Halrule and Windes.

While the likes of the Armstrongs, Nixons, Elliots, Routledges and Crosiers were burning and raiding relentlessly under the English, the Tynedale and Redesdale crews were similarly employed along with the Berwick garrison as Teviotdale and the Scottish East March also put an orange tinge to the night skies with embers glowing in the black throughout 1544. Mind, the Tyne and Redesdalers weren't that fussed about nationality either. When a raiding party came under attack, they left the others behind and 'after their accustomed fashion, made off with the booty, leaving the rest of their company at a disadvantage' so they were notorious for a disdain in national interests and only concerned with their own crews. Self-preservation and looking after your own affairs were very much part of the reiver mindset. This was displayed again at the Battle of Ancrum Moor in February 1545 when the 700 'assured' Scottish reivers in the English army went turncoat and switched sides mid-way through the battle.

The Scottish victory didn't quite put an end to the 'Rough Wooing' period although Ralph Eure and Sir Brian Layton, the Captain of Norham who had led many burning parties into Teviotdale, were killed in the carnage with around 800 English bodies scattered on the field four miles north west of Jedburgh and around 1,000 taken prisoner. Three months later Christie Armstrong and 30 other assured Scotsmen burned a town in Annandale, drove away horses and brought back four prisoners, all of whom were injured, and the English soldiers at Langholm burnt houses and corn in Teviotdale. When they were pursued they left a number of Scotsmen injured and killed their horses. They also took Watt Scott, a near kinsman of Buccleuch, and four others prisoner.

By 1547 there were still 40 Armstrongs serving the English and 160 other Scotsmen taking pay from the now King Edward VI, who was just ten years old, with his uncle Edward Seymour, the Duke of Somerset, leading the Regency Council and defeating a huge Scottish army in the Battle of Pinkie Cleugh near Musselburgh in the September of that year where some 14,000 Scottish soldiers were massacred by a bombardment from English ships offshore, artillery, German arquebusiers (precursor to the modern rifle) and long-bowmen.

The reivers were involved as light horsemen under the Earl of Home and they'd harassed the English army as it marched north up the Scottish East Coast, but they were probably more interested in what they could steal than with doing it any serious damage. During the battle itself, Borderers from both sides were spotted by the English lawyer and observer William Patten wearing other intricate markings than the crosses of St. George or St. Andrew on handkerchiefs wrapped around their arms and on their helmets, talking to each other, then putting on a show of fighting when they were seen.

The authorities decided to draw a line quite literally on where the Border ran through the Debatable Ground in 1552 when they created the Scots Dike, a double ditch that divided the land into English and Scottish territories from the Sark to the Esk which left 'the stone house of Thomas Graham on its west side, and the stone house of Alexander Armstrong on the east.' The French ambassador Claude de Laval, lord of Boysdaulphin, had the deciding say along with Lord Wharton and Sir Thomas Chaloner for the English and Sir James Douglas of Drumlanrig and Richard Maitland for the Scots. It didn't have a great deal of effect and in 1560 the Grahams were squabbling amongst themselves as John Graham of Canonbie had a dispute with George Graham, a son of Richard Graham of Netherby. The Lords of Scotland intervened in on behalf of John and left Wharton scratching his head over what to do with the case at Berwick.

Richard Graham of Netherby handed over a list of the names of the Graham clan to the English West March Warden Lord Dacre in 1561 as they sought a pardon 'for doing good and honest service against the Scots', which was granted. The 250 names were mostly Grahams, but also included some Fosters, Armstrongs, Taylors, Hallidays, Redpaths and Richardsons and noted a number of nicknames such as Gruff, Shag, Flaggon and Redsleeves.

The following year, Lord Maxwell was complaining about Lord Dacre as he accused him of failing to keep an indenture for redressing Scottish bills and refusing to 'make answer for the attempts which are made daily upon this realm by Andrew and Richie Graham, the sons of Hutcheon Graham; Fergus Graham, son to Matthew the Black; Jock Graham, and his son Jock; Willie Blackburn, stepson of Richie Graham of Medhope, and other Englishmen, rebels of Scotland.' He was also furious that Dacre hadn't upheld a law passed at the foot of Sark water that 'if any Englishman occupied any ground of Scotland within the West Wardenry he should pay double the principal' and although Willie Graham of Fauld, Geordie Graham, son of little Tom, Will Graham of Carlisle, Tom Graham of Galloway, Fergus Graham of the Mote, Richie Graham of Netherby, Gib Graham of

Sark, and his son Geordie, Quentin Graham of Sark, Fergie Graham, son of Matthew the Plump, and other Grahams, noted as Englishmen, were on his lands, they were not paying up. Maxwell was similarly infuriated that he'd had no response to his demands for compensation for thefts done by Hutcheon's son Andrew, Black Jock Graham, Sim Taylor, Robin Foster, Little Tom's son Geordie Graham and others. The Grahams were also in trouble because Willy 'Braid's Willy' Graham had fired into a party of Scots that had followed them across the Sark at a May truce day that year.

It was back to business as usual and the Armstrongs and Elliots were causing such disruption by 1565 that Sir John Forster had to place twenty gunners at Harbottle castle to fend off the five hundred men of Liddesdale, all of whom were proclaimed rebels, that, with some fugitives from Tyne and Redesdale, came to within a mile of the stronghold and assaulted his man in charge of the castle. Forster reckoned that the Northumbrian fugitives 'would not have dared take upon without the Liddesdalers.' They were also raiding and spoiling in Tynedale where four of them were taken prisoner. 'As the numbers of the evil increase so do their devices,' he wrote to Sir William Cecil.

The criminal fraternities of the Armstrongs and Grahams have become synonymous with the whole reiving period, but it is wrong to think that the border mafia simply disappeared sometime after the 1620s. They changed, certainly, but they are still there. On Old Year's Night in 1993 the Tyneside hard-man, doorman and underworld figure Viv Graham, whose friends and close associates included people by the name of Bell, Scott and Armstrong, was gunned down and killed in Wallsend and when the Newcastle-upon-Tyne daily newspaper the *Evening Chronicle* listed a number of the biggest names in the North East underworld who had been ordered to pay back millions of pounds under the Proceeds of Crime Act in 2011, two were named Graham and another Armstrong.

The descendants of Dick the Devil's Bairns are still riding today.

4. SIR WALTER SCOTT OF BUCCLEUCH

THE SCOTTS produced not only great leaders but some of the choicest rogues and riders on the Borders and Sir Walter Scott of Buccleuch had a real reiving pedigree.

There are records of the family in the area as far back as the early Twelfth Century and it is claimed in some quarters that the clan were descended from Ireland, the Scotti being a name for a tribe of Celts.

Sir Richard Scott was appointed the Ranger of Ettrick Forest sometime in the late Thirteenth Century and he built the first tower at Buccleuch. His son Sir Michael Scott was a follower of Robert the Bruce and was a great fighter for the Scots in their defeat at Halidon Hill. Sir Michael was, however, less fortunate and was killed at the Battle of Durham some thirteen years later.

Michael's son Robert is reputed to have died from his wounds sustained in the Battle of Otterburn. The Scotts weren't afraid to don their fighting gear and take up arms for the country but they were also heavily involved in all of the reiving action from the earliest of times.

By 1493 Walter Scott of Edshaw was accused of traitorously talking to the thieves of Leven and Walter Scott of Howpaslot was also implicated for bringing in some of those 'Traitors of Leven' named as William Scott called 'Guide,' and his brother John, and resetting – basically taking the stolen goods, feeding, watering and restocking the raiders – Henry Scott and others. The Leven was part of the notorious 'Debatable Land' south of the Liddel water where gangs of 'broken' outlaws rendezvoused before raids and it would become the most troublesome spot on the Borders throughout the time of the Reivers. The men in the Leven were being called traitorous because they had gone down to Carlisle to swear allegiance to the English King Richard III in around 1478.

The Scotts were up to their necks in the trouble and John Scott of Dalloraine was assisting noted thieves such as John Reid (an Englishman), John Scott, known as 'Scot-Stow' in Tushielaw, Hector

Armstrong and other reivers from Liddesdale, Eskdale and Ewesdale; he had also murdered a man known as 'Colthride.' Adam Scott in Auldinnischop was similarly charged with assisting the Traitors of Leven.

Later that year Alexander Scott in Hopton 'barbarously oppressed' an Andrew Taylor and rode his mare so hard that he killed it while Walter Scott of Edshaw stole 13 oxen from Robert Laidler. The then Sir Walter Scott of Buccleuch was also protecting the thieves in the area and gave a bond to free a raider called George Young at Edinburgh in 1498.

The affair rumbled on and in 1502 David Scott called 'the Lady' was bringing in the Armstrongs, still known as the Traitors of Leven, to reive nine score oxen and cows and 20 horses and mares from Synton. Adam Scott in Hawchesters was implicated in stealing six score of sheep from the Laird of Minto with George Rutherford and being involved with Archibald and Ninian Armstrong and William Scott 'the King's rebels.'

Adam Scott in Hardwoodhill's son, Patrick, had reset Richard Armstrong called 'Skaw' in his thefts, including lifting 200 sheep from David Pringle of Fechane, along with an Alexander Scott.

In fact, by 1569, the Scottish East and Middle Marches had famously declared themselves 'enemies to all thieves of Liddesdale, Annandale, Ewsdale, Eskdale and especially to all Armstrongs, Elliots, Nixons, Crosers, Littles, Beatties, Thomsons, Irvines, Bells, Johnstones, Glendennings, Routledges, Hendersons, and Scotts of Ewesdale' in a letter to the Privy Council. It didn't stop them raiding with them, so it was probably just a piece of bureaucratic paperwork.

The litany of Scott larceny continued apace in 1502, however, and Walter Scott, the son of Walter Scott of Edshaw, stole sheep from William Kerr, the Abbot of Kelso and Ralph Kerr while William Scott in Thirlstane broke the King's Protection of Sir Patrick Creighton and occupied his land. Buccleuch became surety to protect his kinsman. Two years later Thomas Scott in Priests Dykes was charged with intercommuning with the Armstrongs and in 1510 Belted Robin Scott called the Lady of Buccleuch as lawful surety at Jedburgh. He did not appear himself and was denounced at the horn with his goods confiscated.

The Scotts murdered John Murray of Fallowhill that year and Thomas Scott in Aikshaw also lost his goods as he and his fellow-accused William Scott in Hawick, George Scott in Goldielands and David Scott in Whitehaugh repeatedly failed to show at the Jedburgh court.

But these were all petty local affairs compared to the turmoil that Scotland was about to be plunged into when King James IV was killed in the carnage of the disastrous Battle of Flodden Field in 1513. The captured Scottish combatants William Scott and John Foreman were taken to Berwick to identify his body before it was embalmed and taken on to Newcastle and a long journey South to London.

Walter Scott of Branxholme and Buccleuch was knighted on the field of the slaughter that day when many of the Scotts are said to have joined the Monarch in losing their lives to the nimble billhooks of the English army on the boggy ground at the foot of the slope that they had charged down.

The King's son and successor, the young James V, was to find the Scottish Borderers a similarly bad headache but he was so determined to put a stop to the lawlessness that he levied an army to deal with them when he finally took full control of the Crown for himself in 1528.

Adam Scott of Tushielaw was such a notorious leader of sheep and cattle raiders that he earned the nicknames 'King of Thieves' and 'King of the Border' and he distinguished himself with the most 'reckless and daring treasons and robberies' and James was keen to make an example of him to scare the others into line.

Adam Scott was born sometime in the late Fifteenth century, a son of David Scott in the forest of Ettrick, who had gained possession of the lands at Tushielaw sometime between 1480 and 90. Adam was granted a charter by King James IV to the forest stead and lands of Tushielaw 'with the right to build a tower and fortalice' in 1507 for a yearly payment of £24.

His brother, William, was also a reiver who in 1502 was one of the 'Traitors of Leven' riding and committing 'stouthreifs, slaughters, burnings and other crimes,' with Archibald and Ninian Armstrong. Adam specialised in taking 'blackmail' – protection money – and it appears he was still demanding money with menaces even while imprisoned in Edinburgh in May 1530 along with fellow villain William Cockburn, the Laird of Henderland.

He also stood accused of murder, theft, receiving stolen goods and 'maintaining thieves' - read being the head of a crew. So forget the romantic view of Scott being hung from a tree in his backyard that was popularised by Border Balladeers; it seems that he was actually lifted, tried and executed in the capital city.

The then 19-year-old King James V of Scotland had consolidated his power in 1529/30 with a clampdown on the Border families that also saw the Earl of Bothwell banished and the Lords Maxwell and Hume and Lairds of Buccleuch, Cessford, Ferniehurst, Polwart and Johnstone, among others, imprisoned. This was probably in response to the fact that the Border warlord Archibald Douglas, 6th Earl of Angus – his stepfather – had held the teenager virtually prisoner and exercised power for him for three years until 1528. Buccleuch had actually tried to free the young King in 1526 during what became the Battle of Melrose and when one of Scott's riders killed the Laird of Cessford, it led to a long running and bitter feud which would eventually cost him his life.

Adam Scott had been previously jailed in Edinburgh castle in 1505 but had broken out and, perhaps most tellingly, in 1525, he agreed to assist the Earl of Angus in 'staunching theft, reiving, slaughter, etc.' Most likely this would involve them actually controlling the reiving activities and it was this connection with Douglas that made the young King probably see Adam as such a threat that he had to go. Adam Scott and William Cockburn were publicly hung, then beheaded and their heads fixed on spikes at the Tolbooth in Edinburgh. Soon after, the King descended on Ewesdale and Eskdale with estimates of up to 12,000 men and hanged another 48 well-known reivers – including the infamous Johnny Armstrong of Gilnockie. A William Scott was also hanged in 1538 for 'breaking the Act of Parliament against Leasing-makers.'

Buccleuch's Branxholme Tower was burned out by the Earl of Northumberland in 1532 but Scott launched a huge counter-raid of 3,000 men over the Border in response. Three years later he was locked up in Edinburgh after being accused of assisting Lord Dacre, the English Middle March Warden, and although he was released, he found himself imprisoned again in 1540. It wasn't a new experience for Scott however; he'd also been locked up at Edinburgh castle as early as 1524.

'Wicked Watt,' as he was known, was one of the leaders of the Scottish army that beat the English, their foreign mercenaries and 'assured Englishmen' from the Scottish Borders at the Battle of Ancrum Moor in 1545 and was in action again at the Battle of Pinkie Cleugh two years later.

Scott was made Warden of the Middle Marches in 1550 and Warden of Liddesdale a year later. But in 1552 the Kerrs finally took their revenge for the killing of Cessford 26 years earlier when they hit Buccleuch in broad daylight on the High Street in Edinburgh. John Hume of Cowdenknowes rammed his sword into Buccleuch's guts and encouraged the Kerrs that he was with to join in. Buccleuch was made of tough stuff; he survived the initial attack but as he lay in a pool of blood and attempted to drag himself along the ground in a vain attempt to get away, his killers came back and stabbed him repeatedly to finish the job.

In 1557 a number of the Scotts – up to 200 - came dressed in full battle gear to the Church of St. Mary of the Lows and smashed the doors open as they hunted down Sir Peter Cranston to murder him. Robert Scott of Allanhaugh, Adam Scott of Burnfoot and his son William, Thomas Scott of Haining, Walter Scott the young laird of Synton and his brothers Robert, William and James, Walter Scott, the son of Watt Scott of Harden, Robert Scott of Thirlstane and Robert Scott of Howpaslott were the ringleaders of the assassination attempt and terrifying display of power. The Scotts were flexing their muscles and were not to be messed with.

Buccleuch's grandson Walter Scott, Fourth Baron of Buccleuch, became the headsman at only three years old as his father Walter had died before the murder of 'Wicked Watt' in Edinburgh. At just 17 he was made the Captain of Newark Castle by Queen Mary and in 1570 his tower at Branxholme was blown up with gunpowder by the Earl of Sussex during his invasion and harassment of the Scottish Borders in retaliation for a devastating raid into England led by the old foes Scott and Kerr of Ferniehurst.

Scott began rebuilding Branxholme in 1571 and died there three years later – but not before he had killed 'Hopshawes,' a great chief of the Elliots, as his swansong.

In 1566 Tom Scott, a sheriff of Lord Ruthven, was hanged for his part in the murder of David Rizzio and died 'very well and stoutly,' as would be expected. Rizzio was an Italian courtier of Queen Mary, her private secretary and if the rumours were to be believed, her lover. Ruthven was a Protestant and despised the Catholic Rizzio, which may have also played a part in his death.

The business of reiving was keeping the rest of the family busy and in 1568 William Scott of Tushielaw was accused of 'stouth and reset of stouth' and not bringing official letters along with Robert Elliot of Belleie and Robert Scott of Horslehill. That was small fry compared to when John Scott called 'the Tinkler' and his son Andrew 'the Breadie,' with Adam Scott called 'Little Peck' and some 500 others launched a huge day foray on Percival Clennell in May 1587 and they drove away 80 kye and oxen, seven horses and mares, insight of £20 and took and ransomed eight prisoners. In 1595 Auld Watt of Harden was raiding with Anthony Carleton at Tredermayne with a band of Armstrongs, Elliots and Hendersons to reive 60 kye and oxen and six horses and mares.

Walter Scott was born in around 1565 and by the time he was 24 he had renewed an old feud with the Ferniehurst Kerrs by killing four of their men in Edinburgh; though nobody was apprehended for the crime, there can be no doubt that Scott was behind the 1589 hits. The Scottish crown were worried that the incident could divide the clans of the Borders as the Kerrs and Humes were strong in the East and would hold together while the Johnstons and the Maxwells in the West were similarly strong and would follow Buccleuch. The feud was ended that November however with a marriage as Ferniehurst took the hand of Buccleuch's sister. Buccleuch, Sir Andrew Kerr and old Laird Cessford were said to have become good friends while young Cessford – Sir Robert Kerr – stuck fast to King James. More trouble was brewing as the Humes 'mortally hated' the Earl of Morton and while it was felt that the Hepburns would join with the Hamiltons, the Davisons, Pringles, Youngs, Burns and others of Teviotdale would go with the young Lord Cessford. Scott himself had married Sir Robert Kerr of Cessford's sister Mary in October 1586 creating a powerful bloc with both him, the Scottish West March Warden Sir James Laird of Johnstone who was in turn his cousin, and Kerr of Ferniehurst, who was now also a brother-in-law. Whether these matters were influential in the decision or not, a year later, Scott the Laird became Sir Walter Scott of Buccleuch 'The Bold Buccleuch' when he was knighted and then appointed Keeper of Liddesdale on the 28th of July 1591 by King James VI.

Scott had resigned the post by 11 August and in September he was sent away to Flanders by the King, but he wasn't going to make the mistake of entering England by Carlisle or the West March. His journey was to take him through Berwick and Sir John Forster noted that he was to 'pass through England to some foreign country.' The King promised Buccleuch that as soon as his cousin – and Buccleuch's stepfather - Francis Stewart, the Fifth Earl of Bothwell, who had been the Liddesdale Keeper from 1587, had passed out of Scotland he would be 'called home with all favour.'

Bothwell was accused of plotting to kill the King in an armed uprising in 1589 and April 1591 he was accused of Witchcraft and trying to do away with the Monarch through black magic. He was imprisoned in Edinburgh castle but broke out two months later and went on the run.

Buccleuch was out of the country until November 1592 when the Queen allowed him leave to return. Buccleuch was 'known to be of high courage and much favouring Bothwell, and it is wished that he may be well allured to cherish the peace on the Borders, wherein he is able to do many good offices.'

He took on the tough job of Keeper of Liddesdale again on the 10th October 1593 and when he moved into Hermitage he told the English officials that he would only answer for offences committed by the Liddesdale reivers from that date. He also brought the Armstrongs and other 'chief men' to his house 'to protest their true services to him' and threatened to hang anyone that 'dealed in any way' with Bothwell.

Buccleuch was a formidable raider himself - in 1587 he had led 200 men on a foray into Redesdale where they murdered John Dunn and burned Woodside; he was also a leader along with Kerr, the young Laird of Cessford and the Laird of Johnston as they combined the forces of Annandale, Ewesdale, Eskdale, Liddesdale, Teviotdale and the town of Jedburgh to take 3,000 men into Sir Cuthbert Collingwood's land in north Northumberland. As well as spoiling, they killed over twenty men – 'so cruelly mangled as they were not to be known who they were' - and took 160 prisoners. This was in response to a fateful raid by Collingwood in Teviotdale where he found nothing as the Scots had been tipped off in advance.

A year later Buccleuch was at the head of 200 horsemen that charged on Bewcastle and spoiled the Routledges, Nixons, Nobles and others of 200 kye and oxen and 300 sheep. He was back in Gilsland a month later with the young Laird of Whitehaugh, Sim Armstrong, and 120 others 'armed with jacks, steel caps, spears, guns, lances, long staffs and daggs, swords and daggers' who descended on the house of Willie Routledge and took 40 kye and oxen and 20 horses and mares. He then set an ambush to assault the following hot trod and killed four soldiers, maimed many others and drove off twelve horses belonging to the pursuers. He may have been a criminal godfather, but he liked to get his hands dirty and Scott's personal feud with the Tynedale Charltons saw himself and William Elliot of Larriston, with 300 men, kill four of the Boughthill Charltons in 1593 and he was back murdering a number of Charltons and Dodds again in 1594.

Perhaps his hatred of the Northumbrian riders had a more deep-seated and psychological aspect; when he was just three years old, in 1568, the men of Tynedale and Redesdale had raided his father at Buccleuch and 'overthrew him and all his company, and took him and 260 others prisoners.' Six of the English were killed in the action, with 'many Scots slain and many hurt.' It must have been a traumatic event for a young child to witness with panic spreading throughout the tower and the fear he must have felt when he father was taken. Whatever the reasons, Sir Walter thrived on revenge.

5. SIR ROBERT KERR OF CESSFORD

LEGEND HAS IT that the Kerrs were descended from the Norse Vikings that invaded France – the Old Norse word 'kjrr' meaning 'marsh dweller' - and were part of the Norman conquest of Britain in 1066. Two brothers of the name were granted land in Lancashire before moving North to Teviotdale. The Kerrs of Ferniehurst were said to descend from Ralph and the Kerrs of Cessford from Robert. So, Sir Robert Kerr's ancestors were no less embroiled than the Scotts in all of the action along the border line for centuries. His great-great-grandfather and great-grandfather were both murdered; his namesake Sir Robert being killed at a Truce Day by Heron the Bastard of Ford, Lilburn and Starrhead in 1511 which was one of the reasons that Scotland gave for their invasions of England two years later that led to their crushing defeat at Flodden Field. It was also cited as the reason that the English had to go into Scotland first to seek assurance on a Truce Day from then onwards as the Scots refused to come on English ground for justice.

Kerr's great-grandfather Andrew of Cessford was targeted by the English Lord Warden Surrey during his campaign in the Borders in 1523 and suffered the indignity of having to negotiate to get a bag out of Cessford castle as the English attempted to blow it up. On Monday the 18th of May around 2,000 English troops assembled in Glendale and marched on the Kerr place at Lochtower and pulled it down. They then razed the fortress at Linton on a morning attack on Cessford, described as 'the strongest place in Scotland except Dunbar and Fast Castle.' The English opened up with a barrage of guns that had little effect on the thick red walls of the Kerr stronghold, so a number of men scaled the walls with ladders and entered the barbican under a hail of stones and arrows. Another artillery barrage opened a hole in an old window and four barrels of powder were thrown in, but the Scots set fire to their own tower and in the ensuing explosion a number of the English attackers were hurt.

Andrew Kerr was a mile away looking on and surrendered the

castle, much to the relief of Surrey who wrote to King Henry VIII that 'if the defence had continued, he could not see how it could have been taken,' stating that the walls were 14 foot thick.

The English toppled and destroyed as much as they could then threw down the nearby Whitton tower. His men and their horses were left weary and exhausted from their exertions in the cold and rain that fell all day, but Surrey reported that they were 'very joyful at the destruction of the fortresses, thinking it better than if Edinburgh and three of the best towns in Scotland had been burnt.' Such was the power that the Cessford Mob exercised over the local area. The campaign continued, and the Earl of Surrey also pulled down Ferniehurst in the September, where he was met with fierce resistance. There was a financial aspect involved and the men of the bishopric of Northumberland and Cumberland were rewarded with £835 4s 4d for pulling down Cessford and other fortresses in Teviotdale.

The following year Andrew Kerr signed up in a bond with the other Border barons to assist the Earl of Angus in controlling the theft, reiving and slaughters in their areas with Walter Scott of Buccleuch, Andrew Kerr of Ferniehurst, Mark Kerr of Dolphinstone, George Rutherford of Hundalee, James Murray of Fallowhill, William Kirkton, Walter Scott of Sinton, Robert Scott of Allanhaugh and Robert Scott of Howpaslot also putting their names to the document.

Cessford, the Scottish Middle March warden like his father before him, and the laird of Buccleuch found themselves imprisoned later that year. In 1526 a feud erupted between the two families as Andrew was run through by a spear and killed by James Elliot when Buccleuch attacked a party near Melrose in an attempt to free the then 14-year-old King James V from the clutches of the Earl of Angus. His son Walter Kerr bound himself to keep the castle of Edgerston that year (receiving the profits from the land for his trouble, of course) and to apprehend the owner Robert Rutherford who had been denounced a rebel. Two years later he was charged along with James Douglas of Cavers, Andrew Kerr of Dolphinstone, John Rutherford of Hunthill and George Rutherford of Hundalee for assisting and protecting the gangsters Robert Rutherford (who he was meant to arrest), George 'Cockburn' Rutherford and John 'Jock of the Green' Rutherford who were committing thefts, reives and slaughters within Scotland.

By 1531 the Teviotdale riders were 'making nightly depredations' into England and the heavyweight bosses of the gangsters Walter Kerr of Cessford, Dand Kerr of Ferniehurst, George Kerr, Dand Kerr of Greenhead, Dand Kerr of Grayden and Lance Kerr turned up at the Redding Burn and 'expressly refused to make redress' to the English officials assembled there.

The following year 3,000 of the Scottish borderers gathered to attack north Northumberland in a well-organised and planned night raid. They sent 300 to plunder Roseden and laid an ambush on the edge of Cheviot for any pursuers; they then sent two more raiding parties into the countryside, one down the Breamish that attacked Ingram, Revel, Brandon and Fawdon and the other to hit Ryle and Prendwick.

When the attackers were pursued by a trod, the Earl of Northumberland reported to King Henry VIII that they saw three standards displayed – those of the lairds of Cessford, Buccleuch and Ferniehurst with the ringleaders being Walter Kerr, the Warden, Buccleuch, John Kerr, the son and heir of Dand Kerr of Ferniehurst and Mark Kerr with all of the headsmen of the Ettrick Forest, all of Teviotdale on horse and foot, 400 'tried men' from the West, all of Jedburgh Forest and the 'tried men' of Moorhouseland and Lauderdale. The raids drove off a number of prisoners and 'a great number of horses, nolt and sheep.'

The raid was possibly made in response to the King of Scotland pardoning all offenders except the Earl of Angus, his brother and their crew and interestingly, at the same time, he banned Scotsmen from speaking to Englishmen on pain of death. If the offender possessed land or goods, then half would go to the lord warden and half to the informer. Northumberland was frustrated and begged that he be given the 'same authority as Dacre in the West Marches to redress the injury.'

In 1542, following the Battle of Solway Moss, the English made a list of the most important Scottish Earls and their houses, naming Bothwell at Hermitage, Angus at Tantallon, Kerr of Cessford's house at Haliden, Mark Kerr and Dand Kerr his son of Littledene, Walter

'Watt the Thief' Kerr of Grayden, Kerr of Linton, Lord Buccleuch Sir Walter Scott at Branxholm Hall, the Rutherford lairds of Hundalee and Hunthill, the laird of Johnstone at Lochwood and the Lord Maxwell at Caerlaverock.

These men were flexing their muscles in the December of that year following the death of King James V with the laird of Cessford and Mark Kerr, with his son Dand entering the house of Kelso and taking all of the King's goods and sheep for themselves and kicking out William Hamilton who was their keeper; Dand Kerr at Ferniehurst took heavy guns from Jedburgh to use at his own house against Mark Kerr as they were in dispute, while Buccleuch took Melrose Abbey and all of the King's sheep there, saying he was doing it as compensation for the sheep of his that had been taken by the King. He said he was having the ground that they were kept on as well.

Who was going to stop them? With the King buried and his heir Mary just days old, the Border crime lords figured that Edinburgh was powerless to prevent their deprivations. The Ferniehurst Kerrs had done likewise when James' father was killed at Flodden and they had Dand Kerr made Abbot of Kelso under the pretence that he would hold it as a defence against possible English attacks when in reality it was a land and power grab as the country's rulers were in chaos. Opportunistic, ruthless, ambitious – the Border mafia bosses had nothing to learn.

They were hit hard by the 'Rough Wooing,' however, with Cessford castle, Jedburgh, Crawling Grange, Otterburn, Cowbog, Morebattle church and other places being burned by the English East and Middle March wardens with John Musgrave and 100 men of the West Marches in June 1544. The Teviotdale men responded the same day by burning Heaton, Tillmouth and Twissell; the English spotted the flames from Kirk Yetholm and took 200 prisoners from the Scottish raiding party with Alexander and Patrick Home narrowly getting away.

The burnings and harassment continued and in April the following year Cessford's barns were burnt out but the Kerrs did hit back and Walter's brother Andrew Kerr launched a counter attack on Wark where they were beaten off by John Carr. Andrew was badly injured in the November as he was set upon during a reive on Wooler.

Dand had recovered enough by the April of 1546 to be involved in a major skirmish with a returning English raiding party near Farmington as the two crews rode into each other while driving their stolen beast. The English retreated to the ford at the Tweed under heavy attack 'with great cries and shouts, after their fashion' but managed to beat them off with 'great slaughter.' The English reported afterwards that the Master of Hume, the lairds of Cessford, Cowdenknowes, and Milestoynes, the abbot of Jedburgh, Mark Kerr and Dand his son, Robert Kerr, junior, the brother of Ferniehurst, and 'other gentlemen of Scotland who were there fled and saved themselves.' The following month Dand Kerr's son Walter with Sandy and Edward McDowell of Stordrike were taken prisoner by John Carr of Wark while old Mark Kerr narrowly escaped.

Robert's father William Kerr of Cessford was born around this time and by 1566 he had gained a notorious reputation of his own by murdering William Kerr, the Abbot of Kelso, with the brothers of the Laird of Ferniehurst. They apprehended the Abbot, who was the brother of Sir Andrew Kerr of Littledene, on his way to Kelso and cut off his arms and head in a savage assassination of a complex inter-family nature.

Six years earlier his father old Walter and Ferniehurst were telling Roger Heron that they would keep their word with the Governor of Scotland and cause no disorder in England. They'd also told Sir John Forster that they would declare to Lord Grey, along with the Laird of Hunthill and the Rutherfords, while Sir Andrew Kerr of Littledene and the Laird of Greenhead promised that if an English army entered Scotland, then they would burn and destroy in Glendale.

Kerr of Littledene was also demanding that Sir Henry Percy, the Earl of Northumberland, be delivered as his prisoner to avoid this happening; Buccleuch and the Scotts were suing the Governor to intercede for them with Lord Grey and the Turnbulls of Rule Water along with the Redesdale men were making promises to Earl Bothwell as peace deals were attempted. Lord Grey, however, was suspicious of Cessford and Ferniehurst and felt that they couldn't be trusted and preferred to talk with the lairds of Hunthill and

Greenhead, the Rutherfords, Sir Andrew Kerr of Littledene, Buccleuch and 'others who are suitors for the friendship of England.'

This was an affront to Cessford and by 1565 he was unable to answer over 100 bills and had to deliver his cousin as a pledge to the English. He promised to undertake a raid 'with 500 of the thieves of Teviotdale' in revenge. The Earl of Bedford, a son-in-law of old John Forster and a border official, was reporting from Berwick that the Teviotdale men had attacked on a market day and stolen, then when chased on a trod following another raid on a market had set an ambush at Chirnside where they badly injured several of their pursuers and took seven prisoners. Nicholas Harrington wrote to the English Privy Council that 'the thieves of Teviotdale continually make spoils. They will burn and destroy in England, and thereby break the peace so that all their attempts are stricken and not to be answered for.' During the chaos, Cessford rescued his cousin.

Mary, Queen of Scots, pardoned the young Cessford for murdering the Abbot but the Earl of Morton, the laird of Whittingham and George Douglas were still in trouble and the Queen was to be at Jedburgh on the 17th August 1566 which caused John Forster at Alnwick to gloat that 'the evil sort of the borderers' were afraid of her coming. Forster met with Cessford later that month, but the Queen had sent along the Lord of Trebrowne to keep an eye on him and see that he did justice; Forster reckoned that 'the cumbers are such by the slaughter of the Abbot of Kelso as he (Kerr) is not able to do what appertains to his office.' Mary, however, was forced to abdicate the throne just a year later and had to flee south into England to seek protection from her cousin Queen Elizabeth I. The Battle of Langside in May 1568 saw the Kerrs divided as Sir Walter of Cessford and his men fought in support of her son while Sir Thomas of Ferniehurst was a follower and supporter of Mary.

Sir Robert Kerr was born around 1570, making him a close contemporary of the young King James, and three years later his grandfather Walter was noted as being paid just '£16 by year, and yet his wardenry great and troublesome, and he of a good mind' as the Scots tried to sort out the boy King's finances and security by upping the pay for 'the better discharge of their offices.'

William took over the Warden of the Scottish Middle March role from his father in the 1580s but the feud between the two branches of the family were intensified as Sir Thomas Kerr of Ferniehurst unseated him in 1584; he was fearful of the reaction by the East Teviotdale crime families, however, and demanded pledges to stand for the crews loyal to Cessford. Ferniehurst's Catholicism was to prove his own downfall and he fled after failing to appear in connection with the murder of Lord Russell at a Truce Day. He was reported dead in Aberdeen in February 1586 and John Forster regretted that 'he and some betters had not been hanged.' The Cessfords were back as warden, provost of Jedburgh and keeper of Jedburgh forest in his absence.

Sir Robert Kerr came to prominence and in one of his first major actions at just seventeen led an invasion party of 3,000 men of Annandale, Ewesdale, Eskdale, Liddesdale and Teviotdale with Buccleuch and the Laird of Johnstone into Northumberland as far as Eslington. They murdered around 15 of Sir Cuthbert Collingwood's men and took Captain Bellas prisoner. Just a few days later Kerr was to be married to the Scottish chancellor Lethington's daughter at Dalkeith but King James forbade the union; it didn't bother Kerr too much as a couple of days later he married the lass anyway at his uncle's house at Newbottle. The King imprisoned him in Edinburgh for his trouble and also sent Bothwell to bring Buccleuch to be imprisoned in Blackness 'or some other prison.'

By 1595 Robert was executing the Warden's role on behalf of his elderly father, and his opposite number Ralph Eure noted that he received no pay for the role so 'his main estate of living forces him to befriend his clan, overlook outrages, and support lawless men about him who serve him without charge.' John Carey, the Governor of Berwick, worried about Cessford's 'daily plottings' to murder Englishmen and his crew were 'lying by dozens, and twenty, and sometimes forty, in secret places to murder any riding by themselves so that no man dare go about his own business or stay in his own house.' Kerr was a notorious killer and murdered his cousin William Kerr of Ancrum in 1590. Four years later he rode on Wooler with 80 men to murder two people and another at Kilham on the way home. He was back at Twissell looking for Storeys to slaughter soon after, sending all his men home apart from two and drinking in the local taverns. He caught up with one of the Storeys in January 1596 and murdered him in his house at night; the East Teviotdale gangs under his protection racked up 200 murders at the time in the general certificate 'and no restitution of 'quick for dead' by March Law,' wrote Eure. They were even falling out amongst themselves and two of the crews (unnamed) were in dispute with each other over the spoiling of one of Lord Northumberland's tenants with one family wanting to raid him and the other – he must have been paying them blackmail – not. He was left badly injured and nearly killed along with his wife, and the crew that wanted to spoil him returned anyway in revenge with 25 horsemen and 'totally beggared' the town. Kerr's gangs also saddled up to plunder Rugley and Glanton and broke into John Selby's house in Tynedale and cut him to pieces 'without known quarrel.'

Cessford was being bothered by Sir John Forster at Alnwick for not delivering William Elliot of Larriston for a Tynedale bill in 1593 and was given eight days notice to either deliver Elliot, himself, or a gentleman to stand for the charges while the following year both Cessford and Buccleuch were gaining favour with King James VI by 'professing ill will' towards the Earl of Bothwell. They had taken Kelso between them and the King was also promising them the Earl of Angus' lands.

Sir Robert often used violence as a means to an end and pulled a dagger and knocked about Sir John Kerr in the Edinburgh Tollbooth in 1595 to impress the Royal circles that he and Buccleuch were moving in and they were promised the disgraced Bothwell's land between them as both sought higher title. It caused some jealousy and distaste among their fellow headsmen and the lairds of Littledean, Ferniehurst, Greenhead, Hunthill and Hundalee quietly offered their service to the King as a 'counterpoise' to protect him if Buccleuch and Cessford 'should presume to 'over-high matters.' But with Scott, Kerr and Johnstone all becoming strong fixtures in the Establishment circle and attending Royal events such as visits by the English Queen, they were becoming virtually untouchable.

6. A PLAGUE ON YOUR HOUSE

THE YEAR 1597 was a bad one in the Borders. The Plague was back with outbreaks in Newcastle that spread to Hexham, Berwick, all over Northumberland, the Merse and Teviotdale, Edinburgh and Carlisle. Black death had come in on a boat at the port of Tyne and caused an agonising end of fever, splitting headaches, pains in the limbs and back, huge dark lumps oozing blood and pus, projectile vomiting and internal bleeding for thousands down as far as Richmond in Yorkshire, Penrith and Kendal in the west and Dumfries up in Scotland. The reivers, however, seem to have avoided the worst of the epidemic with the rural seclusion of their peels and bastle houses and the old volcanic hills of the Cheviots providing them with some protection.

With the crime in the area also at epidemic proportions, the authorities took steps towards brokering a peace in the troubled lands by the 'exchange of the principal malefactors as pledges, to facilitate business.' A Border Commission was set up with the Scotsmen the Bishop of Dunkeld, George Hume of Wedderburn, Andrew Kerr of Fawdonside and George Young and their opposite numbers in England the Bishop of Durham, William Bowes, Francis Slingsby and Clement Colmore. The Commission would handle the delicate business of gathering the men and dealing with the compensation that they owed for thefts and plunder. They also set out 36 articles in a Treaty signed at Carlisle in May which dealt with everything from good ministers being placed in every border church to matters of murders, deadly feud and even banning 'broken borderers from keeping idle persons and none such to remain in a border village or alehouse, or they shall be 'billable' for doing so, as if they had resetted stolen goods.' A number of rules were also set out at the meeting for the entry of the pledges: firstly that two or more of every branch of broken men be entered for bills filed, on them and their branch; that the warden himself would enter a gentleman for similar bills on those not of any known clan; that their entry to be to their opposite officer between the day of the dissolving of the commission and 1st July next; commissioners to be appointed in each March to see their entry effected; to be kept by 'indifferent' men when entered, at their own expense, not with any with whom they are at feud or variance; that they should remain no longer than the bills for which they were entered were duly satisfied; if any died, another broken man of his clan should take his place; the pledges should be kept no longer than a year and a day after the commission was ended and, if the bills against their branch were not redressed, the opposite principal, if he chose, could take his life and call for another to lay another year on the same conditions and, most menacingly, that the pledges should answer at their peril for any attempts committed by their clan or surname while they were lying in ward.

Three months earlier the chief mover behind the taking of hostages, Sir William Bowes, had sent a letter to the Scottish officials detailing his motion as to the delivery of the pledges which he claimed that 'they seemed to like well,' and had dispatched George Young to Edinburgh to get the King's order to put it into action. Bowes felt at the time that the greatest barriers to peace were dangerous wardens (he was obviously having a pop at Kerr and Scott, who were becoming known as 'the two firebrands'), the boldness and unity of the riding surnames and their support upon other men's goods. He confided in Thomas Burghley that he thought Cessford and Buccleuch should be imprisoned by King James and 'more peaceable men placed in their offices,' that the chiefs of the border surnames should be interchangeably delivered without condition and that redress for bills be proceeded with at once.

The chief men that were demanded read like a veritable Who's Who of three and more centuries of conflict, bloodshed, theft and violence. They couldn't have selected a more representative group of rogues and villains and that was the whole purpose of the exercise.

The pledges demanded from the English side were - from Tynedale: Gib Charlton of Boughthill, Lowrie and Lyle Robson, Rowie Milburn of the Comb and Jock Dodd of Greenhaugh. From Redesdale: Rob Hall, younger of Monkridge, John Hall of Gressonfield, John Reed of Troughend, Allan Hedley of Hatherwick, George Wanless of Durtrees, Percy Pott of Yardhope, Tom Coxson of the Woolawe and John Snowdon, and from the West March: Will's Arthur Graham of Netherby, Will's Geordie of the Fauld and John Graham of West Linton, the Goodman of the Mote (Graham), Tom Storey of Howend, Sim Taylor, Rowy Forster of Kershopefoot, 'Little' George Hetherington of Brownhill, Dand's Quintin Nixon, Richie Routeledge of Cancroupe, Anthon's Edward Armstrong of Willgavy and George Bell of Bowbank, for the Bells of Gilsland. Two pledges were requested by George Home and George Young from the English East March as well – William Selby, the Laird of Pawston, and Ralph Reveley of Aykeld, although Selby disappears from subsequent lists.

The Scottish pledges were – for the West March: John Armstrong of Hollows, Jock Armstrong 'Kinmont's Jock', Geordie 'Kang' and Hobbie Irvine, Will 'Red Cloak' Bell, Edward Carlyle of the Limekiln, Will 'Clothman's Willie' Graham and David Johnstone of the Redhaugh. For Liddesdale: Sim Armstrong Laird of Mangerton, Sim Armstrong of Whitehaugh, Will Elliot of Larriston, Will Elliot of the Steel, Archie Elliot, the son of Martin Elliot, and John Nixon of the High Eshes. And for Teviotdale: Ralph Aynsley of Cleethaugh, Jock Burn younger of Cote, Ralph Burn, Robert Frissell, Laird of Overton, Will and Ralph Hall of the Sickes, Dand Davison, Ralph Mow of Mow, William Tait of Cherrytrees, Dand Pringle, younger of Hownam, Jock Robson of Oxnam, James Young of Feltershaws and James Young of the Cove.

Getting criminal underbosses of this calibre to submit to imprisonment was always going to be a tall order and it was a bold move towards ending the reign of the Border mafia for good; the Bishop of Durham noted that both Cessford and Buccleuch were against the idea of taking pledges as 'their best followers are among the worst headsmen of these broken clans.' They had been selected as the 'most notable offenders' by their opposites and the commissioners were concerned by reports that 'insolent borderers of the greatest clans are combining to defeat the negotiation, and openly say that the pledges 'will not enter for King or Kaiser" so they feared that the plan could be sunk before it was even implemented.

The delivery of the pledges was scheduled for ten o'clock on the morning of 25 June 1597 at the West Ford of Norham and Sir Robert

Carey felt that 'if things are done as they ought to be, the borders will be in good quiet.' They weren't, of course.

Sir Robert Kerr and Sir Walter Scott did show up but they hindered the meeting with 'frivolous delays' until eight o'clock at night. Four of the English West March pledges were missing and all of the Scottish West March pledges, two of the Liddesdale and three of the Teviotdale men weren't there either. The English contingent were keen to hand their pledges over to Lord Hume but Carey reckoned that when Cessford and Kerr were pressed for theirs they told the commissioners 'that they would not deliver them, and that none else shall deliver them, except if the King himself did it.' The English weren't blameless; they had known as early as the 13 June that they would struggle to take Anton's Edward Armstrong and were putting plans in place so that 'the next best of the kin of such fugitives to be delivered in his stead, that we may be able to satisfy the King and this Estate,' and urged Lord Scrope that 'no occasion of complaint should be given to the Wardens Officers in Scotland.' They didn't give him the details of the location for the transfer until three days beforehand either. Buccleuch hadn't been that willing to show up himself, but the King had rounded on him and 'so sharply threatened to surrender him to the Queen if he failed to deliver his pledges that Buccleuch hurried back from Falkland to Edinburgh to obtain the help of the Council to procure a longer time for the delivery of them,' according to Sir William Bowes. He also said that at the meeting, following a 'secret conference had by some discreet men of ours with them of Teviotdale and Liddesdale I was advertised that they stood resolute to deliver no pledges, and grounded that assurance upon special warrant from the King.' The meeting broke up as nightfall descended.

Plans for the re-delivery of the pledges were re-drawn in early August with King James stating that if any of the Scottish pledges were missing then the warden himself should be delivered to Queen Elizabeth. The English wardens were to have men ready to place instead of any that were missing on their part and as the laird of Johnstone had been removed from the West March wardenry, a separate 'long day' for the delivery of West March men was to be arranged for a later date. There was some intrigue at foot as well as

Sir Robert Kerr had met with Ralph Eure at Stawford and 'protested his willingness to serve Her Majesty by quieting the borders.' He wouldn't write it down and wanted to let it be known by 'secret words.' He also told Eure at a later 'secret conference' that it was impossible for some of the borderers to make satisfaction for the bills filed against them and others were discontented at having to give pledges. He said that 'if the Queen showed him favour' then he would not only tell her who the disturbers were but would also 'show how to suppress them and be an actor himself therein.' It seemed that Cessford was using the pledges as a bargaining chip for his own purposes while playing both sides in time-honoured Border fashion. Buccleuch was detained in ward by the King until he delivered his pledges and a new date for delivery was set for the 29 September, again at the Norham West Ford. It was another farce; two of the English pledges were missing, four from Liddesdale and six from East and West Teviotdale so a new delivery date of Saturday 8 October was implemented. Eure said that one of his pledges had been grievously wounded by the Scots and another was seriously ill so they couldn't attend while Cessford had spent the best part of the day negotiating with the likes of Sir William Bowes, John Carmichael, Ferniehurst, Lord Hume and Sir George Hume on the Scottish side of the ford, which had been swollen to a raging torrent by rain, until nightfall again broke things up.

Tempers were getting frayed by the third meeting, which was broken up by foul play. By the time that Cessford and Buccleuch got to the West Ford it was getting on for three o'clock and the Scots contingent were still causing delays. Finally, Buccleuch was called forward to deliver his pledges and he replied that he couldn't get them and would deliver his son instead; Sir William Bowes wouldn't allow this, so he offered himself as a pledge. He was taken over the water to the English side and the Scots then asked for the English Middle March pledges, who were sent over with those of the East March. When the English called for Cessford's East Teviotdale pledges, he crossed over with them and 'made a show of delivering them' but one of his riders fired a pistol and another slumped forward on his horse crying: 'slain! slain!' with another shouting: 'treason! treason!' and it all kicked off.

Darkness was drawing in and the English soldiers, that had attended from Berwick garrison, fired off some shot across the water in the general confusion without hitting anyone while a fray of general fighting broke out. Lord Hume protected Sir William Bowes by gathering him in his arms and saying that they'd have to shoot through him to hit Bowes as the rest of the Humes swept down to guard their chief and the Teviotdale riders also charged down to the ford. Cessford was blamed for the disorder and Bowes felt that the East Teviotdale men wanted to kill him – one had a dagger at his back during the mayhem, which was pulled away by the Hume Laird of Eaton, and he'd been hearing whispers that they 'desired to cut me off from stinging them anymore.' He wrote to Burghley that 'this desperate people will leave nothing untried to hinder the general justice.' A week later Bowes was trying to induce Kerr to hand himself over in place of his pledges though the Warden was 'exceedingly wary' of doing so and the commissioner swore that he would only deal with Lord Hume.

Buccleuch had been taken back to Berwick by the English party after the fray on the transfer day and by the 18 October the Governor of the town wanted him off his hands with safer places such as York or Hull being suggested as possibilities to detain him, as he had been housed with William Selby, the burgess of Berwick, whereas the English pledges that had been delivered across the Ford were dismissed by Hume.

Two days later Bowes wrote to the Humes demanding that Kerr be handed over in place of his pledges before the 5 November at a meeting near Foulden, which was ignored. Selby reckoned that Kerr was uncertain what to do and wrote to Cecil that Cessford 'was sometimes minded to enter himself and not his pledges, and other times his pledges not himself' and felt that his 'good entertainment' of his brother-in-law might induce Kerr to submit himself.

But by the 26th the King himself had written to Bowes requesting that Buccleuch be released on bond due to a technicality – the Scots hadn't received anyone from the English side for the Liddesdale Keeper, so the treaty had been broken – and Buccleuch would enter his only son in his place for a while, so that he could have the time to hunt down his pledges, who were now declared fugitives. James had also ordered the Teviotdale pledges to be placed in his hands so he could have them ready for delivery at any new meeting. But the English pledges were gone and in hiding, Wedderburn and Bowes were discussing the possibility of naming new pledges, and the whole episode had left Bowes 'almost past hope of getting any pledges.'

It was never going to be easy and all the while the raids continued. The Bishop of Durham questioned why 'the Scottish and English thieves are quietly allowed to ride from the head of Liddesdale through Redesdale to the very seaside at and around Warkworth…throughout Northumberland, over and over, again and again, without impeachment' and 'wished himself once quit of these troublesome border affairs.' They would try the patience of a Saint, so a Bishop was no different matter and old Toby was well and truly sick of the whole affair.

King James rode on the Scottish West March and hanged 18 men of surnames for 'being common spoilers of the country' before taking pledges back to Edinburgh with him 'for the quiet of Scotland' though it was noted that none of the West March pledges demanded by England were among them, while Buccleuch remained detained with William Selby in mid-December and the Englishman was complaining that Scott was 'troublesome and very chargeable,' in other words costing him money, and he still wanted him out of his hands. By late January 1598 Buccleuch was offering Bowes that he would enter his pledges 'or demolish their houses, destroy whatsoever is in their possession and expel them and enter another that was given to him in lists in their place' if he could be released for a reasonable time to apprehend them as the row over pledges rumbled on and on.

On the 4th of February an agreement was signed at Edinburgh for the delivery of pledges at the fourth attempt at Foulden and the Scots moved that as Buccleuch was detained in Berwick, he would enter his own son as caution and deliver the indented pledges for Liddesdale before the end of April. All of the old English East and Middle March pledges were to be delivered and for any absent Sir William Bowes would enter to Lord Hume or his deputy, Henry Bowes for Tynedale and Ralph Mansfield for Redesdale, to be held until the missing pledges were entered.

Sir Robert Kerr was to deliver the Scottish East and Middle March pledges that had been formerly agreed upon to Berwick the following day and the Governor John Carey, Robert Carey or Bowes himself, with Kerr to hand himself over to one of the three if any of his pledges were missing. The Scottish West March pledges had escaped and 12 new names of men from the same original clans were to be delivered on March 1, with the English West March at the same time and place. It was signed by King James.

The exchange of the English pledges took place at Foulden with Henry Bowes, and Ralph Mansfield also being held in place of those missing but the Teviotdale men didn't show at Berwick. The English waited until sunset when Lord Hume sent a man with a message and met with Bowes up on Halidon Hill where he handed Kerr over in their place. Buccleuch was freed and his son 'about ten years old and a proper and toward child' delivered to John Carey in his place.

The English Queen wanted Kerr transferred to the Archbishop of York, but the Godfather still had cards to play and told the newly appointed Middle March Warden Robert Carey that he had all his pledges ready before his own entry, and he could get them now at a day's warning and 'free himself at his pleasure.' Cessford reckoned that he'd only submitted himself to 'let the Queen know his willingness to satisfy her displeasure by his humble submission' and that he was ready to right past wrongs. He had earlier told his pledges not to enter as he would sort things out 'some other way,' so who knows what plans he had; he was granted an audience with the Queen in March, while still detained at Carey's, and by early April Buccleuch delivered five pledges to Henry Leigh and an English official noted that although Kerr was still held for the default of East and West Teviotdale, it was 'uncertain how long he would lie until their entry was performed.'

On 3 June 1598 Kerr delivered his pledges at the Norham West Ford at the fifth time of asking and they were handed over to the new Governor Lord Willoughby who took them to Berwick, describing the crew as 'beggarly knaves' who were much esteemed by Kerr and pointed out that Cessford wanted to 'have as much favour as Buccleuch, for reputation's sake.' They were transferred to York on the 22nd June and committed to the custody of Robert Redhead, the keeper of York castle.

Kerr told the Queen and Council that his men were 'the best and chiefest of their surnames' and their detention would be 'a special means to bridle the rest from outrages' but warned that 'if any hard measure was offered to them 'unpawned' they would be stirred to exceed all former malices.' He also asked the Queen a favour by stating that he 'could better keep the peace if assisted by some of those men detained, than in their absence; for being wiser than the rest, more obedient to him, and well effected of the common sort, they would possibly keep these in good behaviour and give him information to further preservation of peace,' adding that it was King James' desire as well as his own. Buccleuch was giving similar warnings about the Liddesdale pledges and wrote that 'where there is no hope, there is no fear.'

7. THE ENGLISH PLEDGES

Tynedale

Gib Charlton of Boughthill

A knight named Sir Thomas Charleton was captured alongside Lord Montague (John Neville) in a bloody battle during the War of the Roses in 1462 which saw around 3,000 men killed on both sides. He was lucky; Lord de Bonneville and Sir Thomas Kiryel were taken and beheaded.

There were Charltons (original spelling Charleton) in Tynedale from before 1293 when Adam de Charlton was making a claim on his grandfather's lands. Edward Charlton built their first tower at Hesleyside in around 1343 and the family were ever-present in the reiving history of North Tynedale.

Alexander Charlton of Shitlington Hall stabbed and killed Alexander Elliot at Epsleywood in 1518 and importantly, in 1521, the Charltons killed the chief of the Scotts of Buccleuch and took his sword. In 1595 Walter Scott was naming that incident as the reason behind his blood feud with the Charltons and complaining that they refused to give his grandfather's sword back. Buccleuch was there when his men killed four Boughthill Charltons in Tynedale two years earlier 'for revenge of an ancient feud' – the killing of his grandad and the taking of his sword. Buccleuch also said he'd come back and kill some more; he had earlier been at Greenhaugh looking for Charltons to kill but had to be satisfied with burning a widow's house and her corn.

The fact that the Charltons were 'the sufficientest and ablest men' on the Borders, according to John Carey, and had not only taken back their goods after an earlier raid by the Scotts but had 'encouraged their neighbours to do the like and not be afraid' no doubt also got Buccleuch's back up.

In the March of 1596 there was an appeal 'to all Christian people' to put an end to the 'deadly and detestable feuds' existing between the Ogles, Widdringtons, Fenwicks, Herons, Ramseys, Selbys,

Shaftoes, Mitfords, Ridleys, Erringtons, Lawrences, Thorntons, Aynslyes, Clennels, Pawstons, Halls, Reeds, Hedleys, Potts, Charltons, Robsons, Hunters, Dodds, Milburns and Redheads of England and the Elliots, Armstrongs, Crosers, Lawrences, Hendersons, Beatties, Simpsons and Littles of Scotland. It didn't have much effect; just fifteen days later the Charltons, Milburns, Robsons and Dodds launched a retaliatory raid on Buccleuch's lands.

The Charltons had always been in the thick of the action and in 1523 Willie Charleton of Shitlington and his brother John, with their wives and children, were to be banished from Tynedale along with Willie Ridley and Percy Green or be delivered to the warden, lieutenant or sheriff for justice.

A year later William Charleton of Bellingham and his brother Roger were executed alongside two of the Robsons who had been captured with Robert Robson of Bindmyrehill. Thomas Charleton of Caryteth was acquitted while the aforementioned Percy Green 'a noted thief' who fled into Scotland was to be hung in chains.

The Charletons and their neighbours weren't averse to teaming up with gangs of Scottish reivers to wreak havoc on the countryside and in 1527 after Sir William and Humphrey Lisle had been broken out of prison at Newcastle they joined 'a band of thieves called the Armstrongs' and with the Charltons, Nixons, Dodds, and others, they burned Humshaugh. All of those involved were proclaimed rebels and outlaws.

The rebel Charltons were raiding with the Armstrongs again in 1528 and Will Charlton, late of Shitlington, with James Noble, Roger Armstrong and Archibald Dodd robbed the parson of Muggleswick. They were chased along the swollen waters of the Tyne as far as Haydon Bridge and finally apprehended. Charlton was killed by Thomas Errington and Noble was also killed. Roger Armstrong and Archibald Noble were taken prisoner and later hung at Newcastle and Alnwick. Charlton's body was hung in chains on a gallows at Hexham and Noble's at Haydon Bridge.

Will Charlton was named as the head rebel of all the outlaws and when news of his death and the fact that Northumberland was threatening to invade Nederdale if Angus did not give them up reached the others, they surrendered at the parish Church at Alnwick.

William and Humphrey Lisle with 15 others, in their shirts with halters draped around their necks met the Earl as he was coming from mass.

Despite their frequent involvement in the troubles, the Charltons were important enough to appear before King Henry VIII at Hexham in 1535 and give bonds for the delivery of future offenders. The headsmen present were Edward Charlton of Hesleyside, Thomas Charlton of Howkupp, Rynie Charlton of Shitlington, Roger Charlton of the Bower and Tommy Charlton of Newton.

In a muster at York a year later Edward Charlton of Hesleyside and Cuthbert Charlton of Bellingham appeared for Tynedale, while Northumberland was represented by Sir Thomas Percy, Sir Cuthbert Radcliffe and Sir John Widdrington and the Hexhamshire representatives were George Ogle, Oswald Shelley and John Ridley of Corsenside.

An interesting list from 1537 gave the officers, and their wages, for 'the keeping of the East and Middle Marches safe from Scotland, Tynedale and Redesdale.' Sir William Eure was to be deputy warden of the East March on 200 marks a year with assistance from Sir Roger Gray, Sir Robert Ellerker, Thomas Forster, Thomas Gray, Ralph Etherington, John Carr, Thomas Heburne, Richard Folberry, Edward Mustians, John Selby of Branxton, Thomas Hoborn of Hoborn, William Strother, Lionel Gray and Thomas Carr. Sir Roger, Thomas Gray and Ellerker were paid £20, the rest £13 6s. 8d.

Sir John Widdrington was to be deputy warden in the Middle March at 200 marks with the following to assist him: The lord Ogle, £50; Sir Cuthbert Ratcliffe, Sir John De Lavale, Sir Wm. Ogle, and Sir Reynold Carnaby, at £20; Robert Collingwood, John Ogle, George Ogle, John Horsley, and John Ogle at £31 6s. 8d.

Where it gets interesting is when it comes to the appointment of the Keepers of Tynedale and Redesdale. They were valued positions for ambitious men outside of the gentry and were awarded to Roger and George Fenwick at £26 13s. 4d. The head men of Tynedale were made assistants at £10 each – Edward and Cuthbert Charlton, Henry and Geoffrey Robson and Christopher and David Milburn.

John Hall of Otterburn and Sandy and Anthony Hall got the Redesdale positions at £10 each. It stirred up some resentment and

Roger Fenwick was murdered with the Charltons being accused of the deed. The King was unperturbed and showed how out of touch they were down in London when he dismissed claims for 300 soldiers to be sent to the Borders, telling the council of the Marches to 'apprehend the two Charltons and send them up forthwith.'

The Law attempted to stamp their authority and sent word to Tynedale that they were to apprehend twelve of the most notable local offenders; Tynedale sent word back that they wanted fifteen days to answer. The authorities feared that they would flee into Scotland and set about harrying the countryside; Robert Collingwood, the sheriff of Northumberland, 'sent ten light horse to Waterfall Rigg on Fylton More, between Tyndale and Redesdale, and took some cattle belonging to the people, in hopes that the men of Tyndale would have pursued and fallen into an ambush; but they, suspecting such a thing, did not attempt a rescue.' The principal offenders refused to submit and 'fed their horses and laid watches as men always in dread, being always ready to flee into Scotland.'

Cuthbert Charlton was named as 'one of the causers of the murder of Roger Fenwick, by means of John Heron,' and he died while in detention. An official note stated that they wished 'his fellow Edward Charlton, were with him.' Edward, Ninian and John Charlton, along with John Heron, the illegitimate son of John Heron of Chipchase, and others, were outlawed. The Charltons remaining at Hesleyside were 'doing much harm to the King's subjects' and Charlton of the Bower and others refused to give pledges to the Duke of Norfolk. Sir Reynold Carnaby, now made the Keeper of Tynedale, had put Edward Charlton in place of the rebel Edward Charlton at Hesleyside, but he fled in fear and Hesleyside's family had kept possession of the tower and stead.

Pledges were finally taken from the families and were kept at the Sergeant's house, having to show themselves every day to the sheriffs of the town. John Robson of the Falstone and Gib Charlton were being held and were described as 'two of the most active men in Tynedale' and although they had promised to help bring the fugitives to justice, the authorities began to smell a rat and felt that they'd just stood as pledges to be freed of their promises to the Duke of Norfolk. It was felt best to remove John and Gib to Newcastle '18 miles from their county; for in-coming hither they learn all the bye ways of the country, and are emboldened to steal, knowing which way to escape. We will take them to Newcastle at our going and leave them there.'

The bother wasn't going away and in 1538 a number of Sir Reynold Carnaby's prisoners, including John Stokoe, had died of the plague in Warkworth Castle – except Jerry 'Topping' Charlton, who was described as 'the only accuser of John Heron of Chipchase and the other murderers of Roger Fenwick' was still living. He was accused of a number of robberies and the officials were at a loss with what to do with him. 'Topping' was freed from Hexham gaol later that year along with Clement Armstrong and two of the Dodds by the Liddesdale riders 'together with the English outlaws, Charltons and their fellows.'

They couldn't trust the English so in 1540 a great number of the Charltons ducked over the Border to avoid the Law and John Charlton of Larederburn, Percy Charlton, and Eddie Charlton's sons went to Robin Elliot's while Rany Charlton of the Nuke and John Charlton of the Blacklaw were reset with Clemmy and John Croser. Gerry 'Topping' Charlton had also crossed the Border, but it wasn't specified – or perhaps known – where he was staying.

Three years later two of the outlawed Charltons brought in their Scottish friends the Elliots, Nixons and Crosers to burn Capheaton on the South Tyne. However, a letter sent from officials at Alnwick reported that a widow, one of the Middlemoors of Tyndale, 'sent to her kinsfolk in Tynedale to rescue her goods, and a great fray ensued in which many were hurt on both sides, so that Liddesdale and Tynedale which have been such friends are like to be at feud.'

Edward Charlton was in bother again in 1562 when an Act for the Restitution in Blood was passed against him in London. The same act was passed against Sir Ralph Bulmer, Knight and Thomas Percy.

The Charlton's friendship with the Scots was a distant memory by 1583 when Gilbert Charlton and his son Gilbert, Roland Charlton, Cuthbert Charlton, Ranold Charlton, Thomas Charlton along with two Dodds, four Milburns, two Hunters, two Fletchers and 30 others of Tynedale were taken prisoner by the Armstrongs of Liddesdale and Annandale following a series of massive raids. In that year the

Charltons, Herons, Fenwicks, Shaftoes, Erringtons, Widdringtons, Ogles, Halls and Milburns were all English familes described as being at feud while on the Scottish side the Elliots, Armstrongs, Nixons, Crosers, Turnbulls and Olivers were also engaged in deadly revenge and retribution on whole surnames.

But there were still some ties across the Border and in an episode of intrigue and espionage in 1585 Edward Charlton of Hesleyside was implicated in the murder of Lord Russell at a Truce Day at Cocklaw. Charlton had received coded writings from the Laird of Ferniehurst which were intercepted and taken to Lord Russell, who was later killed. William Kerr of Ancrum, James Kerr of Lintloe and Robert Kerr his brother, Andrew Kerr Laird of Greenhead, John Rutherford of Hunthill, David Moscrop the deputy provost of Jedburgh, a Kirton, the warden sergeant and James Kerr were all 'put to the horn' and denounced rebels by the King of Scotland for refusing to enter England for trial over the murder.

In 1589 Henry Charlton complained that James Elliot of the Binks had stolen a gelding and his furniture (tack) from him and Edward Charlton of Hesleyside, gentleman, was a juror sworn at Hexham in 1596 in an enquiry into the 'decays of the Middle Marches.'

Edward of Hesleyside took delivery of six muskets with rests and handlers and barrels of powder from William Errington, a servant of Sir Simon Musgrave the master of ordinance in 1591 and in 1596 his kinsman and follower John Charlton of the Bower, who was noted as a great thief and 'notorious and infamous for felonies' was paid to serve in Tynedale after being acquitted on two charges and giving bonds for good behaviour. John was a bit suspect to Lord Eure as he was married to a daughter of Anthon's Edward Armstrong of Willgavy in Cumberland who was also noted as a 'great thief and maintainer of many others around him.' Armstrong had married all his daughters 'in the waters of Tyne' and John Charlton himself had several 'lewd and evil persons of name as followers.'

Interestingly, Anthon's Edward Armstrong moved from Cumberland into Liddesdale shortly after and was 'offered living by Buccleuch' while John Charlton escaped a gaoler and fled into Scotland to join his father-in-law and the Scottish Armstrongs. He was soon raiding Northumberland with Rinion Armstrong, stealing a black cow from John Dodd of Greenhaugh.

Lionel Charlton of Thornburgh was described by Ralph Eure as 'one of the greatest thieves in the Middle March' and he was captured in 1596 for offences including assisting both English and Scottish outlaws and burglary. Lord Eure reckoned that 'there is none like him,' and sent him to prison in Durham for trial.

Christopher Charlton 'another thief' went to London to see the Queen and ask for a pardon for himself and Lionel. It must not have worked as Eure was putting on the pressure from Hexham but it didn't seem to matter much to Lionel and Christopher, along with Roger Fowberry, Laird of Fowberry and Thomas Charlton, Laird of Howkupp, who were all at large after escaping from Durham gaol. When he was on the run, Lionel, along with another famous thief called Eddie Hall, bought two grey geldings in Yorkshire and took them over the border to sell to Sir Robert Kerr.

The pledge Gib Charlton of Boughthill was a reiver in the traditional style; in January 1596 Buccleuch wanted either him or Jock Dodd, called 'Jock Pluck,' in exchange for William Elliot of Hartscarth after they'd made raids on each other. The details were important enough to have been sent in a letter from King James VI to Eure. Gib had filed a bill at Berwick against the Laird of Buccleuch and William Elliot of Larriston a month later for the murder of the four Charltons in 1593, so was no doubt high up on Scott's wanted list.

In 1597 Matthew Charlton of Ellingham Rigg filed another bill against Robert Elliot of Thorlshope, Henry Nixon of Kilford and Hob and Alexander Armstrong. It was noted that Robert Elliot was already in Hexham jail and the others were unknown. Edward Charlton of Hesleyside and Isabelle Charlton of Boughthill (possibly Gib's wife) also had bills heard at Carlisle that year.

Gib Charlton may not have even gone into Scottish custody – it seems that he and the rest of the Tynedale pledges had been dismissed by Lord Alexander Hume in October 1597. Sir William Bowes said he did not know where they were, and when it came to rounding them up again, Bowes had to be satisfied with 'getting as many as he could.' To be fair to Hume, he had other things on his mind; Ralph Eure said he was 'very sick' back in the March of that year and 'the French disease' (syphilis) was hinted at while Sir George Hume of Wedderburn was critical of his Chief in a letter to Bowes as they discussed the pledges. By November, Lord Hume was thought to be infected with the Plague and several of his household had died from it as the Black Death reappeared in the Borderlands.

In 1601 Edward Charlton of Hesleyside was found guilty by lack of appearance on a bill of the Laird of Egerton's for 40 old kye and 10 oxen sworn by Andrew Rutherford of Blackchester and handed a hefty fine of £80.

Thomas the Laird of Howkupp, nicknamed 'John of the Hills,' who been a fugitive since his prison escape, was raiding again in 1602 with Tom and William Thompson of The Aspes; they broke into and burgled the dwelling of William Wilkinson at Newton, stealing from him nine sheep hoggs. The notorious John of the Bower 'with various other unknown persons' – most probably his Armstrong in-laws – was back and broke into and burgled the house of a widow called Margaret Elrington of Espsheiles and stole 15 cows from her in November 1603.

Lowrie and Lyle Robson

The Robsons of North Tynedale had a long association with reiving in the valley and as far back as 1293 a Thomas Robson was killed by Ralph Bond at Newbrough when he caught him in the process of burgling his house during the night and struck him twice with his sword. The other burglars escaped into the darkness.

A William Robson from Tarsethope was beheaded for killing Alicia, the daughter of Bernard the Miller. Robson fled but was captured and tried by the coroner William de Bellingham.

The Bishop of Durham excommunicated the riders of both Tynedale and Redesdale in 1498 but Lawry, Davey and Sandy Robson – along with a number of Charltons, Milburns and Dodds - were eventually released from the religious ban on condition that weren't allowed to 'wear a jack or helmet nor ride a horse worth more than 6s. except against the Scots or the King's enemies nor enter a church or a place consecrated to God with any weapons exceeding the length of one cubit.'

Also, in that year, David Scott, called Lady, in Stirkshaws, was charged with 'treasonably in-bringing' the Robsons, Dodds and Charltons to burn Adam Rutherford's place at Hirdmanstone. Never ones to miss an opportunity, they also lifted a number of horses and mares and burned his corn.

When Lord Dacre demanded pledges from the four North Tynedale heidsmen, naming William, Roger and Thomas Charlton, and Robert Robson of Byndmyrehill, the Robsons held out and refused to hand anyone over at Bellingham church. Seeing this as an affront, Dacre, who had made his name at Flodden Field, sent out a night-time snatch squad and captured five of the Surname including the named Robert Robson. He had him executed immediately as an example to the others. The King sent word that he 'was pleased with the execution of Robert Robson and wished him to deal likewise with the rest of the four Robsons that he had in ward.'

Displaying again the cross-border ties developed during raiding and the disdain for the laws of the respective countries, in 1520 the Robsons and Potts teamed up with the Scottish Rutherfords and Douglases, bringing with them 'sleuth hounds' to spoil the town of Kilham and lifting 500 sheep, then hurting the 'poor men and women following their goods.'

Henry Robson of the Falstone was being held prisoner at Morpeth in 1528 alongside Sandy Yarrow, Clement and Ralph Charlton of Carroteith, 'Dumb' Davey Milburn, one of Eddie Dodd's sons and Will Charlton, the brother of Gib of the Bought Hill.

A Robson and two of the Yarrow family were killed in April 1537 when a party of Armstrongs, Fosters and Routledges, numbering 200, launched a raid on the Charlton's tenants and lifted 12 score oxen and kyne and 12 horses and mares.

The Robsons were long at feud with the Armstrongs, the Elliots and the Grahams; the famous and oft-repeated legend being that when the Robsons once launched a raid on Grahams and brought back their sheep, they had scab and infected their flock. The Robsons rode back, hanged four Grahams and left a note saying: 'Next time gentlemen come to take your sheep, they are not to be scabbed.'

Also in 1537 John Robson of the Falstone was named as 'one of the most active men in all Tynedale' along with Gib Charlton. One year later John, Jeffrey Robson, Archie Robson and Henry Robson of the Hall Hill were signatories with the Charltons, Milburns, Dodds, and a Wilkinson, in making oaths to the Duke of Norfolk 'for injuries done during the late rebellion.' They did, however, state that they might not abide by a new order that had come down from the commissioners.

Three years later John Heron of Chipchase, in a letter to the council of the North, wrote that he'd been in Tynedale to try and apprehend Belling and Falstone; he caught John of the Falstone's cousin James, who he reckoned was 'the sharpest man of them' and put him in jail in Newcastle but 'Cold Lyle' 'got away in his shirt'. He feared that the outlaws would steal away into Scotland, and he was right.

John Robson of the Falstone and his sons Lyle, Renye and Dudde, Archie Robson, Lyle Robson called Cowld, John Robson and his father Henry, brother to James Robson, Jock Robson of Newton, Henry Robson of Croshels and Willie and Henry Robson, 'sons to Broked Davie,' were named in a list of English rebels reset within Scotland – the Tynedale thieves using the Border line to their advantage as a number of Scotsmen were also listed as reset in England. The Robsons were staying at Clemmy Croser's place in Liddesdale.

The following year thirty of the Scottish Turnbulls murdered Geoffrey Robson, who was described as 'one of the head men and best ordered of Tynedale' and fired his house hoping to draw the rest of the Tynedale riders into an ambush waiting near Gamelspath.

The omerta that persisted in Tynedale was evident in 1543 as Eddie Robson killed a man that was going to Lord Norfolk but got off by pleading self-defence. It was noted that men were ready to inform on each other but 'shrink from appearing at open trial against gentlemen or men of great surname, insomuch that at last sessions in Northumberland many evil doers were quit for lack of evidence.' The following year Percy Robson had cattle taken by the Armstrongs and Nixons of Liddesdale when they were riding as 'assured' Englishmen during the Rough Wooing with Sir Thomas Wharton. The Nixons also murdered a Tynedale man called Bartie Young because he'd been a guide for Sir Ralph Eure when he burnt Mangerton tower. Eure was unsure whether to take revenge for the attacks or not as the raiders were assured but threatened that if he heard nothing from Suffolk then he would 'do them or some of their friends like displeasure unless he heard to the contrary.'

The headsmen of the Robson 'graynes' in 1559 were Symont Robson of Langhaugh, Andrew Robson of the Belling and Hobb Robson of the Falstone.

An English rebel named Robson, alias 'Foulmouth' had been fugitive in Scotland for seven years and committed many spoils in England during that time but was handed over for justice at a Reidswire truce day in 1563. At another truce day in 1575, which became known as the 'Battle of the Reidswire,' Henry Robson of the Falstone was killed along with a man called Simonson, Mr. Fenwick and Robert Shaftoe as the proceedings went horribly wrong.

When the Robsons and their allies the Charltons, Milburns and Dodds were accused of driving over 1,000 sheep out of Buccleuch's Liddesdale territory in March 1595 and the Keepers of Tynedale and Redesdale of lying in ambush to attack the Scots following their goods, the retaliation was premeditated, two years in the planning, and vicious.

The English Middle March Warden Eure denied that such a raid had even taken place but on Sunday 17 April 1597 Buccleuch raided the North Tyne and caused carnage – 19, including William Robson, were 'slain violently,' five, including poor little Cuthbert Robson, who was only five, were 'burned innocent' and two of the Dodds, including 2 year old Ralph Dodd, were 'slain innocent' in a sickening attack. William Robson and Richard Oliver were taken prisoner. The houses and steads of Thornburn, Donkleywood and Stokoe were burned.

There was a similar raid in 1611 on the Robsons which is often noted as one of the last large-scale invasions on the Border. A wild crew from Liddesdale including Robert Elliot of Redheugh and his brother William, Robert Elliot of Copshaw and his brother Francis, Robert Elliot of Dinlabyre, and his two brothers Gavin and William, William Elliot, called 'Rinyons Willy,' Robert Elliot, called 'Martins Hob', of Prikenhaugh and Christopher Elliot, his son, with Lancelot Armstrong, of Whitehaugh called the 'Young Laird,' Alexander

Armstrong, of the Roan, brother of Lancelot, Francis Armstrong of Whitehaugh and his son Lancelot, Robert Forster, called the 'Young Laird of Fowl Shields,' William Elliot of Prikenhaugh with John Shiels, Archibald Roger, John Elliott called Black John and Robert Elliott of the Park, men to Robert Elliot of Redheugh, with around 70 others, descended on Tynedale to slaughter and maim.

Lyle Robson of the Small Burn was killed by a single shot through his heart. Elizabeth Yarrow of Stannisburn was shot with a bullet through each of her legs, breaking her right thigh, and died; Walter Robson, of the Old Side, had his left arm broken in two places by bullets and Thomas Robson, of Yarrow Hall, was hit in the back and haunches with shot. Another bullet went through his pants and just missed his skin. James Robson's wife Mary was shot in the breasts and the pregnant wife of Geoffrey Robson, Elizabeth, was hit in the head by a stroke of a bow. Rinyon Robson, of the Belling, injured his hands after being shot with a bullet and an arrow from a long bow.

Robert Charlton of Boughthill, James Charlton of Boughthill, Francis Robson of Stannishburn, William Robson of Yarrow Hall; Henry Robson of Well Haugh; Anthony Robson of Crosse Hills; Rinyon Robson of Falstone and John Dodd of the Riding were all lucky to escape unscathed as bullets went through their clothing but didn't hit them.

William Robson was taken and ransomed by a gang of Elliots, Crosers and Nixons in 1589 but John Robson of Woodhouses was raiding Liddesdale in 1597 and another 30 bills were heard at Carlisle from the Armstrongs and Elliots against the Robsons, Charltons and Dodds as the reiving across the moors above Kielder went in both directions.

Lyle Robson did not appear at the West Ford meeting but the choice of one of three others of the surname were offered up to Lord Hume to take his place and they, along with Laurie Robson, were released by Lord Hume in 1597 and vanished.

The Robsons maintained their reiving heritage during the pacification of the Borders and in 1605 John Robson of Charleton, the son of William Robson, stole a grey horse from Michael Hunter at a place called Waterhead near Bellingham.

In 1611 Geoffrey Robson of Yarrowhall and James Robson, called

Auld Thom's Jamie, of Barnsteet, were charged with poaching when they broke into the King's forest at Kildare in Tynedale and shot a stag with a gun then carried away the body.

A year later John Robson of Charleton was back in action with Roger Robson of Charleton, William Robson of Charleton and John Robson, alias Sharpe, of Charleton when they broke in and stole 'one hawked cow, one branded 'guye' and one branded stott' from John Stawper of Whitton at the Dean Burn, Rothbury.

Rowie Milburn of the Comb

Rowie Milburn was a relative – a brother or a son - of the celebrated North Tyne reiver Bartie Milburn of the Comb.

Bartie is often mistakenly said to hail from the nearby pele at Bogg Head but was definitely from the Comb in the Tarset valley. Legend has it that Bartie and his neighbour 'Corbitt Jack' or probably Jack Corbett, went on a hot-trod to retrieve some stolen cattle from the Scots' side and added a few from another flock on their way back. They ran into two Scottish riders heading in the other direction while picking their way through the hills home and squared up to each other. While Jack Corbett was killed, Bartie finished off both of the Scots reivers and as he sliced one of their heads off with a powerful blow from his blade is said to have recounted that it 'sprang across the heather like an onion.' He took Jack's body home and laid it at his front door as was customary.

The tale may be fable but Bartie was a very real character and in 1583 he and Jenkyn Hunter of the Waterhead complained that Tarstet had been hit by the Armstrongs – and hit hard.

Kinmont Willie, Eckie and Tom of the Gingles, John Forster, son of 'Meikle Rowie' of Greenhaugh, George Armstrong called 'Rinion's Geordie' of Arkleton and his sons with 300 others plundered the Comb, the Redhaugh, Black Middens, Hill House, the Water Head, the Starr Head, the Bog Head and the High Field.

The Armstrongs burned the towers and drove away 400 kye and oxen, 400 sheep, goats, horses and mares, took £200 of goods from the houses and killed 6, maimed 11 and took 30 prisoners.

Just a year later, Liddesdale were back in force and Bartie Milburn,

Jenkyn Hunter, Gerry Hunter, Michael Milburn and Lance Milburn of Tarset were seeking justice after Davie Elliot called the 'Carling', Nebless Clem Croser, Sim's Tom Armstrong, Kinmont Will, Hector Armstrong of Hillhouse and 300 others lifted 40 score kye and oxen, three score horses and mares, 500 sheep, burned 60 houses, spoiled the houses to a value of £2000 and killed ten men in another terrifying day foray.

There were thirty Milburns in Tynedale in 1528 and four in neighbouring Redesdale. Interestingly, there were only 403 people inhabiting the barren wilds of Tynedale at the time, and 445 in Redesdale, in a book of names provided by the lord of Northumberland. To give an idea of the people making up the troublesome valleys, the Robsons were the biggest surname in Tynedale, with 62, followed by 54 Charltons and 53 Dodds. The rest of the families were named as follows – Yarrow, Thompson, Wilkinson, Stokoe, Hogg, Rede, Elwood, Hunter, Maxwell, Gray, Sisterson, Jones, Noble, Smyth, Ledderdales, Handwys, Jamieson, Bennet, Burn, Stamper, Willie, Frisell, Kyrsop, Ogleson, Dawson, Allendale, Quilden, Hall, Laing and Carrick.

Will Milburn was part of an international gang with the Scottish riders John Foster of Lyneholmes, Adam Foster, James son of Dowhill, Robin Foster called 'Robbie's Robin of Dobsonclose', Will Graham, called Auld Will, and Henry Scott who took the brothers Adam and James Porteous out of Tallawater in March 1534.

Three years later a Milburn was spoiled by Redesdale men in a raid which surprised the Border officials. It was noted that such a raid had not been heard of before as 'Redesdale was not as powerful as Tynedale.'

That same year Christopher and David Milburn were among a number of men from Tynedale and Redesdale that the Lord Norfolk would not have admitted into pensions as they were thieves or maintainers of thieves. Edward and Cuthbert Charleton, Henry and Geoffrey Robson, John Hall of Otterburn, and Sandy and Anthony Hall were the other notable felons.

Humphrey Milburn was caught up in the aftermath of the murder of Roger Fenwick and in 1538 was one of the signatories on a letter from the Tynedale men stating that they would appear before

Norfolk. Thomas Charlton, Gilbert Charlton, Garret Charlton of Wark, Gerry Charlton of the Bower, John Robson of the Falstone, Geoffrey Robson, Archie Robson, Rynyon Charlton, Henry Robson of the Hall Hill, Henry Parro, John Wilkinson, Henry Dodd and Archie Dodd also signed and when the clans fled into Scotland to avoid justice in 1540, John and Sim Milburn went along with the Robsons, Charltons, Dodds and a number of Stokoes, Hunters and Thompsons.

The Tynedale and Redesdale men were part of the burning and harrying of Teviotdale in 1544 and they took a number of Scottish prisoners to ransom on the way home from Jedburgh. Edward, Eddie, Anthony, Clemmy and William Milburn were part of a crew that lifted 59 men. William Bellingham, Henry Robson, George Charlton, William Charleton of Hesleyside, Wattie Bell, Henry Charleton, Pearce Charlton, George Hall, Tom Pott, and Eddie and William Hall all got in on the action.

As ever there were reprisals and in 1545 16 Scots of Jedburgh forest burned three of the Milburn's houses but they were away at their summer shielings. They intended to draw the Tynedale men into an ambush of 100 men on the waste near Redeshead. The same week, the Teviotdale riders also burned Farnam in Coquetdale in an attempt to draw the Redesdale men and the garrison from Harbottle into another ambush of 160 men waiting on the waste land near Cocklaw.

When George Heron of Chipchase sent Edward Charlton, Harry Charlton of the Larnerburn and John Charlton of Thorneyburn as prisoners to the jail at Hexham in 1559, their fellow captive Thomas Milburn, alias 'Thomas Headman,' was too sick to be taken. The Charltons, along with two Scottish pledges, escaped soon after and the jailer was nowhere to be seen. All the doors in the jail had been left open apart from the one where the jailer was meant to sleep and safeguard the prisoners. It wasn't an unusual occurrence at Hexham where the Tynedale reivers held much sway.

The pledge Rowie Milburn of the Comb was seeking justice in 1595 when the Elliots reived 60 head of cattle from him and Buccleuch told the Middle March Warden Eure that he would sort it out 'conditionally' if the English gave up those responsible for a raid on Will Elliot of Larriston, called 'Hartsgarth.'

Soon after the raid on Rowie, the Scots of Jedburgh forest robbed the widow Milburn of the High Field and took her, her children and her servants prisoner.

Rowie was handed over at the West Ford meeting but was gone with other English pledges that were released by Lord Hume in 1597. Where they had been detained prior to release is unclear, though the Humes often used Fast Castle as a centre for detention and had held John Heron there when he'd been handed over in the place of his illegitimate brother the Bastard following the killing of Sir Robert Kerr in 1511.

The families less troublesome than the North Tynedalers had been detained in the Tolbooth in Edinburgh for at least some of their term of imprisonment – early in December 1599 the Scottish Privy Council noted that George Wanless and Thomas Coxon of Redesdale, Ralph Reveley, John Snowdon, Percy Pott, Allan Hedley and John Reid of Troughend had been placed in the Tolbooth but were relieved 'out of ward' by Patrick Home of Ayton, who stood for Wanless and Coxon; Reveley was released by Sir George Home of Edinburgh, Snowdon, Pott and Hedley by Sir Andrew Kerr of Ferniehurst and Reid by Andrew, Lord Stewart of Ochiltrie. The Privy Council were demanding that the English pledges were returned to the Tolbooth within six days, however, or the men that had released them would have to pay all the damages to the 'parties damnifeit' that the pledges were entered for – but they disobeyed the order and while Wedderburn appeared for the Humes and was fined, Kerr didn't bother turning up and was denounced.

The pacification of the Borders following King James' ascension to the English Crown didn't stop the Milburns being involved in villainy and in 1607 William Milburn of the Cragg shield broke in and stole one red stott from Robert Woodman of Chollerton at the Cruke Bank.

The Milburns were tough stock and even their women could fight; in 1610 Elizabeth Milburn joined in with John Milburn and Rinyon Milburn, all of the Over Leme, and William Green of the Nether Leme to beat the living daylights out of their neighbours Ronald Hall of the Over Leme, John Hall of the Over Leme, Cuthbert Read of Birtley and Robert Hedley of the Heigh in a vicious assault.

In 1614 the farmer Cuthbert Milburn of Doustead stole four branded cows and two black 'quies' from William Glenn of Glantlee as the Tynedale reiving tradition went on in the now quaintly named 'Middle Shires.'

Jock Dodd of Greenhaugh

John Dodd of Greenhaugh was the victim of a raid himself in 1596 when John Charlton of the Bower and his accomplice, named as the 'Scotsman' Rinion Armstrong but more likely than not his brother-in-law from Gilsland, broke into and burgled his house and took a black cow. The Dodds had long been a power in North Tynedale and were signatories on an 'Indenture of Canonbie' made at Coldstream in March 1494.

Robert Dodds and his son Archie along with George and Alex Charlton, Hugh and Richard Wilkinson and William Robson were accused of burning and raiding by John Graham, the bailiff to the prior of Canonbie. A number of the leading officials met to make the peace. Thomas Lord Dacre, John Heron of Ford, Sir John Heron of Chipchase and Edward Radcliffe were among the English officers and William Scott of Blaewearie, Walter Kerr of Cessford, Patrick Hume of Fast Castle, George Hume of Wedderburn and others appeared for the Scots.

In April 1513 an Edward Dodd, of Chirden and Roughside, appears on a Royal Pardon Roll and in 1521 Jamie Dodd of the Burnmouth was named as 'one of the greatest robbers in all Tynedale' and was wanted for his non-appearance at an assize held at Newcastle. He was executed two years later with five other 'very tall men,' but Dodd was named as the most notorious. Surrey complained to the King that: 'the country has been nearly ruined by the continual murders and thefts of Tynedale and Redesdale men,' and wanted out of the job.

In December 1527 Sir William Eure set an ambush at Felton to capture outlaws that had been around that way robbing travellers. Hob Dodd, alias Loosehorn, was killed while being taken prisoner. Percival Dodd and John Stokoe were taken for resetting outlaws. John Merwood of Redesdale was captured after evading an assize at

Newcastle but the gang had put up a strong fight; Matthew Forster had killed one of Eure's men during his taking and was put in prison at Newcastle.

Ten years later Archie Dodd appeared in a number of bills of complaint at a truce day at the Redden Burn and in 1540 Michael and Rany Dodd of the Blakelaw were in hiding across the border with Clemmy and John Croser following the uproar after the killing of Roger Fenwick. 28 other rebels of Tynedale were reset with Clemmy Croser and Robyn Elliot. Nine of the Hunters of Tynedale were at the Rutherfords of Hunthill in Teviotdale and the laird of Hunthill rode to the King to ask favour for them, while Archie Elliot and Robyn Elliot went to Lord Maxwell at Jedburgh, to see about helping the others. Jamie Dodd of Bruntbank, Davie Dodd of the Shaw and his brothers Michael and Dick Dodd were staying elsewhere unspecified.

The Scotsmen that were in hiding in England at the same time were West Teviotdale riders; Robin Rutherford, George Rutherford called Coke Banks, his son, and Hob Rutherford his brother; Gavin Rutherford and his brother; Will Turnbull, Pat Turnbull called 'Cattle' elder, Pat Turnbull called 'Cattle' younger, Jamie Turnbull young Pat's brother, Peter Turnbull called the Monk, Pat Turnbull, Cragwood's son, Hodge Turnbull, Cragwood's son, Ade Turbull, Cragwood's son; Watt Robson and his sons Willie, Jamie, and Lance, Ade Robson of Howstoun, Hobb Douglas of Bonjedward, John Brown, Hobb Robson of Ancrum; Hob Ainsley called 'Clerk Dummont,' Hob Ainsley called 'Fat Collope,' Willie Ainsley called 'White Bonnet', Charlie Ainsley of the Mylne, Pat Waugh, Willie Sklent called 'Ker', a Laidlaw called 'Billop,' a Laidlaw called 'Stronghorn', Willie Oliver called 'Fargus' and Jock Oliver his son. It is not specified where they were reset, but it seems likely that the Hunters in Tynedale were returning the favour.

Uswold Dodd was killed when Kinmont Willie Armstrong, Sim Armstrong young Laird of Whitehaugh, Rinion and Eckie Armstrong of Tweden and 400 men ran a day foray to Tynedale in 1579 to take 40 score kye and oxen, a thousand sheep and 'gate'. Thomas and John Dodd of Thornburn and Lyle Dodd at the Blacklaw were seeking redress for the action.

The Laird of Ferniehurst led 100 men to burn Randal and Tristram Dodd out of Sidwood bastle in 1589 and the Teviotdale riders took both men prisoner into Scotland after firing their corn and hay and taking 100 kye and oxen, 200 sheep, 60 'gate' and two horses and mares.

Tristram Dodd of Sidwood was outlawed in November 1595 along with Nicholas Weldon, of Weldon, Christopher Weldon his uncle, Matthew Errington, late of Stonecraft, Anthony Pott of Carrick, Nicholas Hall, late of Rochester, his brother John Hall and Black William Ridley. The March Warden Ralph Eure denied any knowledge of Tristram Dodd, who was hiding somewhere in the Middle March.

A year later Buccleuch demanded the delivery of Jock Dodd called 'Jock Pluck' and the pledge Gib Charlton of Boughthill – or either one of them – after he'd handed over William Elliot of Larriston 'Hartsgarth.' Scott named Dodd and Charlton as the principal men in a raid against Elliot and the officials hoped that justice could be done to 'remove the grudge between the parties.'

It didn't work and in July 1597 Tynedale launched a revenge attack on Liddesdale and one of the Dodds killed a famous rider called Martin's Gibb Elliot.

Elliot was no mug; he had been a soldier 'trained in War' at Flanders and France and was one of the leaders of the Elliots, being a 'notorious offender.' His son Archie was also named as a 'great rider.'

But the Dodds weren't bothered and broke into Elliot's shiel, assassinating Martin's Gibb and wounding several more of his men. They drove off 200 cattle, 100 sheep, some goats and 20 horses and mares but the feeling has to be that the plunder was secondary to taking out Martin's Gibb.

Jock Dodd of the Greenhaugh was handed over to the Humes as a pledge in 1597 but was also gone when Lord Alexander let them go in the October. The Northumbrian reivers didn't suffer the same fate of deportation on a scale that the Western Clans endured during the pacification, but 100 of them were sent to do military service in Ireland. It didn't concern them too much and by 1618 most of those that had been sent away were back.

In a strange case at Coquetdale in 1598 Thomas Dodd senior of

Whitton, with Hector Dodd of Whitton and James Dodd of Whitton broke into the house of Anne Dodd at Whitton at around 11 o'clock at night and stole four cows and two oxen. What relation the Dodds all were to each other remains a bit of a mystery.

And in 1601 Henry Dodd of the Cragg broke into the fields of Boresheild and stole three goats from Andrew Marken of Tynedale while James Dodd, alias 'Pluck' of the Burne Banks and John Milburn of the Sneep stole six wedders from Henry Widdrington at the Townhouse.

They appear in the records again three years later as Lionel Dodd of Blackelaw, alias Lyle Dodd, son of Archie Dodd, stole £5 in money when he burgled a house in Bellingham belonging to Henry Dodd. Lionel broke into a room at around ten o'clock at night and stole the cash. James Dodd of Blacklaw entertained him afterwards.

The Dodds were thieving from each other again in 1609 as James Dodd of Thornburn and Thomas Dodd of Sidwood stole three lambs from Thomas Dodd of Cragghouse. Edward Dodd of Sidwood was named as an accessory.

Redesdale

Rob Hall younger of Monkridge and John Hall of Gressonfield

The Halls were an ancient family of Redesdale and as early as1288 Ronald de Harle (Hall) was an important official as King Edward I's escheator (executor of wills) for North of the Trent and was residing in Berwick. Thomas Arle (Hall) resided nearer to the home of the Halls and was involved himself in a legal issue regarding the estate of a Richard Hickson who had died in Tynedale during the 1490s with a Gerard Foster and John Raven, the rector of the parish church of Shitlington in Tynedale. Will Hall of Otterburn was hurt in burning and destroying Layton tower in Scotland as part of an invasion force 4,000 strong under William Heron, Ralph Fenwick, Edward Grey, Sir Roger Grey, Sir Thomas Ilderton and John Heron of Chipchase in 1522. The Scots responded with a raid into Harbottle where they drove off a cart horse, two nags from the Peels and half a score of nolt.

Two years later William Heron of Ford and Sir John Heron of Chipchase had to produce the criminal leader John Hall of Elishaw at a court session or forfeit a bond of 200 hundred marks.

By 1528 the Halls were the biggest family in Redesdale with 70 names, headed by John Hall of Otterburn. The Hedleys were the second largest surname with 64, while the Redes had 39 and the Potts 29. The other surnames of the 445 people were Jeffreyson, Ellesden, Don, Nicholson, Spore, Coxson, Fletcher, Lowsdon, Bewkes, Wanles, Dagg, Nixon, Chator, Edgar, Brown, Wilkinson, Green, Hugginshaw, Stevenson, Forster, Wan, Milburn, Hogg, Merwood, Robson, Colwell, Clarke, Robinson, Rawe, Hope, Smyth, Houghton, Wadhawe and Anderson, as recorded in the lord of Northumberland's contemporary book of the inhabitants. This shows that not all of the local families were actively involved in reiving; some were drawn into the action by hot-trod to recover property and others just wanted to farm in peace – when they could.

John Hall of Otterburn, Sandy and Anthony Hall and Edward and Cuthbert Charlton, Henry and Geoffrey Robson and Christopher and David Milburn were 'characterised as thieves or maintainers of thieves' early in 1537 and Lord Norfolk would not have them admitted to pensions – but by the July of that year John Hall of Otterburn and Sandy and Anthony Hall were all keepers of Redesdale with a payment of £10 a year each. Sir John Widdrington was the Leader of Redesdale at £26 4s 4d – he was also making a wage of £133 6s 8d as the deputy warden of the Middle Marches.

It was a tough gig; in 1538 the Scottish Middle March warden would make no answer for attempts on the English Middle Marches by the Liddesdale riders while Tynedale and Redesdale 'continued in their wildness with little regard for their keepers'.

Robert Collingwood and John Horsley complained to London that outlaws remained in Tynedale and 'the head surname of the Halls in Redesdale' and most of them would not attend a head court at Harbottle where the deputy warden of the March was supposed to sort out 'redress' from Scottish raids. They weren't daft and sniffed a trap. Both of the English dales had made attempts on each other, but Collingwood felt that the meetings that they were holding to sort things out amongst themselves were, in fact, making 'a league against their keepers' in case any of them were taken. Suspicion and mistrust were rife.

With the 'Rough Wooing' well under way by 1544, Sir John Heron at Chipchase was discussing with the Scots Borderers that he had on bond with pledges as to what men they could give to serve the English King in France, but they were loath to cross the channel. He was also seeking Tyne and Redesdale riders to fight in the army.

They were certainly doing enough damage at home by burning out Southern Scotland and a number of Redesdale reivers joined up with the Scottish Halls, Olivers, Turnbulls, Rutherfords and Crosers to spoil an area on the Merse and John Hall of Otterburn, with the Redesdale riders and 600 'assured' Scottish borderers, ran a foray to Ancrum. The devastation was horrific – 192 towns and towers were burnt, 403 Scotsmen killed and 816 taken prisoner. Over 10,000 cattle were lifted with more than 12,000 sheep, 1,296 horses, 850 bolls of corn and insight in the thousands.

When Clement Hall was executed at Morpeth in 1567, his brother John joined with 100 Armstrongs and Nixons of Liddesdale to burn and the destroy the house and goods of Cessford's servant John Barrow and drive off 480 sheep in revenge. The English Middle March Warden John Forster captured two each of the Armstrongs and Nixons and had them imprisoned, as well as taking their cut of the booty – 80 nolt and eight horses.

The raids continued and by the 1580s the Redesdale Halls were beginning to wonder if Sir John Forster was in fact in league with the Liddesdale Elliots himself. They had a point – in a number of devastating raids led primarily by the notorious Martin and Robert Elliot and the Armstrong Lairds of Mangerton and Whitehaugh, they had not 'received a penny in redress.' Perhaps Forster was being paid off to turn a blind eye or was pocketing the cash himself. Organised crime can only operate by buying off or intimidating officials and John Hall of Otterburn, the keeper of Redesdale under Thomas Percy the Earl of Northumberland, was certainly being frustrated in his attempts to hit back for the losses; Hall did get a licence from Forster to seek and take revenge on the Elliots of Liddesdale for the losses he himself had suffered and those of his friends and he carried it out by assassinating Robin and Gavin Elliot.

But Foster then had John Hall delivered to the Elliots on a massive bond of £1000 which was 'the utter overthrow and bondage of Hall and the whole of Redesdale.' It was said, in English documents, that if any of the liberty of Redesdale 'did seek or take revenge on Liddesdale or Scotland for their losses, Sir John Foster would either compel them to render the said goods again or deliver the parties to the complainants of Scotland.'

These weren't small scale affairs. Liddesdale was hammering Redesdale and the Halls in particular; the entire village of Elsdon saw 16 men murdered and eight taken prisoner and their houses up in flames when Martin and Robin Elliot with the Laird of Whitehaugh, George Armstrong and 500 others swept in and drove off dozens of cattle, horses and over £500 in household goods and money, then ransomed the prisoners. The people of Farneycleugh were similarly devastated by Sim and Willie Elliot, Willie Elliot of the Falling Ash and Hector Armstrong of the Gingles in another crew 500 strong that burnt the town and took their cattle and goods.

Alexander Hall of Monkridge was spoiled by Dand Elliot, Dand Elliot of Braidley, Martin Elliot of the Hugh House and John Elliot who murdered a Robert Hall and drove away stock. Those same Elliots were also at the Farneycleugh raid. Alexander was also targeted by Thomas Laidlaw, William Laidlaw of the Broom bush, Martin Storey and Willie Rutherford in one raid and Martin Laidlaw of the Heugh and Davie Laidlaw who raided Byrness in another.

Archie Elliott of the Hill, Hobby Elliott, Harry Nixon and Archie Nixon led a gang that raided Alexander of Monkridge and the same crew hit the town of Rudchester three times in succession, driving off all of their goods. Andrew Armstrong teamed up with those desperados to spoil the houses, steal cattle and take prisoners at Rukyn around the same time and the Halls at Monkridge were hit again by a West Teviotdale crew consisting of Robin and John Frissell, Jock Hall of the Sykes, Tom Hall of Foulshiels and others at Cradden Burn, who also rode on Whitestone house in another reive.

Thomas Hall, Jock Hall of the Sykes, Willie Hall of Middleknowes and Ralph Robson also took part in a raid on the laird of Mote and Thomas Pott was robbed by Robin Frissell and Jock Hall of the Sykes at Fawside. Frissell was riding again with David Aynsley of Fala,

Thomas Aynley and Steven Davison in a raid on John Hall of Farneycleugh. Those same reivers were also accused of laying ploughs in England and the West Teviotdale men made inroads on Roger Hall of the Carseylees with the laird of Overton, Thom Aynsley, Ralph Robson of Middleknowes and Jock Hall of the Sykes continuing their own particular reign of brazen theft. The Scottish Halls Jock of the Flints and Tom of the Foulshiel were hitting the land around the English Halls again with the Laird of Overton and Ralph Robson as they took Archie Cook of Rattenrow's cattle from the Sills. They were even plundering from those that they shared a surname with; Gabriel Hall of Ottercopps had his horse stolen by the Scottish James Hall of Heavyside at the Cocklaw truce day when Lord Russell was killed in 1585.

But it was the Liddesdale men that were carrying out the largest raids in terms of scale and violence and Eddie Elliott, Archie Elliott of the Hill, Willie Elliott of the Steel, Archie Croser, 'nebless' Clemy Croser and others including 'Fiddler's Hob' Elliot, and John Noble murdered a number of men and left others with horrendous injuries during a reive on John Hall of Overacres. The Overacres Halls lost another 60 cows and oxen and had two of their name killed in pursuit of the Liddesdale raiders while Ralph Hall of Elishaw was murdered in his bed when they took 50 of his stock and Mitchell Hall of Stellarshiels had 400 sheep and 10 cattle taken with no chance of recovering them.

John Hall of Otterburn was the chief man of the Halls and the keeper of Redesdale but that did not prevent him being robbed himself. He had 40 cows stolen out of Dudleys by 40 Liddesdale men who took 20 men prisoner and stole their horses. He had 50 beasts taken by 20 men of the same crew at Branchave that were never recovered and Ralph Hall of Branchave also lost 20 cattle in the same raid.

When Sander Hall and Tom Pott had 40 beasts stolen from Parkside by 60 Liddesdale raiders and no recovery, they paid their ransoms in Sir John Forster's garden at Alnwick but didn't get any of their stock back; where things get more suspicious is that the chief spoilers were named as Martin and Robin Elliot and they agreed with Forster to have 'daily recourse to his house at Alnwick,' and

'Redesdale dare not find fault with them, besides their goods are licensed to go into England.'

John Hall had fifty light horsemen – all his own friends and surname of Redesdale – but it was felt that he should be able to have 300 able men to pursue goods at Harbottle castle and the 'lack of people to service and countenance' was named as one of the reasons for the 'cause of decay' in Redesdale. The fact that the castle was in a ruinous state didn't help matters, as well as the heavy raiding being endured by the Scots riders. But the finger was starting to be pointed in Sir John Forster's direction too.

The Middle March Warden had taken 40 cattle from Robert Hall of Monkridge under the pretence of a 'bond of surety' and he never saw them again; when the Reeds and Fosters of Redesdale lost 120 cattle a delivery was made for them to Sir John, who never paid the owners and when one of the Potts of Carrick had 20 beast taken by Liddesdale and 'no restitution was made,' Forster imprisoned five men of Rochester for a year. When they were 'armed and quitted,' or released, he took their goods and kept them for his own use, then when John Anderson and Gib Elwood of Elsdon, with eighteen other men, rode into Scotland and recovered 24 cows and four horses, Foster seemed reluctant to let them keep their own goods.

Despite the earlier licence, Forster would also 'never suffer' John Hall to take revenge on one of the Elliots and was accused of an 'indirect' involvement in the deaths of Clement Hall of Burdhope, Roger Hall of Branshaw, Anthony Pott and John Reed of Corsenside and, tellingly, 'not one penny redressed since he had the office.'

Forster did, however, clamp down on some of the troublesome Redesdale families themselves. In 1565 a number gathered in an attempt to break Harbottle jail, and a year later Forster had six beheaded following a Warden Court at Morpeth. In 1568, he captured ten of the principal thieves - Robert Hall of Monkridge, Randy Hall of Colwellhill, John Hall, called 'Anthony's John,' Clement Hall of Burdhope, Anthony Hall of Sharperton, George Anderson of Davey Sheill, Roger Wanless of Durtrees, Mitchell Pott of Clennell, Archie Dunn and George Thompson.

They were held in irons at the decaying Harbottle castle then transferred to the more secure Morpeth gaol for a time before Forster could get them sent to Durham as he felt that Newcastle's prison was too weak and too near the 'evil country' that they hailed from. Forster was also looking to score as he wrote to Sir William Cecil that he had housed them himself (at Harbottle) 'at his own charges…at no little cost, which (he) was compelled to do or suffer the country to be entirely over-run by the evil disposed.' He was obviously looking for some recompense for his trouble.

Sir Cuthbert Collingwood certainly felt that Forster was implicated and wrote in 1587 'if his dearest friends were examined…they could not with credit excuse his faults nor deny them to be true.' Collingwood also appealed at the time on behalf of John Hall of Otterburn, and all of Redesdale, for the authorities not to execute a Turnbull and a Douglas of Rule Water that had been captured while raiding. Hall and his friends were 'in bands for great sums' with the named families and couldn't afford to pay. They were also wary of entering a blood feud if they were killed, which Collingwood noted 'at this instant, they are not able to endure.'

The Rede outlaws began riding with the Scottish Rutherfords and in 1589 Anton Pott of Carrick, George Hall of Birdhope, Anthony Hall of Sharperton and Tom Hall of Dueshill stole a number of cattle from Robert Roddam of Littlehoughton with Andrew and George Rutherford, the sons of William Rutherford of Littleheugh who was protecting the Redesdale men, and Andrew and Jock Douglas who were tenants of the Rutherford Laird of Hunthill.

Ralph Hall of Gressonfield was taken prisoner and ransomed by the Elliots at the Kirk Ford that year – specifically James of the Hill, Robin the Tailor, Will of Fittington, Archie of Ramsgill, Hob the Laird, Mark of the Hill, John of the Hillend, Robin the bastard of Glenvoren, Hob's Davie and Archie of Dewes Leases, Andrew of Blackhall, John the Child and Will Croser of Riccarton, with others. John Anderson of Hatherwick, Thomas Hall of Otterburn, Robert Wintripp, Peter Bell, Hughie Mewers, Clement Hall and Thomas Hedley were the others that lost their horses and had to pay up to be released.

The Halls of Gressonfield were a tough crew. They had helped one of their clan called George Hall to escape over the Border to Jedburgh after he'd killed a man at Durham in 1586, and some of the most notorious members of the family ten years later were Percival of Elsdon, Edward of Yardhope, George of Birdhope (a man that had served in the army in the Low Countries for Sir Phillip Sydney after breaking the law), Uswyne of Raylees, Roger of Rochester and Robert Hall of Knightside, who were all wanted felons. Roger's brother William Hall of Knightside was on a small-scale raid with Oswald Hall of the Rayle Burn and Roger Henderson of Rimside in 1595 when they broke into and burgled the vicar of Muckle Benton, Walter Denton, between 11 o'clock and midnight and stole four black oxen.

Roger Hall of Shilmoor was beheaded by Sir John Forster for a similarly 'small offence' in 1597 and when Richard Fenwick captured the great thief Anthony Hall of Elishaw, seven of his friends landed at Fenwick's door within two days of the capture to offer him 140 score beast for his release. 100 Halls also offered to stand as bondsmen for his life. When Fenwick wrote to complain to Sir George Heron, who was Hall's protector, Heron had to apprehend a dozen of the Redesdale riders who were all condemned and hanged at Hexham. Clement Hall of Birdhope was another famous thief who was strung from the gallows by Fenwick, despite offers of 180 cattle and 'forgiveness for the death of their friends before.' The Halls had long used bribery as a way to attempt to get out of the reach of the Law. When the famous thief Hob Hall was taken by Fenwick to the then-Warden John Forster in 1585 for the murder of two of Forster's servants, he had offered £100 cash to be freed.

When money didn't work, threats of violence were the second option. William Hall of Cartington was the brother of the dead pledge that had been produced at the West Ford meeting in a cart and was described as 'the best of that clan.' He had been arrested by Edward Gray in Morpeth as 'principal of his surname' and meeting with the directions of Sir William Bowes on 'whose estate the Scot's could not object,' so they clearly had ideas of handing him over in his brother's stead. Hall had only been held by Gray for around two hours when Ephraim Widdrington, Ralph Ogle, Andrew Clennell, Luke Errington and John Smith turned up at his house armed with long guns, pistols and swords and demanded that his servant open the iron gates. They asked if Hall was in prison, and when Gray replied that he was, they started cursing him and making threats against his life.

The threats must have worked as Rob Hall, younger of Monkridge, and John Hall of Gressonfield were produced as pledges for the name in his place. But the Halls, like the North Tyne men, didn't bother reappearing after they'd been released by Hume and were gone back into the hills in 1597.

By the time of the pacification there were complaints that the Halls, who had been just as notorious as the Grahams, had not suffered the same fate and been deported to Ireland. In fact, in 1605, the Halls were just as bad as ever; the vicar John Smaithwaite had been placed in the rectory at Elsdon and was complaining that he'd been interrupted in the middle of a communion by Thomas Hall of Branshaw, who was Sir Henry Widdrington's chief officer, and that Gabriel Hall had menacingly grabbed him by the face in the churchyard. He couldn't afford to repair the ruinous house and chancel and 100 outlaws were walking the streets and churchyard at the Sunday market. He worried that he could not 'through his ministry reduce the inhabitants to live in Godly manner,' and put all his faith in the Border Commissioners to bring about change. Probably because the church had no doors, books or communion table and was also in ruins while the merciless locals were stealing from him; they had lifted one gelding, one stoned nag, and one cow, one heifer, 60 sheep, and other things worth £30.

The Halls never lost their wild streak and in 1716 John Hall of Otterburn, better known as 'Mad Jack' for his violent temper, was beheaded at Tyburn for High Treason. He was a Justice of the Peace in Northumberland but had been a major player in the Jacobite Rising of 1715.

John Reed of Troughend

Percy Reed (Reid, Read) went into the history books and folklore as a Border Ballad was written about his murder. Legend says that 'Parcy Reed' was the Keeper of Redesdale and was betrayed by the Halls, who took him on a hunting trip and filled his pistols with water then stood by as the Crosiers cut him down in revenge for the arrest of one of their family. But finding actual documentary evidence for a murder of Percy Reed has proved tricky; a Percival Reed of

Troughend was one of the men involved with John Hall of Otterburn, Roger Fenwick of Cambo and Oswald Fenwick of Middleton that apprehended a gang of 200 Olivers on a hot trod in 1582 - things went wrong and Allan Wanless was murdered as the Scots gang retook the stolen beasts when they were driving them home.

Percival Reed, the young laird of Troughend, was the complainant following a raid by the Elliots in 1584. Archie Elliot 'Hob's Archie,' Eddie of the Shaw, Gavin's Archie, Archie of the Hill and Hob Elliot of the Ramsgill – along with 'Nebless Clemmy' Crosier and 200 others ran an open daytime foray on Birdhope and lifted 200 kye and oxen and 80 horses and mares while taking 80 prisoners and £200 worth of insight. He was one of the English Middle March gentlemen that signed a statement of John Forster's on the circumstances of the killing of Lord Russell at a truce day in 1585 and in 1589 he'd been hit again by a force of Liddesdale riders, mainly made up by Elliots, who seemed to relish targeting Redesdale and Coquetdale.

Will Elliot of Fidderton, Rinion of Dodburn, Robin the Laird of Burnheads, Hob called 'Hob Bully,' Davie 'the Carling,' Rinion Armstrong 'Hector's Rinion' of the Harelaw and 80 others were at his tower at Troughend to murder two men and take 51 cattle, three horses and mares and 60 yards of linen cloth. Reed was still seeking justice for the raid a year later, and he'd roped in James Hedley of the Garretshiels and others to help him. If this was the 'Parcy Reed' of Border Ballad fame, then you would expect him to be seeking vengeance primarily against the Elliots. But why ruin a good story.

It could have been an earlier Percy Reed that had been slaughtered by the Crosiers as the Reeds had been at Troughend from as early as 1400 when Thomas Reed of Redesdale was paying ransom money to William Swinburn for William Mowtrop of Tynedale. The tower at Troughend had originally been in the possession of the Buttycombe family before the Reeds moved in.

Thomas Reed was on a jury at Elsdon in 1429 and the family's reputation was sealed in 1442 when the followers of John Reed, the laird of Troughend, were well described as: 'a ruder and more lawless crew there needs not be yet if well tutored, they might do Her Majesty good service; but their practices are not to be defended.' The

Reeds were obviously a rough and ready crowd involved in organised crime from a very early date. By 1542 the Reeds had considerable power and influence in Redesdale, second only to the Halls, and another John Reed of Troughend was the head of the clan in the 1560s and 'commissioner of enclosures' in the Middle March, while Clement Reed of Old Town was a setter and searcher for Troughend and Garretshiels at the time.

When Percival of Troughend was suffering raids, others of the clan were also at the hard end of the Liddesdale reivers – Thomas Reed called the 'laird of the Burn' had 30 cows and oxen, a grey mare and insight worth 20 marks taken by Archie Elliot of the Hill and his brother James, Martin Crosier and his son Clement and 20 others in 1589 while the brothers Thomas and John Reed of Burradon were plundered of 24 kye and oxen and a horse by a West Teviotdale gang made up of James Hall of Heavyside, younger, James Robson of the Burvens, John Mow, son to Lance, and 20 other men that same year. The West Teviotdale riders Ralph Robson of Middlesknowes, young George Pile and Davie Aynsley of Fala also took a horse belonging to Archie Reed of Blackhope. Those gangsters may have had local knowledge to guide their raiding as Thomas Reed was a fugitive from English justice staying over the Border under the protection of the Godfathers in the area – in 1579 the outlaw Reed was with John Rutherford of Egerton to hit Mark Ogle at Kirkley and steal four oxen. In 1586 Thomas, and another fugitive called Roger Reed, were with the Laird of Overton (Frissell) and stealing from Anthony Twissell of Callerton.

The Reeds were suspicious to the English Middle March Warden Ralph Eure as he noted that they were intermarrying with the Liddesdale Armstrongs; he was also annoyed that the Fosters were marrying with the Humes of Merse, the Selbys with the Rutherfords, the Collingwoods with the East Teviotdale Halls and the Gairs with the Mows. The romances didn't stop the raiding and in 1595 Robert Reed of Dunston was taken for seven cattle and two horses by James Young of the Cove, elder, the father of the Teviotdale pledge, his uncle Thomas and Tom Young 'with the Stowers,' who was a fugitive hiding in the English East March not long after with 'Julian's John' Young.

Two years later James Reed was one of the infamous outlaws of Redesdale named by the gentlemen of the East and Middle marches. Thomas Reed appears to have slipped back over the border at some point as by 1596 he was thieving from Michael Watson of Murraycrook with the laird Manners of Trewhitt and Thomas Errington of Burradon to take a pregnant horse, a grey cloak, a purse with money in it and a sword.

It is possible that the pledge John Reed of Troughend was the same that waited with a pistol to murder a man coming from the market in Hexham; the victim's wife was following behind him on horseback, and when Reed appeared to take his pot-shot she swung up her leg to protect her husband and the bullet shattered her knee. That John Reed was committed to Hexham gaol by Lord Eure in 1596 but broke out of the prison and was also a fugitive, so the chances are that the law could have caught up with him in time to be handed over to the Scots at the West Ford and delivered to the Edinburgh tollbooth before his eventual release in December 1599.

Archibald and Cuthbert Reed of Garratt Sheills stole 14 sheep from Mark Hall of Whitelees in 1605 and Katherine Hedley of Garratt Sheills entertained them afterwards, while in 1615 the Reeds of Alnham – Michael, Edward and William, with Ralph Davison of Alnham and John Snowdon, alias 'John the better' of Farneylaw, stole three heifers from their neighbour Robert Horsley, but it was small time stuff compared to their reiving heydays.

Allan Hedley of Hatherwick

The Hedleys were another Redesdale family that had long lived in the area and been involved and immersed in the reiving culture.

In 1401 a 49-year-old Robert de Hedley appeared with a number of other dalesmen in a proof of age case at Newcastle to prove that Thomas Surtees, knight, was 21 years old. They said that they had been present at an inquisition in Durham with the sheriff for the death of a man in Gateshead when William Bowes, knight, came and told them that Alexander Surtees' son was born.

The Surtees were an interesting Tyneside family, not involved in reiving but part of a story involving one of the Scotts; he eloped with

Bessie Surtees when she dangled from the first-floor window of their Jacobean house onto his horse and they rode off into Scotland to be married. This was in 1772. The house is still standing down by the Quayside and belongs to Historic England. John Scott was the son of a coal miner and considered beneath the wealthy merchants the Surtees. As if to rub it in their faces, in true Scott style he went on to become Lord Eldon, Lord Chancellor of England.

Lancelot Hedley of Ovingham was named on a 1510 pardon roll and in 1528 Eddie Hedley, the laird of Bowershiels in Redesdale, was part of the Lisle gang that assisted the Armstrongs in breaking Newcastle gaol. He, along with Alex Crawhawe, the chief counsellor of William and Humphrey Lisle, John Pringle, Rowly Errington, Gerrard Shaftoe, Edward Bewick of Redesdale, Matthew Stokoe of Tyndale, who had been a pledge that broke free from the Duke of Richmond's council at Pomfrett, Hob Stokoe, William Fletcher of Felton, John Taylor of Felton, and William Middleton, Robert Jackson, Gerard Richester, John Brownwell of South Tynedale, and John Armstrong were captured in a midnight raid at Felton. Nine of them were beheaded following a warden court at Alnwick and five hanged for felony; Hedley and his friends were described as 'most heinous transgressors.'

Another Edward Hedley and William Pott, the 'principal thieves of the great surnames of Redesdale,' along with Rowly Dodd and William Stokoe 'two great thieves of the great surnames of Tynedale,' were also executed at Newcastle that year, alongside a Blenkinsopp and a Nixon. Twelve were killed at Tyneside and twelve at York following an assize.

The Hedleys were also involved in the Catholic Northern Rebellion of 1536 when Sir Thomas Percy was hanged, drawn and quartered at Tyburn in Middlesex for his part in the rising against King Henry VIII. Percy's servant Gerald Reed and his horse keeper John Hedley were both interviewed in the Tower of London.

Two years later a Thomas Hedley of Kellburn brought a message from the Laird of Ferniehurst to the new Earl of Northumberland, Thomas Percy, the eldest son of the executed Thomas, who would also be later executed for treason and beatified by the Catholic Church. The note that Hedley carried was warning that Lionel Grey was a Scottish spy. The Northumbrians passed this on to the Earl of Murray who was the King of Scotland's lieutenant on the Borders at that time. Hedley was up to his neck in the intrigue; by 1540 he was hiding rebel Scottish Rutherfords in Redesdale with Anthony Pott and Gerry Reed. Peter Hall had also been 'resetting' Scottish rebels but was executed at Newcastle.

Fall outs amongst the Redesdale families themselves weren't uncommon and in the 1570s the Hedleys were enraged and at feud for murders that hadn't been sorted out, as were the Andersons, Potts and Weatherheads, with local officials stating that they needed to be kept 'under band and surties for the peace.'

By the 1590s the noted members of the family were John and Anthony Hedley in the Stobs and Archie and James Hedley in Garretshiels. But the most notorious of all was Michael 'Hogskins' Hedley of Hatherwick. He didn't bother to turn up and hear a charge of lifting a grey mare and a black horse from James Douglas of Cavers, the sheriff of Teviotdale, but he probably felt the theft was justified as Douglas, with Tom Turnbull and Tom Turnbull, younger, Laird of Minto, had hit the Stobs and their neighbours William Hall and John Anderson of the Cragg for 50 cows, 30 oxen, four stotts and six wyes previously.

Hogskins had also taken six oxen, two cows and two young 'neat' from the laird of Lowder and his thefts weren't just cattle – he stole two pistols, a sword, cloak, steel cap, purse, silk garters and a scarf from the Laird of Mecarston, some five years after an earlier raid on the same man. You have to wonder who was the more red-faced – Hogskins for the charge or Mecarston for filing it; silk garters on the Border?

It seems that Allan Hedley of Hatherwick would have to be answerable for the raids carried out by Michael and he dutifully turned up at the West Ford meeting and was detained in Edinburgh Castle with the other Redesdale pledges until his 1599 release.

It didn't put an end to the raids from Hatherwick, however, and in 1603 the yeomen William Hedley of Hatherwick and Robert Pott of Carrick broke into John Forster of Benridge's farm and took a brown ox and a red cow. The small-scale thieving continued as John Hedley of Longshaws and Clement Pott of the Cragg took a couple of cows and an ox from Robert Taylor of Shieldykes. But things took a more serious turn as John Hedley of Elsdon murdered his neighbour George Hall in the village in 1611, stabbing him in the head with a long staff that left a fatal three-inch gash. Hall never recovered from the wound and died a little later.

George Wanless of Durtrees

Jacob Wanless of the Birkheads appears in a list of inhabitants of Rothbury Forest with bills of complaint for Thomas Lord Dacre which were collected by Nicholas Thornton of Whitton, esquire, in 1523. The other complainers were John Pott of the Nunnykirk, Tom Birleston and Richard Coots of East Ritton, John Bowman, John Book's wife of the Birkheads, Richard Pott of the Coltpark and James Brown.

With little trace of the Wanlesses in the records, it seems that they mainly stuck to working their land and weren't a huge raiding family, though they do appear from time to time. Roger Wanless (originally Wanles) of Durtrees was one of the ten principal men of Redesdale named in 1568 and the Middle March Warden Sir John Forster had Gregory Wanless locked up in Harbottle Castle for taking William Kerr's sheep in Ancrum. Around the same time, the Coquetdale raider Gawen Readhead was outlawed and took to hiding out in a hollow oak tree near Brinkburn priory. Readhead was said to be: 'as notorious as an Armstrong or Elliot of Liddesdale, or the reiver of Westburnflat.' The Readheads were also inhabitants of Rothbury Forest and are similarly under-represented in the records, though Robert Readhead, and his brother, Edward, of Hollingcrook in the forest, appear in a number of indictments between 1598 and 1609.

By the 1580s George Wanless had been plundered by James Davison of the Burnrigg, Ralph Robson of Middleknowes and George Douglas of Swineside, called 'Pelman,' who drove off 20 oxen and cows in a reive on him.

Michael Wanless of Stewardsheiles in Redesdale complained in 1582 that his kinsmen John and Roger Wanless had been murdered during a large incursion by Archie Elliot of the Hill, James Elliot his brother, young John Elliot of the Park, Hob Elliot of the Park, son to

James, Jock Elliot of the Park, son to 'Scots' Hob,' Martin Elliot of the Heughouse called 'Red Martin,' and 100 others who raided Elishaw and plundered large numbers of cows and oxen, sheep, horses, household goods and a sleuth dog.

The family were hit hard again the following year as Dand Oliver of Hindhaughhead, the laird of Ashtrees, Thomas Oliver of Lustrother, William Oliver of the Slakes and 200 others hit Redesdale and Allan Wanless was killed while pursuing them in a hot trod. Four years later another large-scale raid was mounted on George (the pledge) and William Wanless of Durtrees and Anthony and John Hedley of Stobs. They complained that Robert Turnbull of Barnhill, James Turnbull of Stoneyletch, George Turnbull of Butterwell, Watt Turnbull of Hoppsburn and James Davison of Burnrigg, along with another 200 men, had burned ten houses, taken six prisoners and lifted 80 kye and oxen, 240 sheep, 10 horses and mares and insight worth £10.

In 1585 the Laird of Ferniehurst complained to the King of Scots that an English boy named Wanless had stolen a pair of spurs at a March meeting and his friends had hurt a Scotsman. Kerr also alleged that the Wanlesses were in a dispute with Lord Russell over some unspecified 'displeasure' done to them by him; Sir John Forster denied any such incident had taken place but offered the boy to Ferniehurst to hang anyway.

Robert Kerr of Morebottle had a 1596 bill declared 'foul' by Nicholas Forster of Hethpool on James Wanless, while Will Wanless of Grasslees was named as an infamous felon and 'more fit to be punished than trusted for defence against thieves' by the Northumbrian gentry in 1597.

When George Wanless of Durtrees was released from Edinburgh he went back to working the land, but Gerard Wanless of Hepple long continued stealing horses and sheep, as did Gregory Wanless of Mitford with his violent associate Gerard Coxson, 'the Hint.' James Wanless and Robert Hedley were found guilty of stealing four ewes from Alexander Hall in 1615 as petty thefts among the Redesdale families continued.

Percy Pott of Yardhope

The Potts inhabited Farnham and steads around Hepple, Woodhouse, Yardhope, Lanternside and Sharperton, and a notorious unnamed early member of the family is said to have appeared at the High Court in Durham for having a fight in Alwinton Church.

George Pott of Carrick in Redesdale appeared on a Pardon Roll of King Henry in 1510, though it is unclear what he had done to be pardoned for, while Thomas Pott, a leading man, was executed at Harbottle in 1518 following an insurrection of the 'principal thieves of the highlandsmen of Redesdale' who rioted in an attempt to release him. Ten others were captured and transferred from Harbottle to Morpeth, but when they were being handed over at the Rothbury gate their friends descended and killed the bailiff and six of his men in the escort, took the Morpeth gaoler and four of his men hostage and fled into Scotland.

As well as living in Redesdale/Coquetdale, there were a few Potts on the Scottish side in East Teviotdale who may have originally been fugitives from justice and Thomas Pott of Karslaw appeared in a couple of English Bills in 1537. It wasn't unusual and as late as 1589 Anton Pott of Carrick was reset across the Border staying with the Rutherfords of Littlehaugh and riding with them against his old neighbours. Robert Roddam of Little Houghton complained that Pott, along with other Redesdale fugitives George Hall of Birdhope, Anton Hall of Sharperton and Tom Hall of Dueshill raided him with Andrew Rutherford and George Rutherford, the sons of William of Lytle Heugh; Andrew Douglas of the Brea and Jock Douglas, tennents to the Laird of Hunthill, and their accomplices, and stole 16 kye and oxen from him.

Many of the 'great surnames and headsmen' of Tynedale and Redesdale were executed at an assize in Northumberland in 1526 which was unusual as it was noted that with such a big turnout 'no one was afraid to complain or give evidence.' 16 were killed including Potts, two Fenwicks, Shaftoes, Halls and Hedleys. The report marveled that 'such a thing was never seen before in these parts,' such was the grip of the local gang chiefs.

William and John Pott were named as setters and searchers in

Redesdale in the area around Woodside, Carrick, Elsdon and East Nook by Lord Dacre along with six men on a nightly watch to secure the area from reiving parties in 1552. Mind, in the same year it was reckoned that as well as the Scots the 'surnames as Halls, Fosters and Potts will be as great a terror to the rest.'

Walter Scott of Buccleuch raided Nicholas Pott of Woodside in 1587 and the Liddesdale Keeper took a grey horse, 20 nobles money and insight worth £20, killed a man and burned houses worth £200.

It was a dangerous business pursuing goods following a raid and later that year two of the Redesdale Potts were severely injured when they took part in a hot trod to recover John Hall of Davieshiel after he'd been taken prisoner and all his goods lifted by 30 West Teviotdale riders.

Two Potts were taken hostage in a trod two years later as they pursued Archie and James Elliot of the Hill, Clement Croser 'Martin's Clemmy,' James Douglas Goodman of Yerlside, Thomas Laidler of the Haugh, Jock Henderson of Prenderleth and others who had lifted 16 kye and oxen and £20 insight. The prisoners were James and Renny Pott of Carrick with Robert and John Pott the complainants.

The Elliots launched another raid into Coquetdale that year with James of the Hill again a chief rider. He was assisted by Anthony of the Binks, John 'Half Lug' Elliot, Hobbie the Tailor and 60 others that hit Wingates and took 100 kye and oxen, 3 horses and mares, killed George Hume and left 6 or 7 others severely injured. They spoiled £30 of goods. Thomas Pott, Roger and John Jowsey, the widow Virletson and the widow Hume complained. It was unsurprising, then, that the Potts were one of the Redesdale families noted as being engaged in a blood feud by Sir John Forster in 1596.

Anthony Pott of Carrick was still a fugitive from justice in 1597 but was captured raiding just a mile from Newcastle in 1599 when Thomas Rutherford of Chatto and Nicholas Hall were killed by Henry Widdrington's men.

Jock Pott 'the Bastard' of Yardhope was also riding high at the time and he killed Thomas Middlemist in his own house at Grubet during a night assault with Peter Pott in 1596. Sir Robert Carey said that there were no men called Peter Pott or Jock Pott 'the Bastard' in the East Wardenry when it came to answering charges. He was right;

they were Middle March men and got off on a technicality.

Jock didn't appear to hear a charge of the Goodman of Gateshaw against him and the bill was declared 'foul for lack of answer.' The Bastard appeared on a charge sheet again in 1601 when he took the Laird of Mow for 20 ewes but Jock, again, didn't bother to show up and contest the charges. It was perhaps the crimes committed by Jock that Percy Pott of Yardhope was made to appear and stand pledge for; he was, like the rest of the Redesdale men, released from Edinburgh's tollbooth in December 1599.

Robert Kerr, now styled Lord Roxburghe, was complaining in 1600 that a Scottish Pott named James had been taken by the Goodman of Mote just quarter mile from his house at Haliden. Kerr offered to release him to Lord Scrope. Another Scots Pott called Richard of Ashett had confessed to lifting 5 nags from David Renton of Bylly in 1597.

The Redesdale men were the principal of the clan, however, and in 1601 Gabriel Pott and Michell Pott of Hirdlaw stole three oxen at West Thriston belonging to George Thomlin of Thriston. Soon after, Andrew Pott, alias David Pott of Davysheill broke into the fields of Swarland and stole a black cow and a black calf from a man named William of Long Rowe. The Carrick branch of the family were in bother again in 1610 as Michael Pott, alias Thomas Mac (Stee) of Carrick, stole one black mare from John Younger at Hallindon and the Yardhope Potts fell out among themselves in 1611.

Anthony Pott of Yardhope, Robert Pott of Yardhope and George Pott of Whiteside murdered Jasper Pott at Galley Edge in Redesdale. Anthony Pott was the main culprit, stabbing Jasper in his side with a sword that left a gash three inches long and seven inches deep, killing him instantly. Robert Pott and George Pott were named as accessories and Michael Pott of Elisham entertained the killers afterwards, no doubt getting their stories straight.

Tom Coxson of Woolaw

The Coxsons (Cokesons or Cooksons) first made an appearance in the records in 1357 when John Cokson, William Cokson and Robert Cokson, along with an Adam Breton, were charged in an assize of the Tynedale Ward at Newcastle with stealing beasts from William de Tynedale, William Younger and another from a place called the Green. A John Coxson was a spearman in the King's army at Calais in France in 1513; as he was serving alongside a John Middleton and a man named John Lisle, he may well have hailed from Northumberland.

William Coxson of Elsdon was definitely one of the family; he was taken prisoner with another un-named Redesdale man by Thomas Foster, the marshal of Berwick, in 1523. The Coxsons were in trouble again in 1569 when George Coxson of Woolaw, and others, were arrested by the Warden Sir John Forster for aiding and abetting the rebel Tynedale families.

George Coxson of the Berkhill complained that he'd been raided and lost not only cattle but all his household goods when he was targeted by John Laidlaw of Wadespindles, Davie Laidlaw called 'Todd's Dave,' John and Andrew Armstrong of the Harelaw and others in the 1580s. William Coxson of Bargrave was also raided by Ralph Robson of Middleknowes; he, along with Robert Frissell of Overton, Ralph Hall of the Sykes (the pledges), and Tom Hall carried away 16 oxen and kye and insight, while James and Robert Davison of Burnrigg, William Hall and Ralph Robson of Middleknowes robbed William and Harry Coxson of Bargrave of 20 oxen and kye, which were never recovered.

Matthew Coxson of Heavystones complained that the Elliots with George Nixon of Kellyley, the famous 'Ill drowned Geordie,' had driven away kye and oxen from the common ground at Woolaw and in a similar raid on Henry and William Coxson of Baggray, James Davison of Burnrigg, Ralph and Matthew Robson of Oxnam, Jock Hall of the Water, Thom Hall of Foulsheills and Ralph Hall of the Sykes (the pledge) also rode off with their cattle. The Coxsons and Fosters of Redesdale were also spoiled of 80 head of cattle by 80 men of Liddesdale and they despaired that the bill had been 'redressed' around twenty times and they still couldn't get any justice for it.

In 1596 one of the charges made by the gentlemen of the Middle Marches against Ralph Mansfield, the keeper of Redesdale, was that a Coxson and a Hall were taken out of England and made to fight in front of Buccleuch for his own savage entertainment until that Coxon was killed. Also in that year, Gerry Coxson, alias 'the Hint,' of Hursley, had lifted nine hoggs and sows from Lance Kerr, known as the 'goodman of Gateshaw' and was fined 39s after he failed to appear. Gerry had previously broke into and burgled Richard Forster's house at Blacklaw between 10 and 11 at night, putting the 'whole household in great fear and mortal danger of their lives,' and made off with 13 cows, 8 oxen and a horse. In 1602 he stole two horses from Mark Errington of Ponteland with Gregory Wanless.

The pledge Tom Coxson of the Woolaw, near Otterburn, was held in Edinburgh Tolbooth but released in December 1599.

Thomas Shaftoe of Upper Buston broke into a close of Matthew Coxson of Trittlington in 1602 and stole two bay mares while two years later Edward Coxson of Rea and Roger Heron of West Wheplington lifted two ewes from Percival Brown at Redennes.

Richard Coxson of Milburn Grange in Ponteland was on the opposite side of the law in 1615 when he rescued a sanded grey mare that had been stolen by William Brady, the bailiff of John Clavering, knight, the local Sheriff.

John Snowdon

The proximity of the garrison at Harbottle castle to the 'ten towns' of Upper Coquetdale kept the bulk of the local men in check most of the time. In 1523 Bertie Snawdon (the original spelling of the surname), John Brown, of Wingates and Ralph Brown, who were tenants to Nicholas Thornton, along with a man called 'the Gared Tailor,' were taken by the Ogles while stealing in Northumberland.

Robert Snowdon was involved in an unusual case in 1582 along with Matthew Wilkinson and George Stevenson; the three were on the way to 'the Slyme' together – probably the famous old Slymefoot pub at the head of the Coquet – when they saw a man in an old grey cloak and demanded his name. The man refused to give it, but said he was going to see Martin Croser. The stranger offered them pieces of gold to let him escape, but Snowdon took all his gold, books and letters off him and detained him for the Lord Warden. It was thought that the stranger was a Jesuit priest.

John Snowdon of Linbriggs, the Laird of Varren, with John

Wilkinson of Dunsgreen and George Green of Alwinton, with the rest of the towns of Linbriggs, Dunsgreen and Alwinton, were reived of 100 kye and oxen, 20 horses and mares, had 20 men taken prisoner and their towns spoiled by Will Elliot of Fidderton, Hob Elliot, Laird of the Burn Heads, 'Quintine' Archie Croser, Renyon Armstrong of the Gingles and 200 other Liddesdale riders in 1589.

Gerry Snowdon was a fugitive hiding at Lord Ogle's in Hepple in 1597 but was believed to be in charge and command of the tenants in the village. Snowdon was a notorious rider who was indicted and wanted for murders, felonies, burglaries and March treason. He'd also been part of a large raid on Cavers in Teviotdale with Widdrington.

The Snowdons had a long association with Hepple and in 1523 Sandy Snowdon was one of three men charged with the defence of the village. Local legend has it that a Robert Snowdon of Hepple fought and killed a Scottish champion called John Grieve at Gamelspath when he was just sixteen. Snowdon was later reived of a horse and when he went on a trod to get it back, was stabbed in the side and killed by an unknown assailant.

Nicholas Snowdon of Plenmeller was raided by the notorious Willgavy Cumbrian Armstrongs in September 1597. John Armstrong, alias 'Jock Stowlugs,' Andrew Armstrong alias 'Ingram's Andrew' of Uwmanrowe and Rinian, Thomas and Andrew Armstrong of Willgavy, with Andrew Willie, broke into and burgled his house at Hartley Burn at around ten at night and stole eight oxen, eight cows, a calf and a horse. The same Nicholas Snowdon was with a number of Selbys and Ridleys that gathered to attempt to apprehend a gang of notorious Scottish West March riders that had arranged a game of football at Bewcastle in May 1599. Henry Widdrington wrote that 'the surnames and friends of Elliot and Armstrong that are pledges in York' were all part of the action. Mr. Ridley was determined to catch the Scots on English ground; especially the Armstrongs of Whitehaugh 'who had murdered a number of his friends' and gathered forty together to gain revenge. It all went wrong for Selby, however, and three were killed after having their throats cut while John Whitfield's guts spilled out from another awful sword gash. The Armstrongs and Elliots were drinking in the Bewcastle house after the game but they had been tipped off about the coming attempt and had 200 waiting in ambush.

Just a month before, Robert Elliot of Redhaugh, Gilbert Elliot of Hardlisdale, Gavin Elliot of Brough, Simon Armstrong of Mangerton, Lance Armstrong of Whitehaugh, John Armstrong of Kinmont, Lancy Armstrong son to Simon Armstrong of Whitehaugh and Francis Armstrong, brother to Simon Armstrong of Whitehaugh had offered in a letter to Lord Scrope, the English West March Warden, that they would 'place pledges for our friends into his hands...on bonds to his lordship of £500 a man...that they should remain true prisoners in Carlisle, or wherever else in his wardenry.' But following the raid, the deal was well and truly off.

Just a year later, Nicholas Snowdon of Plenmeller was involved in a murder himself. He smashed his sword into the head of Robert Martin of Westerhouse's at the Abbey Gate in Hexham giving him two gashes, one five inches long and three inches deep and the other four inches deep and three inches long. Martin survived the wound for around three weeks before he died in Hexham. Martin's wife, Elizabeth, was paid 38 shillings by Hugh Ridley at Newcastle castle as part payment from £15 received by an unknown man to conceal evidence against Nicholas Snowdon.

The pledge John Snowdon of Bickerton was released from Scotland in December 1599 with the rest of the English prisoners and was raided himself in 1608 when Robert Tait of Cotewalls and Andrew Tait of Sopwithhaugh stole seven ewes from his farm at Hebdon.

The Snowdons had long farmed the land at Bickerton. In a list of the freeholders in Northumberland in 1628, Percival Snawdon of Bickerton was described as a gentleman with Alexander and William, both also of Bickerton, being yeoman in the Coquetdale ward. Ten years later Percival was dead, and Alexander and William were both gentlemen farming that land.

The family links to reiving continued and in 1604 Christopher Snowdon of Tosson was with Gerard Wanless of Hepple and Adam Laign of South Middleton when they stole 16 ewes and 'Dynmans' from Oswald Wallace at Ilderton.

Ralph Reveley

The Reveleys were an old family of the East March in Northumberland and often held positions of power and influence on the Border, but it didn't stop them getting involved in crime and murder.

Archibald and George Reveley were indicted along with a Lawrence Beal for the murder of Thomas Reveley of Chatton in 1521. Beal fled to Scotland, while the two Reveleys went on the run in England but were captured by Dacre and locked up for treason. One died in prison.

The Reveleys were important to Dacre and he had ten men placed in Ralph Reveley's Langton Tower 'for the defence of the Borders' the following year. But the repercussions of Thomas Reveley's killing rumbled on. 18 years later Ralph was still seeking justice for his brother's life; he went down to Durham intending to apprehend Beal, who was seeking sanctuary at the church. The Earl of Westmorland had him apprehended and 'committed to ward' with sanctuary forfeited. Ralph Reveley's blood was up – Beal had been a servant of Sir Roger Gray (who was also indicted) and had, with four others, murdered Thomas and Thomas Bond 'of pure malice.' Beal had been hiding out in Scotland and, it was alleged, 'adhering to the King's enemies in time of war.' But he had returned across the Border to stay with Edward Mustian and sometimes at North Shields with Richard Beal, alias Gray, always moving around places like Durham, South Shields and Monkwearmouth while outlawed for the murder at the suit of Thomas's widow Agnes. However, at the hearing a man called William Armourer, who was the keeper of Alnwick Park, said that after the murder of Thomas, Lionel Gray reckoned that he hadn't consented to the death of anyone but a John Aynsley. In 1544 William Selby of Norham, alias William Selby of Berwick, merchant, was pardoned for the murder of Ralph's son Edward Reveley at Berwick.

In 1563 Thomas Dacre released John Reveley, a 'man well allied in this part of the country' on a bond with £400 in sureties to appear and hear charges. Dacre reckoned that putting Reveley under March Law would 'touch him very nigh' and wanted straight execution. He felt that Northumberland received 'more danger by rumours of Scots amongst themselves than they do by the Scots and thieves of the opposite borders' and the following year Sir John Forster was happy to indict Reveley on the charges that he was facing. Five years later a John Reveley was captured and taken prisoner by the Scots reivers at Pawston. The East Teviotdale men had ridden on Hethpool at three o'clock on a Saturday afternoon, killed a man and driven off 80 cattle. Captain Robert Carvell from the garrison at Norham and the Selby's took up a hot-trod and followed the raiders as far as Yetholm but couldn't get the beasts back as the Scots quickly gathered 700-800 men together. The following morning some of the mob attacked and 'shot through the drum head with an arrow and threw stones among the soldiers' but the fire was returned, and they left.

The family did not have much luck. Richard Reveley of Chatton had been mortally wounded and died at a truce day at Stawford while Robert Reveley was involved in the famous feud between the Grays and Selbys at Berwick churchyard in 1597, on the side of the Grays. He was assaulted along with John Bell and Edward Gray while Bryan Horsley was killed when Ralph Selby plunged a long rapier in his back. Around the same time John Reveley of Humbleton was named in a bill of the Laird of Hopriggs for a band of £240 Scots money, which was referred to the commissioners.

While Robert Reveley was fairly fortunate to escape unscathed from the showdown in the churchyard, Ferdinando Reveley wasn't as charmed. He was murdered by the East Teviotdale rider Thomas Hall who smashed his sword into the top of Reveley's head and nearly cut it in two with a gash eight inches long and six inches deep that splattered blood and brains everywhere. Andrew Hall was named as an accessory to the murder at Beneley. Unsurprisingly, the Reveleys were at feud at the time with an unspecified family, and there were also quarrels among the English Rutherfords, Wallaces and Scotts. An unnamed Reveley with a reputation as a 'very honest man' was murdered soon after by one of the Northumbrian families and Willoughby requested that the case be heard in Newcastle so that they couldn't 'find means by their clans and allies to escape commonly unpunished.'

The pledge Ralph Reveley was a victim of a raid by the Burns and

Youngs at Berwick in 1588; he was handed over at the West Ford and retaken after being dismissed by the Humes to be detained in the Tollbooth in Edinburgh until December 1599. His standing as a gentleman of the country was reflected by the fact that Sir George Home of Edinburgh stood the bond for him.

English West March

A list of the worst 'freebooters' on the West Marches who were responsible for 'committing the cruel outrages of plunder, burnings and murder upon the neighbouring counties' was presented to the Lord Bishop of Carlisle in 1586 and it makes for interesting reading. Simon Musgrave, the Lord of Pattinson, Will's Arthur Graham, Will's Jock, Richard Graham of Akeshawhill, Adam Graham of Hall, Richie of the Bush, Fergie's Willie Graham, Geordie's Christie, Black Jock's Johnny, Geordie Graham of Sandhills, Geordie Armstrong of Catgill, Hector of the Harelaw, Emmie of Gingles, Muckle Willie Graham, Richie's Geordie, Geordie of the Gingles (alias Henharrow), John Nelson, the curate of Bewcastle; Jock of the Lake's Christie, John 'Longfoot' Noble, Red Rowie Foster, Will Graham of the Rosetrees, Will Graham, Hutcheon's brother, John Musgrave of the Catterlin, Gib's Jock's Johnny, Tom's Robbie, Patie's Geordie's Johnny, young John of Woodhead, Richie Graham, son of the Goodman of Brackenhill, John 'Gleed John' of the Side, Young laird of Graitney, Archie and Jock of the Gingles, Dick's Davie's Davie, Black Jock's Leonie, Will's Jock, Richie Graham younger of Netherby, Sandie's Ringan's Davie, Gibb's Davie's Francie, Watt Graham 'Flange tail,' Will 'Wimble Willie' Graham, Will 'Muckle Willie' Graham and Will Patrick, the priest of Bewcastle, were all named.

It was no surprise then that three of the Cumbrian Grahams were demanded as pledges for the West Ford meeting a decade later; what is surprising is that eight of the twelve actually bothered to turn up. Anthon's Edward Armstrong and Red Rowy Foster were definitely no-shows and the other two weren't named by officials.

Will's Arthur Graham of Netherby, Will's Geordie Graham of the Fauld and John Graham of West Linton were named as the pledges to stand for the clan, who were already in serious hot water for their involvement in breaking Kinmont out of Carlisle as well as their numerous and incessant raids, feuds and organised criminality.

John of West Linton had led a raid on the town of Annan earlier in 1597 where he and his men drove away 30 cattle and 24 prisoners and, although they avoided being sent down to York, Will's Arthur Graham was a fugitive by 1606.

John Musgrave was disgusted and dismayed in 1602 when the notorious Richie Graham of Brackenhill was being primed to take a higher position of office in Gilsland by the noted troublemaker Lancelot Carleton. He was gutted primarily because he'd lost his job as land sergeant and Carleton was replacing him with Roger Widdrington, the brother of Carey's deputy Henry. This wasn't because he was an upstanding citizen, however, but because he had attempted to kill his brother for capturing Francis Radcliffe and sending him down to York gaol.

Richie Graham was a well-known protection racketeer, murderer, counterfeiter, horse thief and reiver who was also employed as the bailiff of Gilsland for over 20 years (where he ran up huge debts.) He was summoned down to London to appear before the Privy Council for his part in the rescue of Kinmont with Walter Graham of Netherby, William of the Mote, William of the Rosetrees, John 'Willie's Jock' and Hutcheon 'Richie's Hutcheon' Graham. Brackenhill's part wasn't a minor one; he'd been named as a chief player in the plot and was threatening to murder witnesses, while one of his daughters was married to Jock Armstrong of Tundmouth, whose uncle had killed the Scottish West March warden Sir John Carmichael. Richie was 'lately deceased' in 1606 and his widow claimed that Brackenhill had been purchased by his father from Sir Thomas Dacre as she attempted to retain possession of it.

Musgrave felt that giving Graham a more official position would 'give such encouragement to the Grahams and other border thieves in friendship with them, as the state of this country is likely to be very lamentable.' Sour grapes or not, Musgrave had a point. The Grahams had tried to murder him two years earlier; they also intimidated witnesses with death threats and refused to appear before the lord warden on any charges. Over 60 of the Grahams were recorded in the sessions of Cumberland and Westmorland as being outlaws for murder, burglaries and raiding, yet they went about unafraid of justice and were keeping a number of Scottish fugitives safe with them.

Musgrave was also aggrieved that one of Carleton's gang, a fugitive for murder from Scotland, had shot a 'piece charged with two bullets' at a Scotsman during a warden meeting in a botched assassination attempt. By surrounding himself with such mobsters, Carleton was becoming a crime Godfather in his own right. The family were long established in Cumberland and had come over with William the Conqueror when Baldwin de Carleton was granted land near Penrith. The Carletons could always spot an opportunity and Lancelot's son young Lancelot went to Fermanagh in Ireland after a number of the Grahams had been deported as part of the King's Ulster Plantation to set up business there.

*

Tom Storey of Howend, near Arthuret, avoided being detained at York as a pledge, like the others of the West March, and in 1606 he was selling £8 worth of corn on behalf of his neighbour and friend George Graham of Mill Hill ahead of his deportation to help him get some cash together for the trip.

Tom was the son of Walter Storey and had been indicted alongside a number of Grahams and others for the murder of George 'Percival's Geordie' Graham in May 1584. In 1588 Tom rode with Willie Irving of Graitney Hill, Fargie the Plump, John Storey of Stagmire and Will Graham of Milehill to burn the houses of George Herries and Cuthbert Geare in Scotland and drive off 80 cattle and a number of horses. Four years later he hit the town of Annan with John Storey of Stagmire and Tom's Willie, Ally's Willie's John Storey, Fargie the Plump and Black Jock's John where they stole 40 horses and took 16 prisoners, stripping them of their horses, armour, purses, gold and silver while killing Thomas Brown and mutilating John Brown. The fact that the bill was excused by the Grahams Rob of the Fauld, Will of Rosetrees, Hutcheon's Andrew and Richie's Will gives an idea of where the orders for the assault came from.

George Storey of the Holme was named a fugitive in 1606 and the Northumberland branch of the surname, who quit the Debatable Lands in 1528, were just as troublesome. In 1605, Nicholas, Christopher, Thomas and Mark Story of Roddam and Richard Story of Wooperton, with William Routledge and Francis Clarke of Wooperton, 'arrayed themselves in a riotous and warlike manner' with sticks, swords, staves and lances to assault James, Ralph and Edward Allison at Roddam.

*

Sim Taylor and his family were at feud with the Scottish Armstrongs in 1583, most likely because Cuddie and John Taylor had twice raided the laird of Mangerton for 200 cattle, insight and £20 while John and Adam's Jamie Taylor had lifted 800 sheep from Sim Armstrong of Whitehaugh. It was a big mistake; the old laird of Whitehaugh, Sim the young laird, Sim's Tom and Jock of Copshaw then rode on Matthew Taylor and slaughtered Martin Taylor, John Dodgson, John Skelloe and Matthew Blackburn then drove away 140 cattle, 100 sheep, 20 'gait' of crops, and all of their insight worth £200 in retribution. The Bewcastle Taylors had offended the Armstrongs some years earlier when one of them stole some important papers from the laird of Whitehaugh and when he sent one of his men to get them back, Taylor burnt them in front of his face rather than hand them over. The Armstrongs weren't the forgiving type and burnt him in his house as revenge.

The headsmen of the Taylors, along with the Grahams, Fosters, Routledges and Hetheringtons, had to give bonds of assurance in 1593 for their good behaviour and those under them due to their intermarriage with Scots.

Sim was also implicated in the Kinmont breakout; Richie Graham of Brackenhill, Will's Jock Graham and Andrew Graham had met on the hill above his house at Carvinley, with the Carleton brothers and Thomas Armstrong, before riding into Scotland to meet with Buccleuch, Rob's Gib Elliot and old Watt Scott of Harden, five days before springing Will Armstrong.

Will Taylor was one of the Carleton Crew and described as their chief man in a mob of 600 Liddesdale and rebel riders that raided Gilsland and took 200 cattle, 40 horses and a number of prisoners in 1597 while the Liddesdale man Andrew Taylor and West March Englishman Tom 'the Laird' Taylor were both declared fugitives in 1601. Tom had been noted as a 'common thief' protected by the Grahams a year earlier.

*

'Red' Rowy Foster of Kershopefoot was one of those named in the Bishop of Carlisle's worst freebooters list in 1586. In the November of that year he'd been taken for 200 cattle and 200 sheep and 'gait' along with his neighbours by Richie Maxwell of Cavens and Scottish soldiers from Langholm. His daughter was married to young Sim Armstrong of Mangerton, while the laird of Mangerton himself was married to a daughter of John Foster's of Kershopefoot, so the Fosters were tied in with the chief Liddesdale riders as in-laws and relatives. That in itself was enough to implicate them in the Border Mafia, but they also had blood kinsmen living in Liddesdale.

The family were described as 'dear neighbours' of the Scots and a number of their men were in turn married to the daughters of the Elliots and Armstrongs and more than happy to raid with them as well as carrying out jobs of their own.

The authorities were not able to get their hands on Red Rowy to deliver him as a pledge at the West Ford. After the others had been brought back from the second unsuccessful meeting, they were either 'broken away or suffered to escape from the Blacknest' where they had been committed on their return. Henry Leigh felt that there could be some 'disquiet' from the pledges being on the loose but 'was as ready as them' to put it down.

George Foster of Birkbush, Laurence 'Laurie' Foster of Greenlaw, Rinion Foster and Arthur Foster were all included in Lord William Howard's 'black book' of executions during the Border Pacifications of the early 1600s.

*

Edward Aglionby wrote in a note during 1592 that the Hetheringtons, Grahams and Fosters that lived by the Leven and Kirklinton were the 'only men that ride both into England and Scotland' on the English West March.

The pledge Little Geordie Hetherington of Broomhill was one of the riders of the family that inhabited the land from Hethersgill almost down to Carlisle under William Musgrave of Scaleby castle in the 1580s. It is possible that he was the Geordie Hetherington who was taken prisoner by a party of reivers named as young Christie Armstrong of Barngleish, Geordie Kang Irving, Watty Curry, 'Prior's

John's' sons Hebby and Jock, Sim of Fingland and others that also took ten cattle, four young nolt, a sleuthhound and nine other men from Willy Graham of Leven in January 1589. He may also have been the Geordie Hetherington at West Linton who had two horses and his insight stolen by 'Tom of Tolshiels' and some soldiers in 1601.

Thomas 'the merchant' Hetherington was an enforcer of Richie Graham of Brackenhill who was charged with collecting protection money with menaces for him along with William Hayer – mostly from other Hetheringtons around Gilsland, Sandy Sike, Lanercost and Walton – in 1596. Hayer, a 'special factor' of Graham's who used 'evil speeches and threatening to make them pay' published a book of all those that were paying up which was displayed in Arthuret church in England and Canonbie in Scotland, just to intimidate a little more.

John 'Jock of the Rigg' Hetherington was hanged in the West March in August 1623.

*

The Nixons were found on both sides of the Border and Dand's Quintin Nixon was selected to stand as the hostage for the families residing on the English side of the line.

They resided mostly near the Leven and in 1583 Thomas Musgrave named the principal riders as Clem Nixon of the Hole, Archie of Kendal, Mally's Hobb, Davie's John, Henry's Tom, Watt's Archie, Will called 'Beksword,' Cudd 'Blanket luggs,' Will 'Byntaby,' Charlie's Clem, Hector and John of the Shate, Christie's John, Jenkin's Adie, John, Will's John and John Nixon of the Park.

The Nixons, Routledges, Nobles and others of Graistangflatt were reived of 200 cattle, 300 sheep and 'gait' in a raid of 200 men led by Scott of Buccleuch in 1588. By 1592 the raiding had taken some toll as the Nixons, Fosters and Crosiers of Bewcastle were described as 'sore decayed.'

In 1560 Willie 'Gimmerhorn' Nixon of the English crew was being held prisoner by the Laird of Ferniehurst when John Haliburton of Murrayslaw attempted to kill him. Haliburton was locked up in Edinburgh castle and not charged until the authorities knew that Gimmerhorn had recovered from his injuries or not.

*

The English authorities had to bring forward an 80-year-old man called James Noble of Kirkbeckmouth in 1538 to ascertain when the Routledges had ended up on their side of the Border. Old Noble said that Cuthbert and John Routledge, Robert Elliot and Gerard Nixon had been let all the lands at Bewcastle when the Liddesdale men 'came into England and were sworn to King Richard III at Carlisle' by Sir Richard Radcliffe and three others of the King's Commissioners 'sixty years since.' Noble stated that before that the lands had for a long time lain as waste ground and the four Liddesdale men paid no rent but were placed there to 'maintain the King's interest during wars and to keep the Borders there.' That's why the Liddesdale men that moved in became known as the 'Traitors of Leven' and were hit so hard by Scotland at that time. The officials – the Musgraves – also spoke to 70-year-old John Routledge of Kinkerhill, who backed up what Noble had said.

Ten years earlier Dacre had been in the Debatable Ground looking to burn out Grahams and Armstrongs and had drawn out the Routledges known as the 'Quickses' and although they disappeared with their household goods into the woods and mosses at the head of Tarras, he drove off 80 nolt, 100 sheep and forty 'gait.'

In 1537 the Routledges rode with the Liddesdale Armstrongs and Fosters in a band 200 strong to Tynedale where they spoiled the Charltons of 240 cattle, 12 horses and mares, and killed two Yarrows and a Robson. That same year William Routledge and his son Thomas, formerly of Lukkins of Leven in Cumberland, were involved in a riot with Will 'Willy Cut' Armstrong and his brother Edmond, Alan 'Bluntwood' Foster and the Scotsmen Jock Halliday and John Gray as a mob of 50 gathered at Hestedhesh in Gilsland where they attacked and murdered Thomas and John Crowe, and Thomas' son Thomas. William Routledge was indicted of treason but acquitted while his boy was found guilty at Carlisle.

There were also Routledges living at Kilham in north Northumberland alongside the Storeys and it is a possibility that they made the journey up there with them when they fled the Esk in 1528. Ninian Routledge of that 'grayne' stole 200 ewes and wedders from the Goodman of Gateshaw in a night raid with John Brewhouse and Robert Moffat in 1596. James 'Rakeshaw' Routledge also hit the Goodman for 40 ewes and wedders in a separate raid. That same year

Andrew 'Leech' Routledge was murdered by the Armstrongs of 'Whittleye' (probably Willgavy, otherwise called Willeva, near Lanercost) in Bewcastle. He was from the branch of the Routledges that had Richie of Cancroupe was standing as a pledge.

*

Anthon's Edward Armstrong of Willgavy has a claim on being one of the most notorious border reivers of them all; in a note in 1607, when the Border Commissioners were attempting to deport him to Ireland, Armstrong was described as: 'the most dangerous person that has lived in these parts and has continued in outlawry for the greatest part of forty years. His return would be most offensive, and of worst example.'

The officials at Carlisle seemed to be apprehensive that they were showing Armstrong favour by deporting and not beheading or drowning him when he had been charged with 12 murders. They wrote meekly to Lord Salisbury that 'Armstrong has friends with whom he desires to live and says he will give your lordship sufficient security for his abode with them, which we refer wholly to your wisdom.'

Lord Dacre was having trouble getting Anton's Edward delivered by Scrope to the West Ford meeting in 1597; he had been denounced an outlaw of England and Dacre wanted to know if he should burn his house, and those of the other appointed pledges that he couldn't get, and what other action he should take with them.

Six years earlier Anton's Edward had been indicted for the murder of the Scotsman John 'Cokespool' Armstrong along with William 'Andrew's Will,' Armstrong and his brothers Rinion and Richie, Andrew 'Ingram's Andrew' Armstrong, John 'Stowlugs' Armstrong and Gresland Armstrong, all members of the Gilsland branch of the family. Their sister was married to 'the laird's Jock' Armstrong of Liddesdale, displaying the complex inter-family ties on the border.

While Dacre was hunting down Anton's Edward, his clan were burgling Nicholas Snowdon's house at Hartley Burn. Jack 'Stowlugs,' Ingram's Andrew of Unmanrowe, Rinion, Thomas and Andrew, with Andrew's Willie, arrived in the darkness at around ten at night and rode away with 16 cattle, a calf and a horse.

They also broke into the dwelling of Robert Wallace of Merse Know in Knaresdale and 'put the whole household in great danger and mortal fear of their lives' while stealing six cows, three heifers and a 'white gray' mare. Walter Graham of Spittal was with Andrew's Will, Rinion, Jock Stowlugs, Sowter's Rinion, Ingram's Andrew and Thomas Armstrong on that raid.

Edward had rejoined his mob by November 1597 to hit John Noble of Knaresdale for five cows and 20 sheep at 10pm with William 'Andrew's Will,' Rinion 'Andrew's Rinion' and Andrew of Unmanrowe. In June 1598 he, along with his kinsmen John and Francis with William and Richard 'Archie's Richie' Orran also of Willgavy, took 11 cattle from Henry Dobson at Byershall during another night burglary. They had stayed at Peter Bell's the day before carrying out the job.

Surprisingly, the following year, Michael Armstrong of Willgavy was riding with possibly the same John Noble, and William Hackneyhead of Bewcastle, when they broke into Jenkyn Blenkinsopp's house and stole three cows from him.

Edward's father Anthony had also been an outlaw named as one of the chief offenders in 1541 after he fled out of Gilsland into Scotland when the Earl of Cumberland was the warden of the West March. His crew killed seven Fenwicks in Northumberland in the Middle March that same week.

Two years later he was still on the run for March Treason by manner of his selling horses to Scotsmen and bringing Scots raiders into Hexhamshire. Thomas Clifford and the soldiers of Carlisle garrison went out to apprehend Anton and although they found him lurking at night in some woods with the Scotsman John Irving, Armstrong had prior warning of the attempt to snatch him and used his local contacts with Thomas Wilson, an officer of Lord Dacre in Gilsland, to get together 60 locals to fight off Clifford's men. Edward had real mafia pedigree and strong family and marriage ties to both the North Tynedale and Liddesdale crime gangs making him a major player in all of the disorder and a trusted go-between for the two.

While the Armstrongs are generally considered to be a Scottish family, there were also more than a few that lived in Northumberland and were English; Simon 'Cudwells' Armstrong of Yearle stole a sheep from Robert Awder at Wooler with James Carr of Middleton Hall and George Rutherford.

The Armstrongs had been in Cumberland as early as 1282 when James de Molton was pardoned for the murder of John Armstrong and the King ordered the sheriff of Cumberland to restore him to his lands, which had been confiscated by the crown for the death. Similarly, in 1377, the English King was bound to 'meddle no further' in Adam Armstrong's lands in Corkeby, which were held 'in fee to him and his heirs in chief by homage by reason of fees' which were paid to Andrew de Harcla.

Some of the Gilsland Armstrongs appear to have moved along Hadrian's Wall by 1601 as Christopher Armstrong of Housesteads, Anthony Armstrong of Thorngrafton, Edward Armstrong of Overhall, Rinian Armstrong, alias 'Andrew's Rinian,' alias 'John Armstrong of Housesteads,' and Clement Hetherington of Plencrosset in Cumberland broke into the spinster Anne Taylor's house at Thorngrafton and lifted 12 ewes and 8 hogs belonging to Edward Foster. That crew became known as the notorious outlaw gang the 'Busy Gap Rogues.'

Rob's Sandy, Ingram's Andrew and Andrew's Will took 13 cows from Cuthbert Wilkinson of Gofton in August 1602 and Rob's Sandy was back on his own in the December to lift 15 hogs from Gilbert Ramshaw. The bulk of the Willgavy crew – Anton's Edward, Thomas 'Geordie's Tom,' Andrew 'Ingram's Andrew,' Richard, Anton's Edward's son Thomas and Jock 'Stowlugs' - were all fugitives and on the run in November 1606, with some of them no doubt being sheltered at the Busy Gap. Two months later Thomas 'Anton's Edward's Tom' Armstrong, Jock Stowlugs and Christopher Irving were pursued as far as Yorkshire and captured. The 'eminent ill-doers' were hastily transferred to Carlisle castle as the officials knew that 'men of their quality are desperate and full of practices.' Anton's Edward himself was captured and put on a boat over the water to Roscommon in April 1607 while Edward's Tom, Jock Stowlugs and Christopher Irving, alias 'Gifford Carlton' were all executed by Lord William Howard. Ingram's Andrew escaped the noose and was raiding again in 1610 with Edward Armstrong of Thirlway and the Scotsman Andrew Henderson of Liddesdale to take three cows and an ox from Hugh Ridley of Whitchester.

At other spots in Northumberland, John alias 'Jock' Armstrong of Harkford was with the Northumbrian gentlemen John Ogle of Rawgreen, John Heron of Hexham and George Humbley of Slaley who set upon Miles Phillipson, insulting him and beating him up during an affray where they also took his horse, some goods and money in 1603. In 1615 Matthew and Henry Armstrong of Brearedge stole two cows from Edward Dodd at Roughside. Nationality was only an issue to the reivers when it came to who was paying or to escape from the law. They were simply Borderers.

*

George Bell of Bowbank was executed by Lord William Howard sometime after his demanded delivery at Norham; he appears third on a list that Howard kept in a diary of those that he succeeded in having hanged behind William Ormsby of Milton and Richard Newton of Lanerton, with Will 'Carlisle Cutler' Bell following him to the gallows. The 68 victims of Howard's tough justice stretch to 1623 and include some of the choicest rogues on the frontier including Simon Armstrong of Twedden, John 'Long John' Armstrong, John 'Jock Stowlugs' Armstrong, Rinion 'Gowdy' Armstrong, Will 'Flang Tail' Graham, John 'Jock of the Rigg' Hetherington and various Routledges, Irvings, Fosters, Dixons, Ridleys, Robsons, Turnbulls, Milburns etc. The final two that he sent to the rope were John 'Cockey' Nixon and Edward Nixon of Moselhaugh at Carlisle.

The Bells were another family long involved in the Border mafia and found in both England and Scotland; the Cumbrian Bells were using their Scottish cousins to evade the law in 1540 when Andrew Bell escaped from Carlisle castle, injuring his shoulder in leaping from the castle walls but continuing to steal while with the Scots. He fled from Carlisle to his uncle Tom Bell's at Gretna, then went from there to his brother Humphrey at Middleby before moving on again to John Beattie's at Langholm. He was riding with Rowie and Nichol Beattie. The Gilsland Bells that George represented had been hit hard by a Scottish Armstrong raid in 1597 which left them 'utterly beggared' and saw 60 taken prisoner over the border. Thomas and James Bell complained to the Privy Council that only they and their friends had been targeted and felt that the Armstrongs were trying to spark a deadly feud on behalf of the dangerous and scheming Thomas Carleton who showed nothing but 'hatred and malice towards them.' Carleton was a high-ranking English official and the Land Sergeant of Gilsland, but he was also related to the Grahams by marriage and he was regularly accused of corruption, inefficiency and collusion with the Border mobsters. He was also a major suspect in Kinmont Willie's escape from Carlisle. Henry Leigh was attempting to assist the Bells but admitted that there was 'neither faith, nor truth, nor manhood' left in Gilsland and felt that the area was almost 'past recovery.' One of the Gilsland Milburns had been killed by Gerard Carleton and two of the Grahams after going down to London to complain on Lord Scrope's behalf.

The Bells, along with the Scottish Elliots and Armstrongs, were said to have been planning to murder Thomas Carleton and all of his kin for his part in capturing and executing the outlaw Christopher Bell, who had 'voluntarily confessed' to 11 murders, in February 1596, and his killing of an Armstrong two years previously. These were, however, the details provided by Lancelot Carleton and are therefore highly suspect. Lord Scrope was dubious himself and dismissed the assassination attempt as false.

Thomas Carleton was murdered by the Northumbrian Ogles and Shaftoes in 1598 when he was harbouring a Scotsman called Davie 'the Carling' Elliot, who had killed William Ogle and others. They knew him well - in 1577 the Carling and John 'Todsfoot' Elliot had been fugitives in England and were 'plainly received among the Fenwicks and Shaftoes.'

The crew got word that he was at a place of Carleton's and 14 of them got together to kill him in revenge. Carleton chased after them when they were riding home and was furious that they had 'killed one within his charge that he had given protection to.' In his rage he almost knocked one of the Ogle's off his horse as he broke a spear over him and fired off a loose pistol shot at another. With a wild-eyed lunatic raving at them and six men in his own company, one of the Ogles had seen enough and coolly and efficiently shot Carleton clean through the head. Sir Robert Carey wrote that Carleton 'fell dead at the instant and never spoke a word.'

8. THE SCOTTISH PLEDGES

Scottish West March

The Laird of Johnstone's pledges were very much demanded on the back of the Kinmont Willie jailbreak at Carlisle; John Armstrong of Hollows, and his brother Christie, were part of the rescue and were partakers in the plot beforehand. John had 300 cattle and 480 sheep driven off his land by the Captain of Bewcastle and five hundred men in 1596. Thomas Musgrave justified this to the English Privy Council by saying that John had been 'the leader of incursions' and he was trying to make restitution to the 'poor men' that he'd stolen from. John put a complaint in for the raid and was seeking compensation for 400 cattle, 200 sheep, £20 in gold and money and £200 insight to a total of £800 at Carlisle on 28th April 1597. The Armstrongs entered an assurance with the Musgraves but hit them with a revenge attack in June 1599 when they killed one man, hurt others and took the Captain of Bewcastle's goods, 120 cattle, 6 horses and 100 sheep. John of Hollows wrote a letter to Lowther after the raid explaining his actions; he penned that at Lowther's desire he had 'done no harm to no Englishman and caused all (his) friends to forebear sense' and was breaking the assurance with the Musgraves. He did, however, sign off 'your friend to use usefully,' and was keen to keep in with Lowther. John was married to Walter Graham of Netherby's sister and was raiding with the likes of Davie 'Bangtail' Armstrong, 'Bungle' Armstrong and the Laird of Mangerton's men Mungo and Jock Armstrong in the 1580s.

*

Jock Armstrong of Kinmont was Kinmont Willie's son and one of the men that signed a letter in April 1599 desiring the freedom of the Liddesdale pledges from York. In 1583 he was riding with Ecky of the Gingles on John Routledge of the Stoneknow and had also saddled up with another Jock Armstrong and Ecky of Stubholme to raid Christopher Bellman of Hedderswood. He maimed and wounded Dick Routledge and his son in a raid on Kirkleventon with Jock of the Calfhills, Jamie of Canonbie and 20 others. Kinmont Jock was a dangerous character with a reputation to upkeep and in 1587 was part of a menacing mob of 500 men including John 'the laird's Jock,' Andrew of Whitehaugh, Hector of the Hillhouse, George of Arkleton and John 'of the Score' Beattie who carried away 600 cattle, 600 sheep, 35 prisoners and £40 insight as they targeted the Ingram valley.

By 1592 he was with his brother young Will of Kinmont, Tom of Rowanburn and 24 others that left a number of men with terrible injuries in an attack on John and James Taylor of Bolton Fell. Later that year Jock, Willie and Christie Armstrong of Barngliesh led the 27 men that kidnapped and kept prisoner Walter Calverlie of the Holme Coltram, while also taking three horses, £10, a gold chain, jewels, gold, silver, writings and household goods during a burglary.

In 1602 Jock was denounced a rebel, with a number of others, for failing to pay taxes to John, Lord Maxwell. Alexander Armstrong of the Craig, Sandy Beattie in the Burnfoot, Ninian, Andrew and Jock of Gingles, Andrew of Langholm, Rob Graham in Brockholes, Christie's Rob, John, Davie and Ally Beattie, Andrew Scott in Rayburn, 'Muckle' Tom Little, Adie Irving, Adam Beattie of the Yards, John Beattie of Ronelburn, Christie Beattie of Bankhead, Archie and Rowy Beattie, John Armstrong called 'Wallis,' Christie Armstrong of the Neid, John Armstrong of Calfhills, Ninian Bell of the Tower, Wattie Bell and Davie Bell, and Jock's brother George all failed to show and hear the charges against them.

*

The 'Kang' Irvings hailed from Stankheugh and in 1592 they were with Geordie Armstrong of Catgill and others that left six people injured in Etterby near Carlisle when they lifted just three nags, so it seems that it was blood they were after rather than goods. The demanded pledge Geordie 'Kang' Irving and his brother Willie, with James Elliot 'Todd' and a crew of twenty, took 20 cattle, 30 sheep, 20 'gait,' a young mare and insight from Robert Forster of Allengarth in 1596. The Kangs were heavily involved in breaking Kinmont Willie from Carlisle Castle; the crew were close to Buccleuch with Willie being described in an anonymous letter to Lord Scrope as his (Scott's) 'own man.'

He was also riding with the Goodman of the Hollows, John Armstrong, one of the other demanded pledges – and 200 men that plundered Anthony Hetherington of 200 cattle and 20 horses while burning ten houses. Then both the Kangs, Geordie and Willie, were with Jock Armstrong of Monkbehirst, Sim's Archie, Pattie of Harelaw, Sim of the Calfhills and sixteen others that burned the houses of George and Roger Hetherington and drove away 40 cattle, ten horses and 40 sheep in 1596.

Hobbie Irving (Irwin, Urwin, Irvine) represented either the Gretna Hill, Bonshaw, Redhall or Kirkpatrick graynes of the family; with Davie Johnstone of Redhall also being demanded, it seems reasonable to assume that Hobbie was from that branch as both were outlaws at the time of the West Ford meetings.

Back in 1535, the English West March Warden Dacre gave refuge and safe conduct to Rockcliffe castle to Jenkin and Robert Irving, Christopher and Andrew Graham, and others named as 'rebels of the king of Scots.' But in 1544 a number of Englishmen were taken prisoner by Scotsmen under the 'assurance' of Wharton; John Musgrave of Bewcastle was taken by Davie Irving of Trailtrowe and Robin Irving, Jenkin's brother, or Willie Bell, with others said to be in the hands of the Irvings, Bells and other 'assured' riders.

The Irvings' relationship with England was a delicate one, and by 1572 the Bishop of Carlisle was urging Lord Burghley to 'loose the reins and let slip against the Irvings of Bonshaw' in a most unchristian manner. The old Bishop, writing from Rose Castle, reckoned there were 'no falser Scot' than them and they were maintaining rebels. He willed Dacre to 'wreak on a Scot, an enemy and a maintainer of traitors, his feud.' Though the man of the cloth said that he 'detested and hated their bloody feuds' he hypocritically used the excuse that he loved his country in encouraging them.

11 years later the Irving allegiances with England were explained by inter-marriages, the Laird of Gretna being married to Fergus Graham's daughter, Watt Irving of Gretna Hill with Robin Foster's daughter and Mungo Irving with William Graham of Leven's daughter; Will Irving of Sark Bridge was with Little Tom Graham's daughter and Edward Irving of the Bonshaw to a lass of Richie Graham of Netherby, while young Edward Irving was with Rob Graham of the Fauld's daughter.

The Irvings, along with the Armstrongs and Grahams, were at

feud with the Musgraves at that time and the Irvings were also long at feud with the Bells and Carlyles. Those of the family that were friendly with England, like the Johnstones, were to be declared outlaws for their allegiances south of the Border. Scrope warned Walshingham that the weakening of the Johnstones would be the strengthening of the Maxwells and was seeking advice on how to handle the situation.

The Irvings and Johnstones had been involved with the Grahams in murdering a brother of Lord Herries (Maxwell) and the Scottish noble was pressing the English authorities to deliver the offenders, around 15 in all, who were 'still doing very many evil actions and committing many thefts both in England and Scotland, to the disquiet of both the Borders and beggaring of many true subjects.' Those were Herries' words, communicated by Lord Scrope, who seemed keen to cut a deal. Treachery was never far away, especially when it came to the law enforcers.

The Irvings and Johnstones were also being pursued by King James who had ridden on the West Border to dole out retribution to the Earl of Bothwell after his raid at Falkland in 1592. They were caught up in the middle of a storm beyond the normal border mafia bounds and paid the penalty in 1597 as all of their property in Gretna Hill was burned out and they were declared fugitives.

*

Will 'Red Cloak' Bell and two of his brothers were at Kinmont's rescue from Carlisle and involved in the masterminding of the scheme beforehand, although an anonymous letter to Lord Scrope claimed that Will 'did nothing but that which Richie Graham of Brackenhill caused him to do.' That involved killing Hob Forster and leaving three other Forsters for dead in the run up, so Willie certainly wasn't as innocent as the writer was suggesting. The fact that Red Cloak and Fergie 'Will's Fergie' Graham had taken 200 cattle, 10 horses and spoiled houses in Sark of £100 with 20 men that year meant he was a major player in the criminal dealings on the Border. In 1586 he was with Watty Bell and the Carlyles burning the mills and corns of the Grahams of Esk while taking £400 insight and then riding with Tom Bell and others to take 30 cattle, 50 sheep, 3 horses and £100 insight from William Graham of Steddalls.

Will 'Redcloak,' Watt and Richie Bell lifted 30 cattle and £100 insight from Geordie Taylor of the Bone Ridings while Will and Tom also hit James Graham and Hutcheon Graham of the Peartrees for 50 cattle, 100 sheep and £100 insight from their houses.

An old feud between the families had been revived four years earlier when the English Grahams crossed the border and murdered two of the Scottish Bells. The Grahams also killed a Scottish Graham who had been part of the Bell crew that had rode on them. Lord Scrope was preparing for the 'greatest feud ever on these Borders' due to the inter-family nature of the dispute with the Irvings and Carlyles also getting involved. The Bells had long been at feud with the Irvings and the Carlyles were Bell allies. With murders going on between the families, in power struggles and simple matters of respect, the West March was in total disorder. In July 1585 the Bells joined with the Armstrongs to drive off hundreds of cattle from Crawford Moor. They killed two of the trod that came after them, injured three more and took twelve as prisoners to ransom. Lord Maxwell was controlling most of the Scots gangs at the time and Lord Scrope felt that they would 'lay waste the whole country up to Peebles' as they ran raid after raid on the countryside of both realms.

However, by 1596, the Bells, Elliots and Carlyles were riding under the banner of Buccleuch and the Scotts and 400 of them, including Buccleuch himself, launched an assault on the English Grahams. They set fire to the doors to smoke the men out of a tower after failing to knock it down and took three of the Grahams of Medhope prisoner. This could have been an attack to prevent the Grahams talking to the authorities over the Kinmont Willie breakout as Robert 'Rob of the Fauld' Graham was beginning to blab and grass up his own kinsmen as well as the others involved.

Humphrey 'the Joker' Bell was a fugitive from justice in 1606 after avoiding a Dumfries court hearing. Red Cloak was the last Chief of the Bells and he died in 1628.

*

Edward Carlyle of the Limekiln led a raid with his associate Geordie Bell of Annandale on William Musgrave of Hayton in 1596. They stole 12 horses and he was named as the pledge to stand for his crew. The Carlyles and Bells were long-term crime partners and often backed each other up during feuds at disputes, with the Carlyles despising the English Grahams.

The Carlyles were heavily involved in the downfall of the laird of Johnstone in 1598 which led to the chaos and non-delivery of the West March men; he had broken an assurance with the gang and one with Drumlanrig, so King James ordered in a proclamation at the market cross in Edinburgh that he 'be defamed and perjured, his picture be drawn in blood, to signify a murderer, and hung with his heels upward with his name set under his head and INFAMY and PERJURY written on his legs'.

The English felt that Johnstone would be enraged at the decision and Sir William Bowes warned that the laird would 'do some great attempt and set that country on fire' on hearing it as he was 'stout and fortunate, and will be desperate.'

The Carlyles and their allies were being hunted down by 1602 with the Scottish King clamping down on the 'great misrule and unquietness of the West March' by asking for complaints against them and the Johnstones, Armstrongs, Bells, Irvings and Beatties 'and other disordered thieves' to be handed in at the market cross in Dumfries. When very few were received, he ordered it done again.

John Maitland brought up an old charge from 1597 to keep the monarch happy. He complained that his boss Sir James Douglas had been at feud with Sir James Johnstone 'with slaughter happening on both parts' that saw the Douglases, Bells and Carlyles fighting with the Johnstones, Grahams and Irvings and Maitland's lands wrecked by the latter gang's raiding. Although Douglas and Johnstone were reconciled, he was seeking payment for the damages. It was a dangerous game as the Johnstones by then were back in power in the West March with Sir James Johnstone of Dunskellie the warden; later that year he was bound to hand over to the Scottish authorities John and Adam Carlyle, Geordie, Christie and Sandy Armstrong for the Kinmonts and Will 'Redcloak' Bell's brother Fergie as pledges for the already detained Francie Armstrong of Kinmont, Will 'Redcloak' Bell and Alexander Carlyle at a meeting on 1 January 1603. He asked to 'borrow them home' on a bond of £2000 each when he did deliver them, however.

By 1606 Hob Carlyle and his brother Willie were on the run after being declared fugitives from a Dumfries hearing of the Border Commissioners as the purges began to kick in.

*

Clothman's Willie Graham was one of John Maxwell, the Earl of Morton's men. He signed up to an Act in favour of Morton in December 1585 along with other Grahams of the West March such as Simon Graham in Howath, Richie Graham of Medhope and his sons John, Francie, Sim, Fergus and Wattie; Wattie Graham of Aikenshaw Hill, William Graham of Beddoskholme, Willie Graham of Blawart Wood, Robert Graham of Longriggs, Geordie Graham, Richie Graham in Woodend, Robert Graham, who lived on the Sark and dozens of others of notable families such as the Armstrongs, Scotts, Littles, Bells and more in the West March.

In May 1586 Lord Scrope was planning a meeting with those Grahams that had favoured Maxwell. The following week there was an attack on the Grahams that had taken the side of the Johnstones, by Morton's followers, and those of Drumlanrig castle.

The Scottish and English Grahams were complexly intertwined. Maxwell was complaining in 1592 that Fergie of Medhope, his fellow Scotsman Francis Irving of Graitney Hill and a number of the Grahams of Esk were violently occupying the lands at Springkell, Logan and Watoun which were worth £2,500 Scots annually to him; the English Walter Graham of Netherby, William and Fergie Graham of Mote and Richie Graham of Brackenhill were also intruding and pasturing sheep on lands at the Harelaw and Canonbie at the time. They were at Kirkanders in Annandale too and Maxwell's main gripe seems to have been that they were doing him out of tax money set by the Abbot of Jedburgh by not bothering to pay – and keeping those that would pay off the land.

The Grahams had certainly started out in the Scottish West March and when an 'Indenture of Canonbie' was drawn up at Coldstream in March 1494, John Graham, the bailiff to the prior of Canonbie, laid a complaint against the Tynedale riders George and Alexander Charlton, Hugh and Richard Wilkinson, William Robson, Robert Dodds and his son Archie for burning and raiding in the Scottish West March. With such venerable leaders as Sir John Musgrave, John Heron of Chipchase and Edward Radcliffe appearing for the English and Walter Kerr of Cessford, Patrick Home of Fast Castle and George Home of Wedderburn for the Scots, it was a formal document of some clout.

*

The outlaw David Johnstone of Redhall avoided going to York with the rest of the West March men but was again being offered as a pledge – either him or his brother James – for the Brumell gang of the large Johnstone clan in 1599 as they made offers of good behaviour to the Scottish Lieutenant.

The other Johnstone crews were named as 'the old gang of Wamfra,' 'the gang of Foullduris,' and the families in Fairholme, Fingland, Dryfe, Kirkhill and Lockerbie, where the chief strength lay.

Davie Johnstone, his son James, brother John and James Johnstone, with Wilkin Johnstone of Eschescshiells and his brothers Robert and William had been entered to appear before the King and Council as early as July 1586, and though the charges aren't specified it seems to be related to the murder of a Maxwell.

The Redhall Johnstones and the Irvings of Graitney were fugitives for the 'cruel slaughter' of John Maxwell and King James was scheming with the English official Henry Leigh to trap them in November 1597.

Gavin Johnstone of Redhall was raiding in Cumberland in 1592, lifting 24 cows and a horse with Andrew and Jamie Rome, David Johnstone of Prescotside, Rob Graham of Langriggs and Geordie's Christy Graham but Davie was the main fugitive of the crew. By 1607 Davie Johnstone may have been residing at Bogedge as he, along with his brother John Johnstone of Redhall, Francis, John and Thomas Johnstone of Priestwoodside, Gavin Johnstone in Cowartsholme and Will Bell had assaulted Edward Maxwell in April the previous year. They cut him up then stripped his clothes and left him lying naked for dead with twelve terrible gash wounds from their swords bleeding all over the ground. Maxwell had recovered enough to complain that he hadn't received justice and the Captain of the Guard was ordered to apprehend them and take an inventory of their goods as they hadn't shown to hear the charges. It wasn't the first time that the Redhalls had been assaulting Maxwells and a year later David 'Stad Davie' and an unnamed brother, with Geordie Johnstone, his brother's son, the sons of Willie of Redhall, were still being pursued for the murder of John Maxwell, the provost of Dumfries – some 24 years earlier - by his nephew Sir Robert McLennan of Bomby.

The long-running hatred and deadly feud between the powerful gang chiefs of the Maxwells and Johnstones contributed significantly to the disorder in the West March with their factions fighting among themselves in a deadly jostle for power, influence and easy access to cash and weapons and peaked in the Battle of Dryfe Sands in 1593 which almost exterminated the Maxwell clan.

Davie of Redhall and his brother Geordie appeared in the list of the final fugitives issued by the commissioners of the Middle Shires in 1618; but that was far from the end of his mafia career – he was again denounced a rebel in 1620 as he joined in a gang of eighty 'insolent persons of the Middle Shires, some of who were declared fugitives and outlaws' heavily armed with jacks, spears, lances, pistols and other assorted weapons to assist Richard Graham of Langriggs and William Graham of Rosetrees after they'd been booted off the £5 land of Langriggs in Annandale by James Lindsay who'd purchased it. They set about Lindsay, and the men who were with him, running him through with a lance, though he survived, badly injured others and garrotted a horse.

Davie remained at large in the Scottish Middle March and in 1622 Francie 'Kinmont' Armstrong, by then living at Nowleck, stood as cautioner for £1000 merks for him to appear before the Border Commissioners at their next justice courts in that he 'shall not escape from the freedom of the burgh of Jedburgh but shall remain in free ward there within.' Gavin Johnstone of Redhall obliged himself to pay a like penalty to free Francie from his caution, thus putting in doubt the notion that the worst of the border reivers were all hanged or deported during the pacification. This simply just wasn't the case as the names turn up time and time again.

Liddesdale

Sim Armstong, Laird of Whitehaugh

Simon Armstrong's reputation preceded him to York. He was described as 'a man of great action and good living, and one that was at the breaking of Carlisle castle,' in the notes written on a parchment for the jailers. The young Laird of Whitehaugh was the eldest son of Lance Armstrong and had a formidable charge sheet; in an early job in August 1583 he was raiding Thomas Swinburn at Capheaton Whitehouse with a crew of 24 others that drove off 80 cattle. The Armstrongs of Whitehaugh, Mangerton and Tinnis alias 'Puddingburn' and the Elliots 'that join with them' were also said to be reiving and stealing in their own country that year 'even to Edinburgh ports.'

The then young laird of Whitehaugh, the Laird of Mangerton and Jockie Armstrong of Kinmont led 600 men to burn 15 houses, take 24 prisoners and cut the hand off one while taking gear worth £900 in a raid on Haydon Bridge and Rattenraw. Sim also saddled up with Tom Armstrong of the Gingles and his son Tom, his brothers Eckie and Ally, Hobb of the Whitehaugh, 'Rowie's Tom' of Mangerton, Adie Elliot of the Shaws, and others, who took ten prisoners to ransom from the Slyme pub at the head of the Coquet. They also drove off 320 cattle, 21 horses and mares and spoiled 30 shielings during the day foray in 1584.

By 1589 Sim was named specifically in a band of the Earl of Bothwell for the keeping of the peace between Scotland and England alongside the other most notorious offenders – his father Lancy, Sim Armstrong of Mangerton, Robin Elliot of Redheugh, Martin Elliot of Braidley, and all others of the surnames Elliot, Armstrong, Nixon and Croser with the Turnbulls and Rutherfords of Teviotdale.

The following year, the Scottish King laid a claim to the Debatable Lands on the West Border below Canonbie. In a proclamation at the market crosses in Edinburgh and Dumfries he requested the following people to make official their stakes on the land – Sim Armstrong of Mangerton, Lancy Armstrong of Whitehaugh, George Armstrong of Arkleton, Sim Armstrong of Whiteside, Hector

Armstrong of Harelaw, David Armstrong of Woodhouslees, Christie Armstrong of Barngliesh, Ninian Armstrong of Byreburn, Christie Armstrong in Broomholme, Christie Armstrong of Auchingavil, Will Armstrong, called Will of Kinmont, Ninian Armstrong of Auchinbadrig, Arthur Graham of Blawatwood, Francis and John Graham in Canonbie and Richie Graham of Rempatrick. The Debateable Land had long been 'possessed by persons disobedient to the Laws' and it was an attempt to bring them under Crown control. Soon after Sim and dozens of other Liddesdale gangsters were to be entered by the Earl of Bothwell and the Earl of Murray for the dozens of English bills that they were filed in as the effort to bring some order to the unruly mafia who were raiding well out of anyone's control but their own.

The Liddesdale crews were refusing to attend days of truce to sort out bills as Buccleuch was in dispute with Cessford and Liddesdale refused to be under Kerr's command. They were described as 'the greatest truce breakers of all Scotland towards England' and a despairing official wondered if it would be 'more convenient' if Liddesdale and Tynedale were just left at liberty to 'do one attempt for another.' In other words, just leave them to it and let them raid, murder and blackmail each other 'like for like and harm for harm,' as he put it.

In 1593 Sim Armstrong stepped up his criminal activities and was one of Bothwell's accomplices named in an Act of Remission and later denounced a traitor by the King. This was after the Earl had forced his way into the Monarch's presence at Holyrood at night to try and intimidate an agreement, with the likes of Armstrong taking charge of the gates, roughing up the courtiers and setting fire to doors. Sim was 'put to the horn' in a proclamation at market crosses throughout Scotland for his part in the rebellion after he failed to show up to hear the charges against him. He was also charged with spending the best part of 1591 and 1592 striking 'adulterated coinage' at his house at Royne in Liddesdale.

Two years later his father Lancy was cautioned as a principal, with Andrew Kerr of Ferniehurst as his surety, that he would be answerable for all 'attempts' (ie. raids) by himself and those he was responsible for – except for Sim and his son, young Lancy.

In 1597 the Lords of the King's Secret Council were meeting to put special measures on hearing cases for the Armstrongs and other 'broken men, thieves and malefactors' from the Johnstones, Bells, Carlisles, Beatties, Irvings and others. They were worried that the Armstrongs could coerce and silence a jury and wanted their bills to be heard by 'the least suspect, most neutral and indifferent' honest gentlemen with two or three of the Council prescent as the gangs were riding on a daily basis into England to commit crimes.

Sim was a hard-case and a major organised crime figure, but his father Lancy was possibly even worse. In 1583 Lance was the head of the Whitehouse Tower Mob with Sim his heir and underboss, but there was also the 'Lady's' Andrew, Archie, and Francis; John, Hobb, Jock, Rinion 'Gaudee,' Rinion, Hector and Jock of Tweden, who were all blood relations and at the top of the pyramid. Old Lancy had murdered Will Noble of the Crew and certainly had more blood on his hands; by 1584 when Lord Scrope captured the head of the Armstrong clan, Mangerton, in his home, he said that he was 'chief and principal of his surname, also the special evildoer in the spoils of this March, next after the laird of Whitehaugh, who I cannot well come by.'

His grandfather and namesake Simon 'Sim the Laird' Armstrong was also a noted reiver who was hung at a gallows in February 1536 for a number of crimes including stealing a couple of oxen from the Laird of Ormistone, a horse from Robert Scott of Howplaslott and burning and fire-raising at the same place; Sim was also accused of stealing sheep from the King's shepherds John Hope and John Hall and 'treasonably giving assistance' to a sworn Englishman known as 'Evil-Willed Sandy' or Alexander Armstrong, and his accomplices, all Armstrongs, Nixons and Crosiers sworn to England. He'd been denounced a rebel three months earlier with Christopher Armstrong, the brother of the famous Johnny 'Black Jock' of Gilnockie, and others. Sim despised King James V for the hanging of Johnny and his followers six years previous and this may have had more to do with his death than the actual offences.

His grandson had a strong outlaw tradition to upkeep, and just two months before he was taken and delivered to York castle as a pledge in September 1597, the Liddesdales under Buccleuch had launched a number of attacks in Northumberland. The most notable was when the Whitehaughs and 24 others went to Turnlippet Moor and in broad daylight attacked several men travelling to Newcastle. They killed two, wounded and mutilated ten others and took 17 horses and mares and all their goods worth £40.

Buccleuch must have eventually talked, or threatened, Sim into going into detention but he had no intention of stopping behind the grim walls of York's dungeons any longer than he had to and was the brains behind a failed breakout attempt in March 1598. They were ratted out as Sir Robert Carey was warning the Archbishop of York that they planned to escape imminently a fortnight before the attempt.

An Englishman named Laurence Canby had been placed in with the Scottish pledges after killing a man in Howden and Armstrong and Robert Frissell soon got to work on him, telling him that if he took their letters to Scotland, then Cessford would give him a horse and gold so he could live better than he ever had in England.

One of the Armstrongs was visiting regularly from Liddesdale to bring cash for Whitehaugh and they had plotted the escape with the assistance of a locksmith called James Dargon of York, who promised them horses. The plan was to hide in the woods and moors by day and travel by night once they were out and eight were originally to go – Whitehaugh, Will Elliot of Clintwood, Overton, Dand Pringle, Thomas Aynsley, Richard Rutherford, James Young of the Cove and Will Hall. Whitehaugh then decided that Ralph Burn, William Elliot 'the boy,' Richard Young and William Tait should go too.

Between eight and nine o'clock after locking up Hall, Pringle, James Young and Rutherford burst through their chamber wall as planned and kicked their way through the dust and rubble up onto the gallery where they used an iron bar to prise the door for Overton, Armstrong, Will Elliot and Aynsley to boot open. The adrenalin must have been pumping as they then broke the bolt on the chamber where young Elliot, Burn, Tait and Richard Young were held and all twelve raced up to smash an iron bar off a window and threw down straw to jump down on. William Hall, Ralph Burn, James Young, Robert Frissell and Richard Young all managed to leap out of the window but the sound of the breaking had alerted other prisoners who began crying out and shouting, so Whitehaugh, Rutherford, Aynsley, the two Elliots, Pringle and Tait had to burst through two wooden doors before they were out into the purple, starry night with fresh air on their faces and onto the walls where they leapt into the darkness and landed with a thud on the sloped grass. Young Elliot didn't dare take the leap and Whitehaugh broke his leg when he landed. But the keeper's men were waiting, and they were all recaptured and spent the rest of their time at York being shackled in irons at night.

It's not clear who the rat was; Canby was passing information to the guards but that was after Carey had sent his warning, so the leak clearly came from the Border. The Youngs and Burns had been trying to meet with the East March gentlemen to settle their bills and get their men out shortly before the attempt, so they didn't know that it was going to go down. Dargon seems the most likely source for the leak as he'd already blabbed about Will Hall's attempts to talk him into getting him a couple of horses for an attempt of his own to Thomas Percy at Alnwick.

They were stuck back behind bars and when the Scottish pledges heard word that their English counterparts had been freed from the Tolbooth in Edinburgh in December 1599, they wrote a letter to Thomas Lord Burghley, the Lord President of the North, soon after asking to be bailed in the same manner or 'place their eldest sons in their stead with sufficient security for their true imprisonment.' They were getting increasingly desperate and offered to enter themselves at any time within forty days of being recalled or pay everyone for the crimes done by their surnames and would be 'so for ever become bound unto your Honour, in relieving them out of this misery, living in irons, wherein they be like to perish, except it may please your Lordship to grant them release thereof.' It's unclear who penned the letter as a number of the pledges, including Sim, couldn't write and signed with a cross but it was an eloquent and impassioned plea that fell on deaf ears.

Sim and Will Elliot of Hartsgarth finally escaped on a Sunday in October 1600 when a notorious thief called Geordie Simpson and three others went to the Castle in disguise under the pretence of supplying them with money and sprung them out. The jailer Redhead hadn't been paid and was probably looking forward to the prospect of getting some cash; when he realised that Armstrong and Elliot were gone he panicked and made up some cock and bull story about having 'a great secret of high importance' that he would only reveal to the Queen. Lord Eure wasn't falling for it and felt it was 'a mere excuse to escape punishment and procure pardon for his offences.'

Sir Robert Carey believed that the escape would bring trouble upon the Borders and 'breed more disquiet than anything that had happened' since his living in the North. Armstrong and Elliot had initially refused to stand as pledges for Buccleuch and he'd had to use the 'strong hand' to get them delivered; now the free pledges were refusing to follow his orders and Carey said they'd 'proclaimed openly that all fugitives, Scots or English, who joined them would be aided and protected, respecting neither their King nor his officers, or any hurt that England can do them.'

Not long before the escape, a two-year-old charge was brought up against Sir Walter Scott of Branxholm for Old Lancie of Whitehaugh, Sim's sons Sim and Archie, Sim of Mangerton and his son, Archibald Elliot, Adie 'the Peck' Scott, Jock 'the Stowre of Quhynecleuch' Scott, Will Elliot, and Dand 'Sweet Milk' Elliot reiving 24 cattle from Corsmondburn and of further later raids 'under his standard and banner' where they'd slaughtered and mutilated. Scott would only admit to young Sim and Archie, and young Mangerton, being his men and therefore part of the Branxholm crew. Mind, he was on a £10,000 bond to keep the Armstrongs under control and he was also dubious of the prices of the stuff that had been stolen and suspected it was the equivalent of an over-inflated insurance claim today.

To give an idea of how the gangs operated, when one of the West March Armstrongs was locked up in the pledge chamber at Dumfries in 1600 following the murder of the Warden Sir John Carmichael, he was described as 'ever being a common and notorious thief, trained up from his youth in reiff, theft and oppression, according to the accustomed trade of the wicked and unhappy race of his father's gang and branch.' Reiving was a family business and a way of life. They knew nothing else.

The reiving days, however, were approaching an end and Sir John

Carey captured six of the most notorious offenders drunk in an alehouse in the East March in April 1602. Lord Scrope reckoned that the men were outlaws that had fled to north Northumberland to avoid justice and steal. Their names were Archie Armstrong of Whitehaugh, Archie Armstrong of the Abbshawe and Jock Armstrong, John Michelson and Robert Story – all gang members of the House of Whitehaugh – with Dandie Armstrong called 'Broad Sword.'

Five months before, Archie had been with his father Sim, brother young Lance, John Forrester, Archibald Elliot of the Hill and his son Mark and 20 other 'wicked persons' armed with hagbuts, pistols, lances and other weapons that arrived in the dark at Bedrule and murdered Alexander Lord Hume's shepherd John Wilson in his bed. They cut off his right foot, stabbed and slashed his head and all over his body then drove off 400 old sheep, wedders and ewes to Whitehaugh's ground in Liddesdale where they divided the booty up. Hume had taken over the land from Hector Turnbull of Barnhills when he was 'put to the horn,' so there is a distinct possibility that it was a killing to frighten people off taking their friend's land, or they'd been paid by Turnbull to carry out the hit. It certainly sent out a message.

Three years later Sim of Whitehaugh was approaching semi-respectability and was out poaching with Walter Scott of Harden, James Gladstones younger of Ormston, Robert Scott of Bowden, John Armstrong of Kinmont (the West March pledge), Robert Elliot of Larriston, William Elliot of Dumboyline (possibly the boy from Dinlabyre, or a relation), and Gilbert Elliot of Horsleyhill, when they were caught in the Cheviots, Kidland, and down into Redesdale taking game without permission from the landowner, the Earl of Dunbar. They were all fined 1000 marks.

Sim was hanged by the commission in 1607, and by 1611 his sons and the Elliots were still hunting in the area and not only 'making a great spoil of the game and destroying the woods,' but trying to stir up trouble with the locals. They were denounced rebels for failing to appear at court to hear the charges. Hob Armstrong of Whitehaugh was also hanged that year while John, Francis, and his sons Lancie and Simon, were all fugitives from justice after failing to show at

Jedburgh for sentencing.

The law caught up with the younger Sim Armstrong, called Whitehaugh, in Meddop, in 1622 when he was charged at Dumfries Justice Courts with stealing a carcass of salt beef from Andrew Little three years previously, a stick of 'fustiane' from the peddler James Linday and his brother, three horses from England in 1616 and a nag from Rob Graham in Howend the year before that. They were petty charges, and Armstrong walked as he was cleared of all the offences.

Will Elliot of Hartsgarth (Clintwood)

Will Elliot was off the Hartsgarth branch of the Larristons, a brother of the Laird of Redheugh, and noted as a man of action and some living when he was sent down to York Castle. He was also a 'cousin' of Buccleuch and was said to be protected – and often joined – by him in his murders, burnings and spoiling.

And Buccleuch's crew were formidable, racking up over 50 gangland murders during the lead up to 1596, including cutting to pieces six Allendale men going to Hexham market and slaughtering seven Charltons and Dodds in their own houses. Buccleuch himself was said to have personally killed 24 Englishmen, including 16 soldiers, and although he had been imprisoned (under house arrest) by the Scottish King, he had made a decent time of it, senior crime figure that he was, by going out hunting and hawking. It was reputed that his crew had robbed to the value of £10,000 out of the West and Middle Marches of England over the previous 20 years and he had 'bound himself' with all the notorious riders in Liddesdale, Eskdale and Ewesdale.

Elliot was one of his underbosses and no doubt kicking some of the take from his raids upstairs. He was burning barns and raiding in Northumberland in 1587, and later hit a farm of Gilbert Park at Wharton. He then murdered two Dodds that he was at feud with in Tynedale. Will was a stone-cold killer and was with Buccleuch and 200 horsemen to murder and burn in Tynedale again soon after and was accused of the murder of Charltons in 1593 alongside his boss, the keeper of Liddesdale. He was riding with Watt Scott of Harden and his fellow pledge Sim Armstrong with 60 men to drive off 300 cattle, 20 horses, take goods and gold money worth £100 and spoil two houses of Robert Graham of the Lake in the English West March.

Will was a high-ranking criminal and had a gang of his own working under him; his man Robert 'Hob' Elliot of Bowholme was condemned to death and hanged at Hexham after being caught red-hand by the captain of Harbottle and two more of his thieves, named as John 'Gleed Larriston' Nixon and Clemmy 'the Clash' Nixon, were with George 'Buggerback' Elliot and others that drove away 80 cows and 12 horses from Quentin Foster at the Hasslegill in 1595.

The Elliots had always proved troublesome for the authorities of both England and Scotland and in 1494 William Elliot, and 85 others of Liddesdale named Elliot, Armstrong, Whigham and Croser, failed to appear at court and were fined.

By 1515 Robert Elliot of Redheugh and his brother William of Larriston with Henry Nixon, James Forester in Greenhaugh and Adam Croser with 11 other kinsmen and associated were charged for 'all manner of actions.'

To give some idea of the criminal activities that they were engaged in, Will 'Side-ears' Elliot had led a cold January raid on Haltwhistle with Will, Gavin and Archie Elliot, Jock Elliot of Thorley's Hope and his sons Rolly, Hob and Willie, Lionel Croser and others, including the Nixons. Willie 'Side-ears' Elliot was a major player at the time and organised Jock, Dand and David Elliot in a crew that burned the village of Unthank and took 60 cattle, 10 horses and insight gear from William Hopper. 'Side-ears' gathered his gang together again and more than 300 of them descended to burn the old town of Hexhamshire; Willie Elliot of Thorlishop, Rolly and Hob Elliot and a Nixon were the ringleaders alongside him in that episode of murder, burning and robbery.

The following year William Elliot of Larriston and seven others 'all kin and friends of the clans and surnames of Elliot' delivered James Forester and 47 others as pledges to the Scottish crown for 'all manner of crimes of treason, slaughter, reiving etc.' who were to be held for one year.

In 1526 a James Elliot was hanged for common theft and reset of theft and treasonably coming with Sir Walter Scott of Branxholme and the 'traitors and thieves of England and Scotland' against the Scottish King at Melrose. The following year King James V was still 'demanding redress' from Liddesdale and made Lord Angus, the Warden, refuse to 'host the broken men' – Elliots, Armstrongs, Nixons and Crosers. The English Lord of Richmond had complained to the Scottish monarch about the criminal behaviour of the named clans and Angus apologised that he had 'fully intended to have invaded the broken men and surnames on the Borders, but had had no leisure.' Whether or not he had the time to deal with the troublesome families is up for debate, but he was promising the 'pacification of the country to the satisfaction of all parties.'

Ten years later John Elliot, alias 'Jock Unhappy' was hanged for common theft and reset of theft and by the May 1543 the Elliots, Nixons and Crosers were looking to Sir Ralph Eure, the keeper of Tynedale, to 'assure them from hurt' and they would 'be bound to take part with England.' The Armstrongs had already signed up to help the English during the 'Rough Wooing' and their confederates were looking to get in on the action and the English money. Eure responded that, while the truce lasted, 'he would not hurt them if they didn't hurt England and kept the truce.'

The English seemed mistrustful of the Elliots; Wharton assured them until the Christmas but unless they, like the Armstrongs, put hostages into English hands then the deal was off. The Crosers were signed up to take part and a side-note stated that the order concerning the Elliots was because they thought that 'all should serve the King (Henry VIII) in like manner.'

They needn't have worried. The Elliots and Armstrongs raided John Dawson's house of Over Howden in Lauderdale on the 19th November and two days later they were at Buccleuch's chief councillor Michael Scott's places at Over and Nether Crishope in the Ettrick Forest, then two days later at the laird of Cessford's town of Newton in Teviotdale as they took to the job of harrying their fellow countrymen with relish.

The persistent Liddesdale habit of taking up arms for the English had long caused consternation in Edinburgh and the English chiefs were similarly sceptical of where the valley's loyalties lay.

The ordinary business of reiving continued and in March 1561

Will Elliot called 'Wedder-neck,' Peter Turnbull called 'The Monk' and Henry Black in Softlaw were hanged for common theft and receiving stolen goods but real trouble was brewing for the Elliots three years later. William Elliot of Horsleyhill, Robert, Gavin and Archie Elliot, Robert's illegitimate son William, Robert Elliot and James Scott, the son of William Scott in Haseldene, were charged with the murder of David Scott of Hasledene and it led to a blood feud between the two families.

The Scotts and the Elliots were 'riding daily and spoiling each other' because of 'some slaughter on either part committed,' and the Elliots made secret advances to the English to protect them in April 1565. They offered not only for their whole surname and friends to become English to Queen Elizabeth I, but also offered her delivery of 'their Sovereign's house in Liddesdale' – the formidable Hermitage castle. Lord Scrope was dubious on taking them up on their offer at first as he didn't want to disrupt the peace between the two countries; the following month Buccleuch was assisted by the Teviotdale riders as they raided the outlaws of Liddesdale, murdered seven Elliots and Crosers and drove off 'a great booty of cattle.' The very same day Liddesdale men were riding near Hawick, killed a farmer who was ploughing a field, and took some cattle.

So, in September, an English Lord, Bedford, secretly paid £50 to the Elliots and stated that 'if they acquitted themselves in the matter as they had begun,' they would get another £50. They were 'holding out well' and still working for the English a month later with the English Warden encouraging them to keep together at the Hermitage stronghold.

The bond didn't last and although a Crosier, a Douglas, and a Turnbull were charged with killing Sir George Heron at the Battle of the Reidswire in 1575, the loose tongues where saying that it was in fact one of the Elliots that killed him during the fray at Carter Bar.

A year later Dand Elliot, called of the Heughhouse, was filed on old and new charges and stealing 31 sheep from the Laird of Cessford and while he was found culpable of the crimes, the sentence was suspended.

Will Elliot escaped from York castle with Sim Armstrong in October 1600. Eight years later his spouse, Jean Rutherford, along with the wives of Gavin Elliot of Stobbs, George Haliburton and Gilbert Kerr of Lochtower, were complaining that William Scott, called Will of Northhouse, and his brother Walter came with a heavily armed gang to Stobbs at night and smashed the doors in, taking all the writs to the lands, and said they'd come back and burn them out unless they handed over the property to them. William Scott was declared a rebel for not appearing to hear the charges against him.

William appears in the records again in 1611 when he stood as a cautioner for his brother Robert Elliot of Redheugh for 300 marks and Archie Elliot, the laird of Foulshiells, for 200 marks while in 1622 a William Elliot was employed by Walter's son, the Earl of Buccleuch, to help bring justice to the 'Middle Shires' alongside a French of Frenchlands, Walter 'Norths' Scott, Walter 'Newburgh' Scott, Thomas Armstrong, Robert Pringle, John Scott, Alexander Hamilton, Henry Davidson and Hector Cranston. Whether or not this was his father's old riding companion and enforcer is unclear; but with nepotism rampant and old favours being called in, it remains a distinct possibility.

William Elliot of Dinlabyre

The young William Elliot was a child of just twelve years old, and 'heir to a man of fair living' called Martin's Archie Elliot who was 'one of the greatest undertakers amongst them', according to Sir Robert Carey. He wasn't exaggerating; Martin's Archie and his brother Gib, their cousin Martin's Gib, Will of the Steel (one of the other pledges initially demanded), 'Long' Jock and Archie Nixon, with others, had raided John Stoke and Edward Armstrong in 1589 to take 20 cattle and two horses, and injure two other horses. Martin's Archie and Will Elliot of the Heughhouse also took eight cows from Robert Younger of Halliden, then he hit Thomas Rutherford of Blackhall with Martin's Gib, his brother John, and Martin Elliot of Prikenhaugh, to steal five horses and a foal.

Martin's Archie robbed £6 insight and 12 cattle from Anthony Greenwell, Thomas Heron and Lancelot Teesdale at Stealie, and in a larger affair with Martin's Gib, Will Elliot of the Steel, younger, Archie Elliot of Larriston Burn, Andrew Kerr, and Clemmy Nixon 'the Clash', they cruelly wounded and maimed Christopher Hewrde of the Whitehall and took a horse and mare and £17 insight.

The same crew, with Dand Elliot and Jenkin Nixon added, reived 16 cattle, 3 horses and £20 insight from William Robson and Matthew Thompson of Allerwesh as the almost constant raiding continued. Martin's Archie was a ruthless reiver and killed John Hunter and John Hetherton while driving off 40 cattle with Sim's Tom, Hob Armstrong of Whitehaugh, Martin's Gib, two sons of Archie's Hob, John Nixon of Larriston Burn, and sixty other Scotsmen.

The raids were co-ordinated and well-organised. On one afternoon in August 1587, as Martin's Archie led a reive with William Elliot of Hartsgarth (the pledge), and 160 other men, to take away insight worth £300 and burn 23 houses and barns in Readpeth and Wyden, Sim, Andrew and Francis Armstrong of Whitehaugh, Archie Armstrong, who was Sim's servant, Eckie Armstrong of Tweden, Tom Elliot of Copshaw, and William Elliot of Gorrenberry, and others, followed up that evening and burnt a further 25 houses and took insight worth £1000 as Featherstonehaugh went up in flames.

His father Martin was also a chief gangster who rode with the likes of the lairds of Mangerton and Whitehaugh to plunder Sir John Forster's lands at Cheplopp and drive away 140 cattle, 3 horses and insight and three prisoners who they 'detained in war-like manner.'

His other sons, John and Gib, were with Watt Scott of Harden, Sim Armstrong of Whitehaugh, and 400 other men 'arrayed in most war-like manner' that drove away 300 cattle, 20 horses and burned 20 houses in a 1596 raid on the Armstrongs in Gilsland where they also took gold money worth £400 and mutilated many of the tenants.

Martin had built a strong tower house at the top of Liddell water against Tynehead which Sir Ralph Eure noted was 'strongly vaulted with open vents for trains of powder', which they had defended when besieged by Lord Scrope and Sir John Forster. When the Tynedale Dodds launched a hot trod on it to recover stolen cattle, they took the opportunity to lift a further 200 cattle, 100 sheep, some goats and 20 horses and mares in reprisal, and killed the former soldier Martin's Gib Elliot to bargain, Eure added that this clan of Elliots were 'great offenders to England, and Martin's Archie was a great rider.'

He was receiving Redsdale fugitives in 1597 and was demanded as a pledge for his clan in the first list issued in June that year. He actually turned up at the first meeting – Sim Armstrong of Mangerton didn't, as he was reputedly locked up in Carlisle castle for Lord Scrope's bills at the time – and the rest didn't bother; likewise, six of the Teviotdale pledges did not show. The Scots' King put Buccleuch in prison until he'd paid £5000 for failing to deliver the Liddesdale men. They had been sent for and were within 20 miles of him but cottoned on to what was going on and flitted before they could be taken to Norham.

Martin's Archie delivered his son to Buccleuch of his own accord and after Armstrong and Elliot of Clintwood broke out of York, Sir Robert Carey offered to have the boy taken out of the Castle and delivered to him; he reckoned that he could use him as a bargaining chip with Buccleuch to settle the Liddesdale bills if he was freed on conditions. He also felt that if he released young Elliot, whose family were in dispute with the Clintwood branch anyway, he would 'get such friendships by the boy's delivery that no attempt shall be devised against my March by the two escaped pledges as I shall have private warning of it.'

It didn't come off and it is unclear when young Elliot was released, but he was certainly still there when Hall broke out in September 1601 and does not appear to have been there a year later when the remaining pledges were sent up to Berwick.

It would be nice to think that he'd returned to the hills of home and pulled some good clean air tinged with meadow grass into his lungs as the rain pattered down on leaves and hugged his mother and father, but young Will seemingly disappears from the records.

   *

Will Elliot of the Steel was taken and held in the pledge chamber at Carlisle castle before he was delivered to the West Ford meeting. He managed to negotiate his way out of being sent down to York, much to Robert Carey's disdain. He blamed Lord Scrope's deputy Henry Leigh for allowing him to go free and the West March warden was to regret it as very soon after Elliot masterminded a raid on Tynedale that took 200 cattle, 30 horses and all of the wealth of the unspecified area that he hit; whether this was to get the cash together to pay someone off is unclear, but he was recaptured by the English and Carey felt that 'no death be bad enough for him to endure' as he urged for hanging and wanted to do the business himself, being mistrustful of the West March officials.

Elliot was a major reiver, as was his father Will before him. Old Will assured for his branch of the Elliots with Robert Elliot of Thorloshope and Archie Elliot called 'Fire the braes' in an unprecedented assurance made by all of the Liddesdale Crime Families at Hermitage in December 1584 to the Wardens of the English Middle and West marches, Forster and Scrope. It didn't stop him from learning his son the trade, however, and they were in a raiding party together in 1588 with 'Long John' Elliot and others to take 30 cattle, a horse, a mare and insight from Hob Tweddle of Birdoswald; in 1589 the father and son were at Catton in Allendale kidnapping and ransoming 15 prisoners while lifting 30 cattle, 4 horses and mares, a 'sleuth dog,' a sword and a spear.

They also hit Percival and William Thirlwall and Lancelot Robson for 16 cows and oxen and spoiled three houses with Jock and Steven Shiel, Archie 'Cowfoul' Nixon, George Simpson (the man who helped free Sim Armstrong and Will of Hartsgarth from York), and others, and rode with the chief Robin Elliot of Redheugh, Martin Elliot and his sons Archie and Hob in a raid on Robert French and Alexander Cragg to steal 60 cattle, two horses and £100 insight while burning five houses and two 'stakes' of corn.

Old Will robbed three houses and took six cattle and three horses from Greenridge in a gang with Archie Elliot, 'Long John' and Martin's Gib, and he was also part of a Liddesdale job on Kirkharle with Whitehaugh's son Andrew, his brothers Francis and John, Archie Elliot of Clintwood, Hob and Gib Elliot, Martin's Gib, Geordie Simpson, 'Long John,' Andrew and 'Red Nebb' Hob Armstrong that carried off 40 ewes and 10 hogs then turned on the hot trod pursuing them and took and ransomed the men Thomas Blenkinsopp, Ralph, Robert and George Wallace, Nicholas Teasdale (father and son), Robert Younger, Henry Robson, Henry Smith, Thomas and Robert Coulthard, John Harrison, William Teasdale, William Harrison, Henry Parker, Richard and Henry Liddell, John and Henry Bell, Richard Gray and Henry Ramshatt, with their horses and gear, and ransomed them back for a bumper £180.

In 1589 young Will led a raid with the Shiel boys and Jenkin Nixon 'Jock' on Roland Walker where they took six cows and a stott, and he was at Over Warden in Northumberland that year with Hob Elliot of Thorleshope, John and Gabriel Elliot of the Park, James Elliot of the Binks, George Simpson, Hob Crosier, 'Ill-drowned' Geordie Nixon, John Nixon of Larriston, and 80 others, that stole 42 cattle, six horses and mares and insight worth £100. When they were pursued by a hot trod, the Elliots turned around and took Arthur Thompson, Robert Stevenson, Anthony Stokoe and Matthew Leadbetter prisoner, ransoming them for almost £24.

Will's thefts and robberies continued, and he was with Geordie Simpson again in 1596 when they rode a day foray on Anthony and Clement Hetherington of Torcrossett with Anthony of the Binks and 100 men to forcibly remove 100 nolt.

Young Will was denounced a rebel in 1605 on an old charge going back to 1597 when he'd taken just three pregnant cows, a young horse and 20 marks of goods from Hector Turnbull of Stoneyletch and his son George in a night raid at Rule. Although the Border Commissioners felt that they had no power in the case as it had 'lain over so long,' it was still enough to see Will of the Steel have to go on the run as a fugitive. He was captured and hanged in 1607.

*

The laird of Mangerton, Simon Armstrong, was the chief of the Armstrong clan and another notorious raider. He was delivered at Carlisle by Sir John Carmichael with John Scott, one of Walter Scott of Branxholm's crew, to Lord Scrope for a major raid on Gilsland the year before. This was in the August of 1597 and should have made Mangerton easy to deliver at the West Ford as his 'detention' came after he'd been demanded as a pledge by the commission. However, Mangerton and Scott were permitted to 'remain at free ward' within the city and 'not to depart without licence from Lord Scrope.' There seems to have been some collusion going as at the meeting at Norham the following month, Eure was under the impression that Armstrong was being held in Carlisle castle, hence his non-appearance; six of the fourteen Teviotdale pledges were also missing from that meeting as a number of stalling tactics were deployed.

Scrope let him walk and in April 1599 he signed an offer, along with Robert Elliot of Redheugh, Gilbert Elliot of Hardlisdale, Gavin Elliot of Brough, Lancie Armstrong of Whitehaugh, John Armstrong of Kinmont, and Sim of Whitehaugh's son Lancie and brother Francis wanting the Elliots and Armstong held at York removed to Lord Scrope's detention.

When you see the 'justice' that he was dealing out, it's not hard to fathom why they were offering £500 bonds each on four men to 'remain true prisoners in Carlisle' and offering to do jobs 'from time to time' for Scrope, while 'always reserving our service to our Lord of Liddesdale' (Buccleuch). In time honoured fashion, they were offering to work for England by killing and thieving but playing both sides as they didn't want to bring down the wrath of Scott.

That all went south just a month later when the football match between the Armstrongs and Elliots and some locals at Bewcastle ended in murders. Within a couple of days, the Armstrongs murdered another and took 12 prisoners in a surprise attack two miles outside Haltwhistle. It seems that their request had been turned down and they were going to make Scrope pay by violent intimidation.

Sim of Mangerton was married to a daughter of Robin's Rowie Foster of Kershopefoot and in January 1584 he was captured in his own house by a snatch squad led by Humphrey Musgrave, the deputy warden of the English West March, Henry Leigh, the steward of Brugh, a captain Pickman and his soldiers then taken to Henry Scrope at Carlisle. Scrope was pleased with himself and bragged that the capture was 'greatly wondered at here, for it was never heard that a laird of Mangerton was taken in his own house in either peace or war without the hurt or loss of a man.' Sim must have talked his way out as in 1590 the Scottish Lords of Secret Council passed an 'Act for the Borders' at Holyroodhouse which principally named him and fifty other Armstrongs, Elliots, Crosiers, Nixons, Beatties and Scotts which had to be delivered to the English to answer for the bills that they were contained in. Bothwell promised to deliver Mangerton to Sir John Forster or 'never look his majesty in the face again if this be not done.' Mangerton's criminal dealings had made him some powerful enemies but in true 'Teflon Don' style, the charges never seemed to stick and although he spent some time inside cells, he never seemed to be there long.

The laird of Mangerton was hanged by 1607 when his brother Archibald Armstrong was denounced a rebel for obstructing King James' men from surveying the Debatable Lands alongside a number of other choice rogues such as Walter Scott of Tushielaw, John Armstrong of Hollows, Francie 'Kinmont' Armstrong and others of the clan with Grahams, Irwins and Johnstones. Archibald was in hot water again in 1610 for going to Alexander, the Earl of Home's lands at Gretna and Holme with 24 men armed with pistols and other weapons to violently take 240 stacks of corn. He was again denounced a rebel for not bothering to show up at the court.

*

John Nixon of High Eshes had been with his brother stealing sheep from Rolly Robson of Allanstead in 1595 and he and his crew were in Cumbria to drive away 20 cattle from Geltsdale belonging to Alan Hudson and Robert Storer of Castle Carrock the following year. John, the laird of High Eshes, seems to have completely ignored the commands for him to stand as a pledge and was one of the riders that fled when Buccleuch took them for a meeting with the Scottish King prior to being stood for York, though it appears that he may have been detained for a while in Carlisle castle with Will Elliot of the Steel.

The Nixons were long on the Border and in 1398 William Nixon appeared as a bond for Douglas of the West March of Scotland alongside the knights Sir John of Johnstone, Sir John of Carlisle, Sir William Stewart of Castlemilk, Herbert of Curry, John of Carruthers, John and Simon of Glendowyne, Nichol Little, Alexander, Geoffrey and Alexander Armstrong while in the early 1400s the Liddesdale branch of the family represented by Archie, Davy, Clement and Quintin were on a bond of 20 marks with Roger the Bishop of Carlisle, Thomas Lord Dacre and the knight John Musgrave. The terms were that 'if the above-bounden persons or any of their surnames, clans, or any other dwelling under them, neither steal, resett, lodge, nor aid stealer or stealers, resetter or resetters within the borders of the same, or if the said persons having stolen any goods restore the same to the owners within eight days after demand, or else within six days after such demand 'enter the said person or persons, stealer or stealers of the said goods to the King's guard, and if it shall happen any Englishman to follow his trod of his goods stolen into any ground where as the said Archie, Davy, Clement, and Quintin or any of their surname or clans have habitation or rule over make restitution of the said goods or else outrun the said trod out of their ground,' then the above bond is to be void.'

This early example of a Border treaty gives an idea of how long the raiding had been going on for and by 1515 the Nixons were still fully embroiled in the Liddesdale action. 'Fingerless Will' Nixon, Will Nixon of the Steel, and Hector and Ingram Nixon were riding with Will 'Side-ears' Elliot's gang alongside Lionel Croser and others including Jock Nixon and Henry Nixon's son Hector.

The following year the Nixons were raiding around Hexham with Hector and Will – the sons of 'Muckle Henry' Nixon, 'Deaf Jock' Noble (otherwise called Nixon) and his brother Dand – the sons of 'Fingerless Will' - and Will Nixon of the Steel's sons William and Ninian, Jock Nixon, James Croser alias 'James Twicks,' and 'the eldest son of one called Bragman, noble Scotsman,' stealing ten oxen and a bull belonging to the convent. They were pursued into Scotland but got away.

This incident was complained upon at a Spylaw truce day in the December of that year, which was attended by French officials as the fall-out from Flodden Field continued – the peace between England and Scotland had ended on 15 May 1515 and officials named De la Bastye, Clarencieux and others were there as witnesses; they also saw Lance Kerr doing a piece of traditional Border provocation - he put a glove on his spear point with a piece of paper with the name of Sir Roger Gray above it as a challenge. His brother Mark Kerr said that they were in contempt of Gray as they'd made him a prisoner in England because he 'entered not to them.'

The hanging of a glove from church railings was also used as a challenge for anyone that dared take it down to fight with the person that had put it there, as was witnessed at Rothbury in Northumberland by the vicar Bernard Gilpin 'the Apostle of the North' in 1570. Gilpin removed the glove without repercussions.

William Lord Dacre complained from Naworth in 1526 that the Nixons, Elliots, Crosiers and other Liddesdale men had ridden in by

Bewcastle and Thirlwall to Northumberland and took a man named John Bell hostage. A trod overtook the raiding party but ran into a waiting ambush of three hundred men that killed eleven and took 30 more prisoners. Dacre claimed that he was 'marked out for vengeance' because he would not allow the Armstrongs (and others) to settle on the Debatable Ground at the time, nor allow them to visit the Carlisle market. He was bitterly disappointed that none of the people of Bewcastle had assisted him and the garrison at Carlisle had refused to come out.

The following year the Nixons, Dodds, Charltons and Armstrongs joined together with Sir William and Humphrey Lisle, who had escaped from Newcastle prison, and gathered a crew of 140 men to burn Humshaugh in Northumberland. The Lisles were riding hard with their Scottish confederates the Nixons, Armstrongs and Crosiers and 'committing daily outrages' according to Sir William Eure. He demanded that well-horsed men be set on the frontier against Liddesdale at Haltwhistle and Hexham 'or else the head of Northumberland and the water of Tyne will be destroyed by Christmas.' This was in the October. He worried that the strength of Harbottle castle was 16 miles away and he 'could not keep both places.' The mayhem was abated somewhat in 1528 by executions and a Nixon was one of 12 hanged at Newcastle, with 12 others strung up at York, while the English Nixons of Bewcastledale fled over the Border.

The Scottish Nixons sent six of their men in the opposite direction to Bewcastle to offer service to the English as 'assured men' during the Rough Wooing in 1541. The Scottish King was said to be on his way down to the Borders from Edinburgh to punish the rebellious Liddesdales, with both Kelso and Lochmaben preparing for the visit; the Nixons weren't alone in pledging to England, however, with 'most of the surnames of Liddesdale and some that inhabit the Debatable Ground' following suit.

The Liddesdale cartel were undoubtedly the most violent and aggressive of all the riding clans and their ability to raise huge numbers to raid in large scale terms made them feared and respected on both sides of the line. But the real power behind Liddesdale lay in the hands of just thirty-one men, the chief mobsters of the valley.

In 1590 when Francis Earl Bothwell was to deliver six people to the English East March warden or his deputy for a devastating reive on Mindrum, an Armstrong, an Elliot, a Crosier, a Nixon, a Scott and a Turnbull were demanded. Helpfully, the English also made a note of who they wanted to answer for Liddesdale's crimes so unwittingly created a Who's Who of the crime families in the area.

They considered the worst offenders at that time to be Sim Armstrong of Mangerton, Sim Armstrong younger of Whitehaugh, Will Elliot of Hartscarth, Archie Elliot, called 'Martyn's Archie,' Archie Elliot of the Hill, Ninian Armstrong of Twedden and his brother Hector; Whitehaugh's other sons Andrew, Francis and Hob, Alexander's Archie Armstrong, John Armstrong, called 'the laird's Jock,' Thom Elliot of Chopschaw, Will Elliot of Gorrunberry, Davy Elliot, called 'the Carling,' Sim's Tom Armstrong, Thom Armstrong, called 'Rowie's Tom,' Ade Elliott of the Shaws, Sim Armstrong, called 'Rakkas,' and his brother John; Anthony Elliott of the Bents, Archie Elliott of the Hill, John Elliott of the Heughhouse, John Elliott, called 'Bowholmes,' Archie Elliot, brother to Will of Falneesh, Archie Crosier, called 'Quintin's Archie,' John Crosier, Martin Crosier of Bastonley, George Nixon 'Ill-Drooned Geordie' the son of Will of Callaley, John Nixon of Larriston burn and Mark Turnbull of Nether Bonchester – the top four all being the heavyweight pledges demanded in 1597.

Teviotdale

Thomas Aynsley of Cleethaugh

As far back as 1493 a Ralph Aynsley was up in front of the courts at Jedburgh on numerous charges; he had, along with Robert Aynsley and Patrick Mow, met treasonably with the former Duke of Albany. Ralph himself was also accused of meeting with an English reiver called Richard Reid and in another incident of driving away of 24 oxen and cows and six horses and mares from Spittal. Alexander Kerr of Ferniehurst stood as surety, which was unsurprising as the Aynsleys were long associated with the House of Ferniehurst.

Ralph was a reiver of the old school from near Dolphinstone and was charged again in 1502 for another raid of 100 sheep and 10 oxen and cows from a John Smith of Glengelt. This time Mark Kerr of Dolphinstone stood his bail to satisfy both parties.

The Aynsleys were another family that straddled both sides of the Border and in 1523 Hodge Fenwick, of Ottercops, was accused of 'keeping' Willie Aynsley, a Scot, for eight days every month. A decade later Sir Ralph Fenwick, the lieutenant for the English Middle Marches, was trying to get his hands on the lands of an Aynsley that had been executed for March treason. The farm, at Shaftoe, was worth 10 marks yearly; the wily Fenwick was offering five.

The Scotsmen William and Dave Aynsley became 'assured' English bound to King Henry VIII in 1544 and when Thomas Kerr of Ferniehurst took the side of Mary, Queen of Scots during the 'Lang Siege' of Edinburgh castle from 1571 to 1573, before finally being blasted out by a ten-day bombardment of heavy English guns, William Aynsley of Fala was a close accomplice of his.

Kerr was jailed before fleeing abroad and Aynsley was representing him among the clans; John Davison of Symmeston was fined £5 for associating with him, as was John Howd of Ancrum, who was also given a financial penalty for fiddling the price of his malt.

William Aynsley of Fala and his son Davie were raiders with the Rutherfords of the Tofts, the Piles of Milnheugh and Jock Hall of the Syckes that plundered Percival Elsdon of the Mote in 1587. Davie of Fala was a notorious reiver who was involved in a number of raids at the time with the likes of Roger Aynsley of Cleethaugh, the Halls, Ralph Robson of Middleknowes and the Piles who hit farms in upper Coquetdale, Redesdale and the Alnwick moors.

In 1595 Ralph and William Aysnley, and others, stole three cows, two oxen and 20 Nobles insight from William Hall and Simon Vaughan of West Newton. The Scottish Rutherfords came into Northumberland three years later and murdered one of the English Aynsleys, named William, as he tried to defend his goods, which they took, and his brother prisoner as well for good measure.

Thomas Aynsley of Cleethaugh was one of the Ferniehurst Kerr's crew and described as a 'man of some living and action' on a jailer's sheet at York. He lifted 16 oxen, 5 kye, 5 mares, 3 horses, a foal and a sleuth dog from William Haggerston at Haggerston in 1596 with Philip's Andrew Rutherford and in 1588 he was with his brother Roger and Tom Laidler of the Haugh to reive 17 kye and oxen, a horse and 20 marks insight from Laird Anderson.

Aynsley was one of the principal men behind the 1598 escape attempt at York castle and in April 1600 signed a letter with Robert Frissell, Richard Rutherford and William Tait that offered to satisfy the bills for which they had been detained at York 'either by payment, or by delivery of men contained in the bills to their value, or by Englishmen's sufficient bonds to satisfy the parties in three months,' and asking to be returned to Scotland. Much was made of the fact that he was Cessford's pledge, but one of Ferniehurst's underbosses, though soon after the four Teviotdale men were transferred to Berwick and chucked in 'Haddock's Hole.'

Sir John Carey was 'looking daily' to see if Thomas Aynsley's friends had agreed his relief by June 1602 as only he and Cessford's man Tait remained in detention there; his brothers Ralph and Roger in Cleethaugh were in trouble at the same time for being part of a large gang of Ferniehurst Kerrs that were killing and burning a house in Jedburgh and Adam 'Red Adie' Aynsley was also wanted by Sir Robert Kerr for failing to appear for a villain called William Henderson in Jedburgh who was wanted by the English.

The period locked up didn't seem to have much of an effect on Thomas Aynsley of Cleethaugh and in 1607 he was spending £1000 for William, Earl of Angus, to buy the legal outfit of arms from Sir Michael Balfour of Burley, Colonel Bartholomew Balfour or their factors. Other graynes of the family remained involved in the trouble, however, and John Robson, the burgess of Edinburgh, had to stand 500 marks each on Lancelot Aynsley in Oxnam and his sons Adam and Patrick not to harm an Adam Murray in Plenderlethtown. In 1611 Tom Aynsley called 'Midirie' was convicted and executed at a Jedburgh Court alongside Mark Elliot in the Hill, Hob Armstrong in Whitehaugh, Hob Moscrop, Archie Roger, Will Laidlaw, David Clarke and Hob Eccles.

During the Jacobite uprising in 1715, a Mr. Aynsley and 16 other Teviotdale men that had joined the rebel Army at Jedburgh didn't fancy their chances and slipped away into the Cumbrian fells as they marched from Penrith to Appleby on their way to defeat at Preston.

Ralph and Jock Burn (junior) of the Cote

The Burns were second to none when it came to matters of retribution and blood feud and in 1596 they slaughtered 17 of Sir Cuthbert Collingwood's tenants because they'd had the temerity to kill the reiver Geordie Burn's brother.

That number was later increased to 35 in a note by Sir William Bowes and the Burns and Youngs were also at feud with not only the Collingwoods but Sir Robert Carey and the officers of the Earl of Northumberland at Alnwick.

Geordie Burn met with the rope himself that year. He'd been raiding and was driving off cattle in the darkness when they were apprehended by Carey and his men. Two of the Burns, described by Carey as the 'principal thieves of Teviotdale', were killed and Geordie was left bloodied and bruised as he put up a fight when captured.

Carey had him hanged a couple of nights later and had a list of good reasons for doing so; he said that Geordie Burn was a 'great spoiler' and reckoned that he'd got a confession from him while he was in his cell. The fact that Geordie Burn is reputed to have said that the number of spoils and outrages committed by himself were 'so great that he couldn't remember the half of them' and that he'd freely admitted to 'several murders of innocent Englishmen that had never offended him' has to make one suspicious. When Carey later beefed up the confession to seven murders, 'laying' with over 40 men's wives and Burn 'spending his whole-time whoring, drinking, stealing and taking deep revenge for slight offences,' it seemed to be a way of justifying for his actions. His brother John Carey stated that Burn was Cessford's chief man, and the incident had taken place just three weeks after Kerr had bust James Young of the Cove out of Swinburne, so it smacked of provocation and a revenge killing by the Officials.

Kerr arranged a 'great football match' to meet with the chief riders at Shelsey and two days later he sent 15 raiders into Norhamshire in the mist of an early morning, then set a trap of 100 for anyone pursuing a hot trod. His men took some cattle from Norham town but nobody was foolish enough to give pursuit. Kerr told his men to drive the cattle back as it 'was not goods he wanted, but blood.' The Teviotdale men were looking for Selbys, Armourers or Ords to murder in retribution for Geordie Burn; those being the families involved in taking him. It just seems implausible that Geordie Burn would talk himself into hanging when he was protected by one of the most powerful men on the Scottish border. Nah nix, say nowt – the old Border code.

The Burns were an old Teviotdale family and John Burn and Hob Burn, his brother, were two of the chief riders in a crew 200 strong that burned Chillingham in 1516. John Burn was also a leading man on a raid on Newton that year. The family steads at Clifton Cote, Elisheugh and Awton Burn were destroyed by fire in an infamous English attack on the Bowmont Burn in 1542 by 2,000 horsemen from the garrison at Berwick led by Sir Thomas Hilton, the warden Ralph Eure, Sir William Boulmer, Ralph Boulmer, Robert Collingwood and John Horseley. The Burns became 'assured' Englishmen to King Henry VIII in 1544 with John and James Burn signing a document to serve the Monarch 'against the Scots and Frenchmen as all other nations.' These events culminated in the Battle of Ancrum Moor in 1545. It wasn't just the border valleys that were being burned and devastated by the Earl of Hertford for King Henry, but the incursions also saw Edinburgh and Leith fired during 1544. Seven hundred of the Scottish borderers that became 'assured' Englishmen joined 1,500 of their neighbours from the English side of the line and around 3,000 German and Spanish mercenaries in the English army that were confronted near Jedburgh by a Scottish Army of around 1,000 lances led by the Earl of Angus and a contingent of fellow Scots Borderers that hadn't assured under Scott of Buccleuch.

When the Scottish army began winning the battle, the assured men in the English ranks – the likes of the Burns, Youngs, Taits, Davisons, Pringles, Turnbulls, Rutherfords, the Scottish Halls and Robsons, Crosers, Nixons, Armstrongs – tore off their St. George's crosses and rejoined their countrymen to slaughter those around them. Sir Ralph Eure was killed in action as the Scots won a decisive victory.

In another English invasion, in 1570, all the farms on the

Bowmont Burn and the Kale Water were burned out again and Sir William Kerr and the clans went to Kelso to request the army to stop; as they refused to hand over pledges, the carnage continued and most of southern Scotland was fired.

Andrew alias Dand Burn of Elishaugh, Thomas Burn in Cote and the pledge James Young of the Cove were all fined £40 each for resetting and intercommuning with Thomas Kerr of Ferniehurst's men in 1575, while Mungo Burn and David Pringle in Lempitlaw were both fined £10 for assisting in an unspecified incident at Edinburgh.

The following year, in a Band of the Clans of East Teviotdale in a Bond of Manrent to Archibald Douglas, 8th Earl of Angus, at Jedburgh, Dand Burn of Elisheugh, Mungo Burn of Lempitlaw, John Burn in the Cote and Tom Burn all signed. The document basically recognised 'the many and great dangers and inconveniences' that the families had 'sustained and been subjected to' and the clans agreed to defend and give and take advice from Douglas on matters in the Middle March.

The Burns were on the rampage throughout the 1580s and in 1587 Jock Burn of the Cote and Tom Burn of Awton Burn, with Charlie and Mark 'Goodman' Burn of Elisheugh took 16 kye and oxen and 20 nobles in money from the Laird of Trewhitt. They were hitting Coquetdale again later that year; Tom Burn of Awtonburn, Mark Burn of Elisheugh, Charlie Burn and James Hall of Heavyside, with others, descended on Cuthbert Ogle at Lorbottle and stole 16 kye and oxen, two nags and £20 insight.

Charlie Burn of Elisheugh and Jock Burn of Clifton Cote's son Jock, the pledge, were part of a gang made up of Youngs, Davisons and Taits that reived Branxton that year and in 1588 George, Charles and Mark Burn of Elisheugh, Gib Burn of the Lough and Jock Burn, with Dand Young of Feltershaws and Richie Frame of Woodend were at Ingram lifting 30 kye and oxen and £5 worth of gear. They also wounded a man called Thomas Tevidale during the raid.

The Burns and the Youngs were involved in a blood feud with the Collingwoods and when you look at the damage that they were doing at the time, it's not hard to tell why. In 1589 Jock Burn of the Cote younger, Tom Burn of Awtonburn, the other pledge Ralph Burn of the Cote, whose nickname was 'Shortneck,' Charlie Burn of Elisheugh and Gib Burn of the Lough reived 24 kye and oxen and a lance from Gavin Collingwood of Berwick.

The Collingwoods were targeted again a couple of months later as Jock Burn of the Cote elder and his son Jock, with Dand Young of Cessford, lifted 24 kye and oxen, three horses and mares and insight worth £10 from Ralph Collingwood, Gavin Collingwood, Ralph Reveley and Thomas Mill of Berwick.

Jock Burn of the Cote and John Pringle of Linburn also took four kye and oxen and a sleuth dog from Sir Cuthbert Collingwood at Hasylriggs. The violence was cranked up a notch when Jock and his son Jock, along with Mark and George (quite probably Geordie) Burn of Elisheugh and Mark and Steven Burn of the Lough came with 30 men to Thornton and murdered three men, mutilated six men and women and spoiled Henry Smith and the township of £100.

The raids were obviously of a tit-for-tat nature and the Collingwoods were committing crimes of their own on the Teviotdale riders. In June 1589, the English Middle March Warden, Sir John Forster, wrote to Francis Walsingham, Queen Elizabeth I of England's principal secretary, that Sir Cuthbert Collingwood was going to deliver his sons and friends to Sir Robert Kerr as pledges to the Burns for their bills of complaint. The matter dragged on for three years, but they were eventually handed over at March meetings at Kirk Yetholm and Kirknewton on the 8th and 9th of March 1592. Forster reckoned that full justice was administered on both sides and that 'there had never been better quietness in the Middle Marches.' It didn't last long.

The Burns and Youngs killed a man called John Selby at Pawston who was defending his cattle and that same night they drove 80 sheep of Sir John Forster's to Awtonburn. A year previously, in 1595, Steven Burn of the Lough, with his brothers Jock and Gilbert, and Watty Young of the Knowe, with others, took 12 kye and oxen, a young horse and a mare from John Strother of Kilham. The Burns were almost certainly part of Sir Robert Kerr's gang of 60 horsemen that killed two men at Wooler and another at Kilham on their way home around the same time.

Ralph Burn of the Cote was described as a stirring man but of small living on the jailer's sheet at York. He was a raiding companion of Richard Young of Feltershaws; they'd done jobs together in the past. Although he'd been part of the breakout attempt at York, no further records can be found of Ralph, so it must be presumed that he languished there until being released in 1602 following Kerr's efforts to have them sent to Berwick with the other pledges.

His brother Jock Burn, however, escaped from imprisonment on the morning of 27 June 1601. Jock was described as 'very dear' to Cessford and he'd received some special attention by being allowed to be detained in Berwick when all the others where sent down to York. Lord Eure, the English Middle March warden, was accused of denying an Englishman called John Brown any justice against Jock in 1597, probably to keep Kerr happy, so the reiver had some clout.

He was taken to the Provost William Breadman's house in April; he'd been detained there for eleven months previously. Breadman reckoned that he'd asked for him to be placed somewhere stronger in the town, suggesting the loathsome Haddock's Hole, but was refused and Burn escaped two days after the death of Lord Hunsdon, the Lord Governor of the town.

There had been whispers of an escape attempt but Breadman said that the now-conveniently dead Carey would hear none of it. A Scotsman called Gray brought a 'boule' of wheat and a nag to pay part of Burn's charges for his keep on 26 June.

Burn rose at around four o'clock the next day, grabbed the horse and leapt on its back, charged past a servant at the gate and was gone, galloping through Berwick and heading off for the hills of home in the distance. The English intelligence pinpointed Burn to be staying at Fast Castle with Sir Robert Logan, the Laird of Lestalrig, a week later. Logan was an interesting character who employed the alleged 'wizard' John Napier to search Fast Castel for treasure. After Logan had died in 1606 his decomposed corpse was exhumed and put on trial three years later. His estates were, unsurprisingly, forfeited.

Having his kinsmen locked up hadn't put Tom Burn of Awtonburn off raiding either and in 1601 he was down at Rothbury forest robbing a widow Spurman of 12 oxen, 11 kye, a grey mare worth £5 and £10 of insight. It remained business as usual for the Burns, if on a lesser scale.

Robert Frissell (Fraser), Laird of Overton

As a West Teviotdale Family, the Frissells raided mainly in gangs containing Halls, Robsons and Rutherfords under the protection of the Kerr Laird of Ferniehurst, a rival branch of the family to Cessford, that had long jostled for the top positions of power in the Scottish Middle March.

In 1582 Roger Milburn of Throphill complained that John Frissell, brother of the Laird of Overton, and Thomas Hall of Foulshiel had stolen 18 oxen from him and in the same year the same two stole horses from John Massill of Little Callerton.

The Laird of Overton himself was in trouble in 1586 for receiving the fugitives Thomas and Roger Read after they'd plundered the stocks from Anthony Twysell's farm at Callerton.

Around the same time, Robin Frissell and Jock Hall of the Sykes drove away 30 kye and oxen from Thomas Pott of Fawside. Robin Frissell was raiding again with David Hemsley of Falls, Thomas Hemsley and Steven Davison to take cattle and household goods from John Hall of Farneycleugh and the Laird of Overton, with Jock Hall of the Flints, Thom Hall of the Foulshiel and Ralph Robson stole 15 kye and oxen from Archie Coxson of Rattenrow at the Sills.

The raids into Redesdale continued and Robin and John Frissell, with Jock Hall of the Sykes and Tom Hall of Foulshiels drove off 30 cattle and stole household goods from John Hall of Monkridge at Cradden Burn. The same crew also hit Whitestone House and plundered dozens of cattle and a hefty haul of household goods.

In 1585 Maxwell, the Earl of Morton, appointed one the Frissells as the Captain of Lochmaben with 100 men for its defence. The castle was one of the King's houses and the greatest strength in the West Border of Scotland, according to Lord Scrope. He was sacked a month later, however. Borderer that he was, Frissell was implicated in a secret plot to execute Morton, who also suspected his own brother Robert and the King of Scots himself of being involved. Morton was similarly paranoid about the Johnstones and jailed their chief in Caerlaverock at the same time.

Andrew Frissell of Overton was raiding at Wharton in Coquetdale in October 1587 when he, along with Dand Rutherford (brother of the pledge Richard Rutherford) of Littleheugh, Jamie Hall of Heavyside younger, Ralph Robson of Oxnam (who was originally demanded as a pledge) and his brother Rinion lifted 28 kye and oxen and a horse from John Davison, Ralph Leighton and Richard Simpson. Andrew saddled up with his brother William Frissell, Andrew and Robin Rutherford, the sons of Jock of the Tofts, and reived 14 kye and oxen from Archie Ayton and Robin Foster of Dalton the following year.

Raiding was always a family affair and in 1589 Andrew and William were descending on Woodburn in Redesdale with Thomas (the pledge) and Ralph Ansyley of Cleethaugh, Jock Rutherford of Edgerston, Davie Laidlaw of the Sunnyside, Martin Croser late of Baxton Lee and his son Clement, Robert 'Hob the Tailor' Armstrong and Eddie Elliot, son of 'the Carling' to take 12 kye and oxen and £5 insight from Bartram Forster.

Sir Ralph Eure was annoyed in 1596 when John and Robert Frissell and Phillip Rutherford of Edgerston all built houses close to the head of the Rede water right on the Border and he claimed that they should be 'defaced and ruined' if the English got 'no redress for past losses or assure of future justice.' Having troublesome neighbours so close to a launching place for raiding was clearly irksome to the Middle March Warden.

When a Rutherford and Ferniehurst Kerr 'hunting party' strayed into England in 1598, and three of their men were killed, it was noted that Fenwick and Widdrington had advised their men that 'none should take (prisoner) or show favour other than the worst (killing) to any Rutherford, Frissell or Hall' on pain of death. The Frissells and their riding crews must have been doing plenty of damage to have such an order passed down.

The Laird of Overton seems to have struck up a friendship with William Tait of Cherrytrees during their incarceration. Not only was Tait the only East Teviotdale pledge to sign the 1600 letter with Frissell, Rutherford and Aynsley offering to deliver on the bills in return for their release, but he was already friends with the Dowknow Taits and after 1604, and for the following 18 years, Overton's sons were reiving primarily with John Tait called 'Chief' of the Dowknow.

In May 1601 Cessford wanted the pledges to be removed from

York and told the English that it had been ordered at Court; by the July Lord Burghley had informed the pledges how their bills were filed. He had shown them letters from the Queen's Agent in Scotland stating that if they settled their debts, they would be removed to the East and West Wardenries and delivered to the people that had filed against them, which made them pleased. They wanted out of hell hole but weren't sure how they would get the money together unless they were first delivered closer to home. They offered delivery of English pledges, or their eldest sons, or both, as security.

Kerr's attitude changed when the Youngs, Burns, Davisons and Pringles complained that their kinsmen remained at York when the others had been sent to Berwick, and began raiding again. Kerr was obviously worried that he was losing control over his henchmen and while Frissell, Rutherford and Aynsley were West Teviotdale men and therefore not directly answerable to him, Tait was one of his Lieutenants.

Upon their delivery Carey wasn't going to make the same mistake of letting them escape from Berwick as Jock Burn had done a year previously and had them imprisoned in 'Haddock's Hole' – something like the Bangkok Hilton only smaller, darker, colder, grimmer and slightly less salubrious. The Hole was described as 'loathsome prison' at the time, so one can only imagine just how disgusting and severe it was.

In April 1602 John Carey complained that Frissell and the other pledges now at Berwick (Aynsley, Rutherford and Tait) were in a worse state than ever and Kerr, Lord Roxburghe, would not 'suffer their friends to come to them nor to treat them with such as they too are faulters to for composition.'

Carey did show some sympathy and reckoned that the pledges 'poor men' were doing all that they could, but Kerr was plaguing their friends 'by calling them to the law and by persuading such as they be faulters too not agree without extremity as they know not what way to work.' 'In so much as yet the poor pledges are in a pitiful state, their friends don't dare to do anything without his (Kerr's) consent, and he not willing that they should be relieved,' wrote the East March Warden. Kerr made a proclamation that 'none of the pledge's friends should meet or tryst with any of whom they be faulter for the satisfying of their bills,' then broke a truce day and sent his men foraying, which so incensed Carey that he trusted Sir Robert Cecil would 'hang some of their friends at York instead of sending them down hither.'

But it was Burghley that got right to the root of the matter and nailed the issue on the head when he said that their own Wardens would never get the prisoners freed as 'they were the commanders of these men and received most of the booty.' The Godfathers were leaving their foot soldiers and underbosses out to dry. It's a scene that was replayed in the bulletproof courtrooms of Napoli and Palermo during the 1990s; the bosses in their suits and dark glasses watching on as their crews press hands against the glass, make gestures and take the fall for long prison stretches.

Robert Frissell was described as a 'man of some action and living' on a paper at York and had been the chief instigator with Sim Armstrong of the failed breakout attempt in March 1599. His friends defied Kerr and risked his wrath on 1 June 1602 when they sorted things out with Sir John Carey, who sent the Laird of Overton to Alnwick where he was received by Henry Widdrington's men and released.

Lord Roxburghe, as Kerr now was, had been away from his Middle March Warden office with King James VI but was back by the August and had taken four of the best of each surname as pledges. He wanted the rest of the pledges still held in York brought up to Berwick to sort out their bills. Sir John Carey remained suspicious of Kerr, however, and although he was going to journey into England and stay at Widdrington's house on the way, the Berwick Governor reckoned that 'he says much more than he will perform, but, if used in his own kind, may be a good instrument.'

Robert Frissell's time at York hadn't affected his standing and he was a signatory on a band of the clans to 'give up all friendship, kindness, oversight, maintenance or assurance...with common thieves and broken clans...answerable to His Highnesses Laws' with James VI at Jedburgh in October 1602 along with Hector Turnbull of Wauchop, George Rutherford of Fairnington, Ralph Kerr of Shaws, George Douglas of Bonjedburgh, Thomas Turnbull of Minto, Walter and William Turnbull of Bedrule, Walter Scott of Goldielands, Walter

Scott of Tuschielaw, James Gladstanes of Cocklaw, Will Elliot of Fallingash, Robert Scott of Stitchells, Watt Scott of Harden, Sim Scott of Bonnytown, William Scott in Burnfoot, Sir John Kerr, Sir Andrew Kerr of Heighton, J. Cranston Hundalee, Andrew Kerr of Linton, Andrew Riddell of that ilk, John Mow of that ilk, Robert Scott of Haining, James Douglas of Cavers, M. Cranston, Gavin Elliot of Stobs, Thomas Rutherford of Hunthill, John Pringle of Buckholme, William Douglas of Bonjedburgh, George Kerr of Cavers, Walter Scott of Stirkshaws, Walter Chisholm of that ilk, Robert Elliot of Redhaugh, Robert Langlands of that ilk, Gilbert Elliot of the Mains, William Scott of Hartwoodmires, Philip Scott of Dryhope, Robert Scott of Thirlstane, Robert Scott of Aikwood, William Scott of Howplaslott, Watt Scott of Whitehaugh, James Scott of Gilsmancleugh, John Dalgliesh of Duechar, Robert Kerr of Ancrum, Adam and John Rutherford, William Brown and John Allison, all bailies of Jedburgh. With such a choice selection of rogues in the room, it marked the beginning of the end for the Border mafia.

Will Hall of Heavyside and Ralph Hall of the Sykes

The West Teviotdale Halls were every bit as notorious as their Redesdale cousins and the Halls of Heavyside had a reiving pedigree stretching back for generations. Robert Hall in Heavyside was a notorious villain who appeared at Jedburgh court in 1510 accussed of a long list of crimes such as stealing four horses and heifers and household goods from William Jackson, a horse and an array of household goods from Adam Edgar, stealing and concealing two oxen from Thomas Johnson and Dougal Wilson, a cow and 11 hoggs from the Laird of Bon-Jedward, five horses and heifers, gold and silver and household goods from William Jackson and a horse, household goods and, strangely, a bagpipe from George Weir.

The list went on; Robert had reset, supplied and conspired with the King's Rebels and had broken into William Rutherford's house in Nether Chatto. He could not find anyone to stand his bail and was given 40 days by the Sheriff to find sureties or face the noose.

Other branches of the family were just as involved, and in 1493 Peter Hall in Newbiggin had stolen a shield and sword from John and

Edmund Hall, who were both also from Newbiggin and probably relations. But Peter had done a lot worse; he murdered John Henderson in Lintonlee and lifted six ewes from Thomas Henderson in Jed Forest, then murdered him too for good measure. David Aynsley stood as surety for him.

In 1537 Andrew Hall, called Fat Fow, and William Hall 'Wanton Pintle', were denounced rebels for stealing sheep from William Douglas of Bon-Jedward and his neighbours, and bringing in English reivers to steal corn from the Douglas place at Cunzearton.

With the English Halls just over the Border, the Halls were again accused of bringing in Redesdale thieves in 1563 to steal from Alexander Lord Hume and Thomas Cranston. Lyle Hall was the guide for the English raiders and was hanged on the Borrowmuir in Edinburgh for his efforts. The Teviotdale Halls had joined up as 'assured' Englishmen in 1544 when Hob Hall of Heavyside signed the document.

Dand Hall of Awtonburn was riding with some large-scale raids with the Youngs in 1587 and in a smaller affair he'd taken nine cows and oxen from John Swinburn of Edlingham with Dand Young of Woodside, William Hall of Woodsidedean and Dand Glenholm of Mow.

The Heavyside Halls were also terrorising the countryside around by descending on isolated farms at the time. James and his brother Robert, with Pat Turnbull of Littleheugh robbed eight cattle, a horse and various household goods including tablecloths, a sword, an axe and a dagger and the burglar's favourite – candlesticks – from Robert Lisley and Thomas Garrett while the Halls of the Sykes were raiding with the Scottish Robsons and the other West Teviotdale crime families.

Jock of the Sykes was named in numerous bills and was on a bond with Thomas Kerr of Cavers in 1588 to appear before Richard Fenwick of Stanton within 15 days, which both Kerr and Hall ignored. Jock was raiding again with Robert and Simon Hall of Heavyside in 1595 and they took a grey horse and a mare from William Strother of Kirknewton. Around the same time the Halls, Youngs, Piles and Aynsleys cut up doors with axes during a violent assault on Haggerston.

Ralph Hall was described as a one of the men of very small action and obscure men on the jailer's sheet and died in York castle a week before the Whitehaugh breakout attempt. Ralph had been on a raid with his brother William and Thomas Douglas of Swineside in 1589 when they stole 12 ewes from Robert Clavering at Callaly, so perhaps his death was one of the reasons behind the escape efforts as his friends looked on and thought they were all going to die in there if they didn't get out.

Will Hall was a 'stirring man but of small living' and was trying to get himself and another – possibly Ralph - out three months before the Whitehaugh attempt. Will had befriended an Englishman called George Davidson who was bringing letters and cash to the pledges from their people through Thomas Percy at Alnwick castle. Hall promised Davidson that 'if the whole of the City of York was his, he would give it to him,' if he would help get him out and asked if he could get his brother Robert 'Hobby' to bring him two horses so that they could escape. Davidson knew Hobby well as Hall had been a prisoner himself at Warkworth castle in Northumberland until 'the house was set on fire' and was released on a bond. William told Davidson to go and see his sister-in-law, who was widowed off another of his brothers and now married to a man in Kirkbymoorside, to get word to Hobby about the horses. It was rumbled and didn't come off, but Will did escape from York castle in September 1601.

Thomas Lord Burghley had noted that York was so full of prisoners every day that there were constant break-out attempts and he saw 'no hope for their delivery or security' as he was getting no replies from Kerr at the time.

The pledges had been manacled in irons every night following the first mass attempt to get out in 1599 and as well as the shackles and chains on the arms, the gaolers were using an iron grate from a chimney used to hold in coals. Hall and an unnamed other broke off one of the bars from the grate and used it to smash off the manacles; the noise alerted the guards but before they could get there, Hall and the other had jumped down seven yards and struck out a light that one of the panicked keepers was carrying. Hall fled into the darkness, but his companion was smacked over the head and badly injured in his recapture. Although Burghley set a watch in the City, Hall was gone. Burghley was the President of the Council at York and seemed a decent man as he was pleading clemency for the others left, writing that they 'were never able to find security' and if they were freed he was 'of the opinion it will prove more honourable than hurtful.' Perhaps he just wanted rid of the headache of keeping them; Robson, Armstrong and Elliot of Hartscarth had all also escaped prior to Hall's flight.

William appeared in a list of Ferniehurst's heavies with his brothers Simon and Thomas that were killing and burning in Jedburgh in 1602. It seems that he may have paid the ultimate price for his escapades, however, as in 1604 a Hall of Heavyside, almost certainly Will, was tortured and executed by Lord Hume. During the torture he had said some things which were undisclosed but prejudiced against Lord Roxburghe (Kerr.) The King declared that Hume had done no wrong in torturing the Hall and that Roxburghe's standing wasn't affected by the confession, which was declared 'unworthy of all credit.' It seems suspiciously like Kerr was doling out punishment for his escape and Hall was being silenced as the Crime Godfather's closed ranks and consolidated their power under the Crown.

When the first lists of fugitives from justice began to appear in 1605 as the Border Commission purges kicked in, the following Teviotdale Halls appeared: James Hall called 'Crowdie,' James Hall, son of Andrew Hall in the Sykes of Heavyside and Jamie Hall called 'the Bastard of Heavyside.' They were also on the list of the 'final' fugitives from justice in 1618 when Sim Hall, son to John Hall in Sykes, was named.

Richard Rutherford of Littleheugh

Thomas Rutherford, the son of Nicholas Rutherford, was denounced a rebel and all his goods seized by the Crown for the murder of Duthac Rutherford in 1495. His cautioner, John Rutherford of Edgerston, was also fined a bumper £40 when Thomas failed to appear at the court in Jedburgh to hear the charges.

Nicholas was a reiver himself and in 1502 he was up at Jedburgh for stealing a cauldron from the wife of Richard Rutherford, a cow from Lawrence Pile, five horses from the Earl of Huntley and a horse from Thomas Hall. The Rutherfords were denounced as 'the King's rebels' at the time and John and Thomas Rutherford produced remission at the same hearing for resetting, supplying and intercommuning with those wildest elements of the family like Robert Rutherford, who had stolen silk, sheets, linen, cloth and clothes from the church in Jedburgh.

The Rutherfords continued in more serious crime and John, the son of Edmund Rutherford in Auchincorth, was hanged along with Thomas Davidson for theft and resetting of theft in 1528.

The family were also found in Northumberland, primarily at Middleton Hall, and an English Tom Rutherford was a servant to Dacre who was doing a bit of spying for him in Edinburgh in 1515, returning to Harbottle castle with his information 'disguised as a Scotchman.' Surrey also had a spy from the family; his man James Rutherford was reporting back to him in 1523 that the Lords of Scotland had left Edinburgh for their houses and if French aid wasn't forthcoming within a specified timescale they would 'take forth the King, give the rule to four temporal lords, Argyle, Huntley, Lennox and Arran, and sue to England for peace.'

That same year the Teviotdale Rutherfords, Kerrs, Davisons and others slipped in by Tynedale to run an open day foray on Haltwhistle; 120 of the locals fought the raiders off, killed 120 and captured 12 others who were executed the following Sunday. Bewcastledale and Gilsland were being blamed for not joining in to beat off the invasion party and there were strong suspicions that the Tynedale men were implicated in the raid as the Scots had passed through their land without trouble in both coming and leaving. Interestingly, it was noted that the official 'was sure that Liddesdale would not have let them pass.'

The magnificently named 'My Hell' Rutherford was a Redden Burn official at Truce Days for hearing charges in 1537 and three years later the Scottish King James V wanted to exchange an Englishman called Doctor Hillard for a 'great reiver, thief and man slayer' called George Rutherford, alias 'Cokebank,' who was held in Carlisle gaol by Sir Thomas Wharton.

The Rutherfords were caught up in the Rough Wooing between the two countries and in 1544 John Rutherford, the laird of Hunthill, placed George Kerr of Gateshaw as his pledge and Richard Rutherford, lord of Rutherford stood John Rutherford of Edgerston as they signed up to assist the English in wasting Southern Scotland. It did lead to some mighty fall-outs in the aftermath, however, and in 1546 John Rutherford of Hunthill, Nicholas Rutherford of Hundalee and Charles and Richard Rutherford and their friends had to sign an order of peace (that all concurred against the English) by the Scottish Privy Council with Walter Kerr of Cessford, Mark Kerr of Littledene, the Kerrs of Graden and their friends.

An agreement also had to be made between Walter Kerr of Cessford, John Kerr of Ferniehurst and the Douglas's of Cavers and Bonjedward with Sir Walter Scott of Branxholm, the Turnbulls of Bedrule, John Cranston of that ilk, James Pringle of Tinnes, William Turnbull of Minto and their followers.

The Rutherfords were named with the Scotts and Humes as 'three great bands of gentlemen' by Andrew Melville who wanted to travel from Northumberland to do business with the West March Warden, Lord Maxwell, and felt that with they would allow him to pass through Teviotdale and Jedwood forest unhindered in 1559.

They were a powerful family and involved in some high-end negotiations between England and Scotland at the time as Hunthill and others of the clan were sitting alongside such luminaries as the lairds of Ferniehurst, Cessford and Greenhead, Sir Andrew Kerr of Littledene and the Lord of Buccleuch as 'suitors for the friendship of England' with the likes of Lord Grey and Sir Henry Percy.

The old rows reared their heads up soon enough and in 1572 Roger Fenwick complained that the laird of Bedrule, the laird of Edgerston, Philip Rutherford of Egerton and William Aynsley of Fala were hiding two English fugitives, John Hall called 'Bransharn' and John Hall of Elishaw, after they'd reived him of cattle at Rothley. Thomas Carr of Old Felton was similarly aggrieved that Andrew Rutherford of Littleheugh and James Hall of Heavyside had also been on the raid at Rothley; Carr had a little more to complain about some 13 years later when Andrew Rutherford and James Hall came to Old Felton and stole his cattle, probably just to shut him up.

John Rutherford of Edgerston was also accused of taking in an English outlaw called Thomas Reed in 1579 after he'd stolen four oxen from Mark Ogle of Kirkley.

The fact that Fenwick had sent 'a defiance' to the Rutherfords in 1576 was also stirring things up and the Scottish Regent Morton 'smelled an intention of some new trouble' by the correspondence. Mind, the reivers were also trying to profit at the time off the back of the 'Battle of the Reidswire' and putting in over-inflated claims for stolen horses. The Regent despaired that they wouldn't bring the horses and goods to an appointed meeting place and would rather 'claim the high prices they had sworn them unto than the horses and goods themselves.'

The headsmen of the Rutherfords in the 1570s were Richard Rutherford of Edgerston, Andrew Rutherford at Hundalee and John Rutherford of Hunthill and they were often the recipients of official letters from Edinburgh, but they had a reputation for harbouring English fugitives and Fenwick despised them for keeping 3,000 sheep six miles into English ground. He said that John Rutherford, the laird of Hunthill and William Rutherford of Littleheugh were 'great Scottish thieves' that had looked after around a dozen Redesdale men on the run from justice for murder and robbery. He also noted that no-one dared place their sheep by the Rutherford's except old Sir John Forster – implicating the March Warden in villainy and corruption once again.

Perhaps this had something to do with the 1598 Redesdale 'hunting' incident as the Rutherfords and their friends, numbering around 60, strayed onto English ground and were attacked 'in warlike manner' by Fenwick, Widdrington and 400 men who chased them back into Scotland and killed three – the laird of Hundalee's brother, Robert Pringle and a Robson of Chatto – while wounding many more and taking prisoner the younger lairds of Bonjedburgh, Hunthill and Greenhead and others. William Selby reckoned that the Scots were cutting down and carrying off wood and hunting 'is if in their own country' without licence from the warden.

Richard and Archibald Rutherford were wounded by Andrew Kerr of Ferniehurst in 1575 and Adam Rutherford in Plewland was fined £4 for talking to rebels. More seriously, John Rutherford, the laird of Hunthill, was denounced a rebel and named a public enemy along with William Kerr of Ancrum and his brother Robert, James Kerr of Lintloe, Andrew Kerr the laird of Greenhead, David Moscrop, the deputy provost of Jedburgh, and others, for refusing to enter England for trial. They stood accused of playing a part in the murder of Lord Russell at the Cocklaw truce day in July 1585 and both sides of the line were threatening to charge anyone that helped them with high treason. He was also in bother with William Rutherford of Littleheugh and James Kerr the laird of Corbett for failing to pay a bond of £30 that they owed the laird of Crawster.

Crawster was relieved of four cows and an ox by John Rutherford of the Tofts and John, also known as Jock, was riding with his son Andrew, Philip Rutherford and his son, also called Andrew, Willie Aynsley of Fala and his son Davie, George Pile of Milnhaugh and his son George, and Jock Hall of the Sikes, to plunder Percival Elsdon of the Mote of 24 kye and oxen and a horse in 1587.

That same year William Rutherford of Littleheugh was part of a crew 500 strong led by Scotts, Laidlaws and Olivers that ran a huge day foray on Clennell and the following year Jock of the Tofts' sons Andrew and Robin rode with Andrew and William Frissell of Overton to reive 14 kye and oxen from the Forsters at Dalton.

Andrew Rutherford of Littleheugh had also raided Wharton with Andrew Frissell of Overton, Jamie Hall of Heavyside, younger, and Ralph and Rinion Robson of Oxnam to take 28 kye and oxen and a horse while Eddie Rutherford of Nether Chatto stole 18 sheep from Jock Sanderson and took 10s sterling from another man.

Thomas Rutherford of Chatto and Nichol Hall were killed while raiding near Newcastle with the Redesdale fugitives Anton Pott, Hob Shaftoe and Hob Errington by Henry Widdrington's men in 1599. Soon after, Sir Robert Carey was demanding that the pledge Richard Rutherford of Littleheugh be delivered from York to him in Northumberland; he was a cousin of the Earl of Huntley and described as 'a stirring man, but of small living' on the prisoner list at York. He first appears in the records with the young James Hall of Heavyside when they stole eight oxen, a cow and a nag, and £3 insight from Robert Mitford of Seghill in August 1589.

A month later he was with his brother Andrew, Andrew Kerr, the laird of Corbett's son, John Douglas of Hownam kirk and William Douglas of the Brae, who took 14 kye and oxen from Robert Roddam at Littlehoughton. He was close with his brothers and joined Andrew and William, and Adam Rutherford of Chatto in May 1590 to thieve four oxen, three cows and a mare from John Horsley of Horsley.

Richard was William of Littleheugh's eldest son and was part of the breakout attempt at York in March 1598, but by July 1599 Sir Robert Carey seemed very keen to have him released after the family had approached him.

Carey said that his friends were a great surname that could 'annoy England more than any other on the Border' and were in deadly feud with many English gentlemen. Carey wanted Richard to make satisfaction on all the bills that he, and his people, were filed for before he let him go; he was also threatening that all deadly feuds would be taken up 'especially if the Scots have the worst of it' and wanted to take bonds for the Rutherford's good behaviour. Carey thought that releasing him back to Scotland would do 'much good and no hurt.'

Carey was to travel down to York himself and have Rutherford delivered to him. The principal Rutherford's were keen to get their man back and in the July were offering to pay up on all bills since Richard had been sent down. Carey was cautious but optimistic and wrote to Cecil that the Rutherford's had assured that they would 'never assist or consent to other Scotsmen annoying England' or he would not let him free from his place at Alnwick.

There was, however, a snag. Sir Robert Kerr became embroiled in a bitter dispute with Carey's deputy Henry Widdrington and he ended up offering him out for hand to hand combat to sort things out. Kerr said that he'd meet him at Havr Craggs on the Border at eight in the morning on 7 September with a 'short sword and wyniard, steel bonnet and plate sleeves' and mocked that he wished 'some spark of courage may make (Widdrington) appear in some form.' You have to admire Kerr's style; the boss wasn't afraid to get his hands dirty and within a couple of weeks Carey was almost pleading Cecil for a way out of the Warden job as he could get 'neither honour, profit, pleasure nor contentment' from it. He was also twining that it was very cold and far from the sun.

So Rutherford was stuck at York until being transferred to Berwick after signing the offer letter in April 1600. He took very sick during his detention in the hellish 'Haddock's Hole' in March 1602 but on 15 April he was finally released blinking in the sunlight to Alnwick and received by men sent from Widdrington after he satisfied all the bills on himself and his surname by the English East March, his friends obviously getting the money together for him. Carey worried that Sir Robert Kerr, by now Lord Roxburghe, might try and keep him at Alnwick as he 'hadn't been relieved by his means,' but Rutherford was the first of the pledges to be finally free after five years of detention in dank, dark, cold and wet stone and iron.

While Richard had been inside his father and a couple of brothers got into trouble at a horse race at Strokestrutther in Teviotdale in 1601 when they, William, his dad, and his brothers Adam and William, along with Thomas, William and Robert Rutherford of Hunthill, Robert Rutherford of the Tofts, George Rutherford of Farington, Nichol Rutherford of Edgerston, Philip's Andrew Rutherford and John Rutherford, younger, of Nether Ancrum had fired pistols at, and been fired upon, by Dandie Young of Caverton and Dandie Young of the Know. Thomas was locked up in Edinburgh castle and the two Youngs in Blackness, while the others denied the charges.

By 1606 the Moscrops were complaining that the Rutherfords were in rebellion against them, and in 1608 the Earl of Mar was attempting to kick the Rutherfords off his land and issued a decree against them as the clearances picked up pace. The powerful Nichol Rutherford of Hundalee, along with Charles Rutherford in Jedburgh, John alias Jock in the Plewland, Charles in Nether Nesbitt called of the Walls, John called Jock of the Slope, Robert 'Hobbie' and his son, Peter in Burn, John 'Jock with the Jadie,' James and Walter, Nichol, Andrew of the Hall, George and Peter of the Know, William in the Overton, Walter, John in the Slope and William Rutherford called of the Plewland, were all named in the action.

Richard of Littleheugh reappears in the records as one of the ringleaders suspected of 'unruly courses' that the Border commissioners felt should be 'confined or removed from their present homes' in 1607. Rutherford and his fellow ex-pledge prisoner Frissell of Overton were to be sent away to Brechin while the younger Rutherford of Hundalee was to go to Kirkcaldy. The other suspects were John Carmichael of Meadowflat, who was sent to Dundee; the master Maxwell to Dunkeld or any part of Fife and Angus; Alexander Jardine of Applegarth and John Carruthers of Holmends to St. Andrews; William Maxwell and Hobby Carlisle of Brydekirk to Montrose; Robert Elliot of Redhaugh and Walter Scott of Goldielands to Coupar in Fife; Hobb Scott of Northhouse to Perth; Walter Scott of Edshaw, because of his inability to sustain himself, could go to the Laird of Reres 'or any other gentleman of Fife or Angus he may please,' and John Kerr of Corbetthouse and Kerr of Shaw went to Aberdeen.

Richard didn't seem to go, or was back, as in 1610 he was on a bond of 1000 marks with William Douglas, the sheriff of Roxburgh, alongside John Rutherford of Jedburgh on 500 marks, not to harm Robert Kerr Lord Roxburghe, William Davidson of Symeston, William Burn, Andrew and Richard Hounam, Richard Davidson, all in Cuthberthishope, and Adam Bell in Hindtown. At the Jedburgh Court in October 1611 Richard of Littleheugh and George Rutherford of Fairnington had to forfeit an astronomical £1000 each for the non-appearance of Thomas and William Rutherford in Tofts. William went on the run and appeared in the list of the last fugitives from justice in the Borders that the commissioners produced in 1618.

Dand Davison of Brownfield

The Davisons (and Davidsons) were another family that could be found on both sides of the Border line, but the Teviotdale family were the more infamous. George Davison of Fowmerdon was a notorious reiver in the period after Flodden Field and he was involved in three huge raids across the Border towards the end of 1515. In the September he was with John Burn, Tom Young of Yetholm, Edward and Ralph Tait, Adam Tait, George Middlemist, and others, 'to the number of eight score horsemen,' who robbed the town of Newton of seven score kye and oxen and the insight. A month later George was one of the leaders of a huge raid by 400 men with Mark Kerr, Laird of Dolphinstown, lieutenant of the Middle Marches of Scotland, Lance Kerr, Laird of Gateshaw, Dand Kerr, Laird of Graden, the young Laird of Mow, Dand Pringle, constable of Cessford, that 'came to Corkleech upon Mylnefield, and put forth their foray, eight score horsed men, to the town called Holborne, robbed it of all the insight and of 200 kye and oxen, 30 horses, and took the principal inhabitants prisoners.'

He was named a leading rider again with Lance Kerr, Laird of Gateshaw, Dand Kerr, Laird of Graden, and the young Laird of Mowe and a crew of 300 that burnt the town of Hessilrig, took 30 prisoners and drove away fourscore kye and oxen, 30 horses, and the insight. The raiding went both ways and Dand Davison of Horsley was taken for 13 kye and oxen by Willie Archibald of Cornhill, and some other of Lord Cornhill's servants and friends in a raid in October 1523 that broke a Truce that had been in place between the Marches.

The Davisons were powerful and influential enough for Robin Davison of Hadderlands to be a Scottish juror at Redding Burn Truce days in 1538 and both he and Tom and William Davison appeared as both complainants and complained upon in the bills that were heard, while in 1542 one of the clan was named as one of the most feared and notorious raiders from the Scottish Middle March.

When Stephen Davison was taken captive as his raiding party where heading over the Border and bumped into an English reiving party of the Lisle's going in the other direction, the Captain of Berwick reckoned that he (Davison) had 'done more harm to the King's subjects than any Scot in Scotland,' so he was quite a catch.

His nephew, young Stephen, and Watt Young were also taken. It is interesting to note that the letter states that with it being very windy and pitch black, the two gangs were on top of each other before they noticed. 'The hardiest of the Scots tarried and the rest escaped in the darkness,' wrote the Captain. Two more of the Davisons were taken prisoner, along with a Bromfield, shortly after by John Carr of Wark, and a few days before the Keeper of Redesdale and Tynedale had led 200 horsemen to burn Nether Clavering in West Teviotdale.

The flames burning in the darkness of the black hills was to become a regular feature of life in Teviotdale at the time as Hertford led successive firing missions to burn out and harry which led to James Davison of Symeston, John Davison and Richie Davison of Hayhope pledging allegiance to the English King with the other East Teviotdale riding families in 1544.

The Crown were putting cash the Davison's way in 1576 as Dand Kerr in Hayhope was distributing money to John Davison and his sons George and Hobbie in Whitton and his brother Thomas Davison; it did however, go back just as fast – a month later all four were fined £3 6s 8d for intercommuning with rebels. Walter Davison in Linton Park and Stephen Davison of Fowmerden were also hit with a hefty £13 6s 8d. fine for 'hoching' oxen and horses that were ploughing Robert Kerr of Ancrum's land in a bill that had taken eight years to be heard, while Andrew alias Dand Davison of Lempitlaw called 'of Whitton' was up for talking to the friends of Thomas Kerr, formerly of Ferniehurst, and done for a fiver. William Davison in Semmeston and his brothers George and William were also implicated and fined for the same offence. William Davison in Graden, George Davison in Linton and William, John and Bartholemew Davison in Denholm Know all faced similar penalties around the same time.

Dand, John and Robert Davidson and Walter Middlemist lifted four oxen and a nag from the powerful Sir Thomas Grey of Chillingham in 1579, and there was hell on about it. Old William Kerr of Cessford was charged by Edinburgh to settle the matter and Dand Tait of the Dowknow became involved in the dispute alongside the March Warden. The Davisons must have driven the stolen stock back home through Yetholm as Tait said he'd seen them going past and could prove it. He didn't appear at the court, however, so Dand Tait of Barearse, along with James Hoppringill in Hownam, Dand Hoppringill his son, Watt Hoppringill in Clifton, Thomas Hoppringill his brother in Halden, Robert Davidson in Symestoun, Dand Davidson son to Wester Will, Dand Davidson called Thankless, James Davidson his brother, James Young of the Cove, Thomas Young of Lempitlaw, Dand Burn of the Loch and Mongo Burn of Lempitlaw were all summoned to appear before the Regent at Holyroodhouse to try and settle the matter. Kerr washed his hands of it all and Dand Tait of the Dowknow must have wished he hadn't bothered as he was made responsible for the bill.

The Davisons were noted as loose men in the Middle Marches in 1583 and were raiding hard into England at the time; an estimation of the forces of the raiders from Scotland put the combined forces of the 'loose men' of East and West Teviotdale – Davisons, Youngs, Burns, Pringles and the Turnbulls, Olivers, Aynsleys and Robsons at 3000. The Liddesdale families – Crosers, Nixons, Armstrongs and Elliots - were estimated at 1000 and the Eskdale Beatties and Ewesdale Gingles (Armstrong) at 300.

In 1587 Hobb Davison of Fowmerdon led the Youngs and Taits with 30 men to plunder Branxton while John Davison of Fowmerdon was with John Burn of the Coat and Hobb Pringle of Clifton, the son of Watt, and George Kerr of Primside Mill on another inroad. The same George Kerr and William Davison of Fowmerdon reived Cuthbert Dunn of 30 kye and oxen, 2 horses and mares, £3 in coin and 40s. insight at Glanton that year. George Davison of Throgden and Henry Davison of the Burnfoot were part of a raid on Lewis Pott of Trewhitt, and Dave Davison of Harden had led a raid on Mark Ogle of Kirkley to take two horses and mares at Hepscot in 1584. A year later, John Davison of Overwhitton, called 'Holl Chair,' and his accomplices, were at the death of Lord Russell and in the ensuing chaos had taken the opportunity to steal a saddled-up horse and a mare from Thomas Carr of Old Felton.

Will Davison of Throgden, Will Kerr of Hayhope and Jock Pringle of Clifton, called 'Jock of Kelso,' stole 3 cows from Michael Turner of the Barn Yards in 1588 and in the following year William Davison of Wooden House reset 114 stolen sheep from Nicholas Manners of Newtown. The Davisons were back at Rothbury forest in 1590 where Dand Davison of Horseley and Robert Davison of Hatherlands drove away 16 kye and oxen, a white mare and 5 marks insight from Henry Rutherford of Middleton Hall.

In May 1596 the English Middle March Warden Ralph Eure captured two of the headsmen of the Davisons, which he noted as 'great spoilers under Cessford,' and held them prisoner to answer for 'all injuries done during their lives by them, kinsmen or friends.' The Davisons had been very active reivers with a mean reputation for violence and blood feud in the 1590s and James Davison of the

Burnrigg raided West Newton in daylight to take five horses and mares. He hit the same place in a night raid that wracked up another two horses, 20 neat and 20 nobles of insight. James was also a chief rider with the Youngs that took six cows from Richard Favors, the master gunner at Wark-on-Tweed, in another brazen daytime reive. Henry Davison of Morbottle was also foraying with James Kerr, the illegitimate son of James Kerr of Corbit House and William Davison of the Craggshiel who stole 40 old sheep from William Selby of Grindon Rigg. William had a great nickname – 'The Devil's Shaft Blade' – and he also took five cows from Thomas Pigg, the warden sergeant, while Thomas Davison of Burnrigg and John Robson of Over Crailinghaugh took 13 oxen and kye from Ralph Gray.

John Davison of Howden took Edward Gray's tenants at Preston for 25 oxen, three cows and insight while one of the English Davisons, James of Linbriggs, was raiding the other way and took eight cows and oxen from James Trotter of Fogo.

While the English demanded a Dand Davison in the original list compiled by Robert Carey, it's uncertain as to which one they were requesting; the second list again just says Dand Davison and the Family had offered a choice at the West Ford meeting in response to the English Robson's offer of three to choose from when Lyle Robson didn't show. Dand Davison of Brownfield is first referred to in the list compiled by Robert Redhead, the keeper of York Castle, when the pledges arrived. Dand of the Brownfield was a decent pledge and described as a man of some living and action who signed a note along with all the others subscribing to pay Redhead 10s 4d a week for their food and keeping in March 1599, just before the breakout attempt. In April 1600 he is on a sheet naming the Scottish Pledges at York as Dand Davison of Primside; whatever his name, he wasn't part of the Whitehaugh breakout attempt in 1599 and was stuck in York until Cessford finally managed to get the remaining pledges sent up to Berwick in September 1602.

The Burnrigg Davisons weren't helping in his efforts to get out, mind. In 1601 James Davison called 'of Burnrigg' and James Davison in Nodday were playing football against three of the Cockburns at Lochtown in Merse and when they fell out, pistols were fired. James Davison of Burnrigg was noted as a common thief and outlaw and they were both denounced for not appearing at the court. The following year Richie Davison of Burnrigg, younger, and Wattie Davison called 'Wattie of Callaly' stole two horses belonging to a James Knight as they were stabled in Jedburgh and Dandy Davison of the Burnrigg was denounced a rebel for being part of a large and menacing gang of Sir Andrew Kerr of Ferniehurst's that broke into John Allison's house in Jedburgh, murdered the people inside and fired it. The court was disgusted that the crew were going to the Church, market and other public places 'as if they were free lieges.' To give an idea of the Ferniehurst Mob, these were the others in it at the time – his brother James Kerr, James Kerr of Lintillie and his son William, William Kerr of Ancrum, George Mosscrop the burgess of Jedburgh and his brother David, George Kerr in Oxnam, John and Andrew Kerr in Redden, Charles Robson in Wollis, George Pile in Milneheaugh and his brother David, Simon Hall in Heavyside, Michael Kerr in Oxnam, Thomas Kerr, the brother of George Kerr 'the Browster,' James Hislop in Eschesteil, Ralph Aynsley in Cleethaugh (probably the brother of Thomas the pledge), Thomas and William Hall in Heavyside, Ralph Robson in Middleknowes and his brothers John and Ninian, Roger Aynsley in Cleethaugh, Dandy Davison, Leonard Kerr, the son of Lancelot Kerr in Oxnam and Sir Andrew's servants George Stewart and Richard Malcolm. It reads like the poster of the New York Italian mafia Crime Families that the FBI produced in a triangle down with Kerr of Ferniehurst at the head.

Unsurprisingly, Dand Davison in Burnrigg and his brother Willie were fugitives from the Justice Court at Jedburgh on the 29th October 1605 as the pacification got underway.

Ralph Mow of Mowhaugh

The Mows were a small but active and powerful family, involved in all of the Teviotdale action, and long held land just West of the Cheviot. There are people named de Molle, the original spelling of the name, recorded in the area back to the 1100s and 1200s.

Despite the major losses suffered by Scotland at the Battle of Flodden Field in 1513, just two years later the young Laird of Mow was involved in two of the major incursions with George Davison of

Fowmerden described previously. Northumberland had attempted to hit back after the third raid and in a hot trod the young Laird of Barmor, the Laird of Holborne, Hector Grey, and others, 'followed their neighbours' goods, and were taken prisoners within England, and with them 40 persons were conveyed to Cessford, to the warden's house, where he kept some, ransomed others and refused redress.'

John Mow of that ilk was a Laird important enough to figure in a trial of John Johnstone in 1542 alongside the likes of Walter Kerr of Cessford, Robert Scott of Howpaslott and Gilbert Kerr of Greenhead. He was described as 'a mean man in substance and reputation' by Shrewsbury. A year later his son was held as a pledge with Sir George Douglas being responsible for his release; he was freed in 1544 in exchange for Robert Collingwood's eldest son. Mow himself had been imprisoned in England at Carlisle Castle with Jock Pringle, who had been raiding with Mark Kerr, Dandy Young and others, and they both just escaped death. The King ordered that Mow, Pringle and 10 of the best prisoners should be 'kept surely and honestly' while two or three that had been the worst offenders were to be tried at a warden court, condemned and executed. Others were to be freed back into Scotland – because of 'the cumberance and cost.' Justice in the Borders clearly had a price.

The Laird of Mow lived up to his reputation in 1546 when he killed Sir Ralph Eure, the son of the English East March Warden, William. Eure sent his other son, Henry, with George Bowes, the son of Richard Bowes, the Captain of Norham, to burn the steads and towers in Mow and Colerust at the head of the Bowmont water in revenge. They also killed the Laird's brother, four of his kinsmen and took 20 prisoners.

This was all part of the wider revenge dished out on Teviotdale by the English following the Scottish pledges turning on their 'allies' at Ancrum Moor and a total of 888 Scotsmen were killed, 1,645 taken prisoner, with 1,813 kye and oxen lifted along with 1,384 horses and nags and over 13,000 sheep.

The Laird of Mow himself was killed at a Truce Day held at Carter Bar in 1575, which became known as the 'Raid of the Redeswire.' Sir John Forster, the English Middle March warden, and Sir George

Heron met with Sir John Carmichael, the Lord Warden of the Scottish Marches and Mowe's friend Sir George Douglas of Bonjedward to settle bills.

The trouble is said to have started when the English failed to produce a wanted man called 'Farnstein', (it's been deduced that this was actually a Robson of the Falstone) and with insults flying it all kicked off, the late arrival of the men from the town of Jedburgh turning a free-for-all into a decisive Scottish victory.

James Mow led a raid on Thomas Collingwood of Great Rile with John Heslop and John Bell of Mow and Robert Heslop of Corrowse when they took 60 sheep in 1584; two years earlier William Mow was with Thomas Marshall, Robert Oliver and Gilbert Atkinson to lift sheep from Collingwood at Alnham common. Robert Heslop, Ronald Burn, and David Hall of Mow targeted the common to take more sheep later that year.

Collingwood was similarly aggrieved in 1585 as Alexander Mow, the son of Stephen Mow called 'the Shepherd of Corrowse', and Dand Hall of Mow stole 26 ewes with lambs out of the west end of Hersdon. William Collingwood was also a victim of the Mows when William Mow, the brother of the laird of Mow, and Thomas Marshall of Mow stole ten old sheep from him.

In 1587 Alexander Mow was in a crew with Thomas Simpson of Sharples (a man of the Rutherford Laird of Hunthill), James Myler of Awtonburn, Thomas Young 'Tom of the Clan,' George Burn 'The Hen,' Tom Denatson 'Short Tom,' and others that reived 10 stotts and whies, and three whies more from Ralph Gray of Ownhame Grange.

They hit Coquetdale again that year as William Mow of Mow Mains saddled up with George Davison of Throgden, Henry Davison of Burnfoot and Tom Young of the Townhead to take six kye and oxen, a mare and insight worth 40s sterling from Lewis Pott of Trewhitt. Two years later, John Mow, son to Lance, was riding with the notorious James Hall of Heavyside, James Robson of the Burvens and 20 other men to take 24 kye and oxen and a horse from Thomas Reed of Burradon, and his brother John, at Farnham.

Francis Radcliffe of Cartington esq, complained that John Mow, the young laird of Mow, had pounced on his men Ralph and Roger

Fenwick and Edward Hall when they were on a lawful hot trod to recover stolen goods in 1598. Mow took them prisoner and robbed them of two horses, a dag, a dagger, a spear and a spear cap.

The Mows often held positions of office and Alexander Mow was the burgess of Jedburgh. He was taken prisoner in the 'hunting party' that strayed onto English soil in 1598. Given that the hunting party contained such luminaries as the Lairds of Hunthill and Hundalee (Rutherford), the Laird of Greenhead (Kerr) and the Laird of Bonjedward (Douglas), the Northumbrians that took them probably had good cause to be suspicious. Three were killed; a Rutherford, a Pringle and a Robson, 12 were taken prisoner and 50 nags stolen in what became a great scandal of the time.

The raiding went both ways and all ways; in 1596 George Kerr of Crookham took 20 kye and oxen in daylight from the Laird of Mow, John Mow of Mow Mains and his friends, and in 1601 the Laird of Mow, who was Cessford's deputy for the Scottish Middle Marches, was robbed of 20 ewes by Jock Pott 'the Bastard' of Yardhope, an illegitimate brother of the Redesdale pledge Percy Pott. The Laird was at a hearing in Morpeth of English bills made at Berwick that year with Thomas Ogle, the English Middle March deputy.

Although it was Ralph Mow of Mowhaugh that was originally desired as a pledge, in April 1600 a Ralph Mow of Linton was said to have died the day that he arrived at York in a note written by William Selby. It remains a possibility that he was replaced by Ralph Mow of Mowhaugh, as in an earlier note he is described as one of the men of very small action and obscure men that did not stir during Whitehaugh's breakout attempt. There are clearly some discrepancies among the English records of the time.

William Tait of Cherrytrees

The Taits had long been involved in the villainy on the Borders and one William Tait was taken prisoner and locked up in Berwick castle alongside a Richard de Eccles by the men of John de Clifford in 1358. Tait was held on a bond of 250 merks until his release the following year.

The family were long-term associates of the Kerrs and in 1493 Sir

Robert Kerr, knight, became surety for William Tait of Cessford Mains and his cousin Robert Burn after they'd murdered Thomas Young at the ford of Kale and stolen his horse, saddle, bow and a satchel and purse. Interestingly, William had stood as surety for his brother David eight months earlier when he had wounded the same Thomas Young in a moonlight assault when he robbed him of his horse, saddle, bow, a pair of spurs and a purse containing an amount of silver coins at the Kale water.

When that same Sir Robert of Cessford, the Scottish Middle March Warden, was murdered by an English trio named Heron the Bastard, Lilburn and Starrhead at a truce day in 1511, two of the Taits were dispatched by his son Andrew as hit-men to York where they caught up with Starrhead, (the unusual name possibly arising from Starrhead bastle in Tynedale, more commonly known as Shilla Hill) murdered him, cut his head off and brought it back in a sack. The Kerrs then had it displayed on a spike in Edinburgh. George Tait of Cessford could have been one of the men in on the hit – he was certainly an active reiver and was charged with lifting 46 oxen that year.

The murder of Sir Robert was one of the reasons given by Scotland as to their fateful invasion of England that led to a bloody defeat at Branxton in 1513. One of the Taits definitely fought on the Scottish side that day; William Tait was there as he complained afterwards that William Turnbull had stolen his grey horse, which he had handed over to a David Strachan, servant to Thomas Dixon, Dean of Lestalrig, his master for the time, as the battle raged. Turnbull was ordered to pay him compensation.

A Dand Tait, with Robert Dalgliesh and his son, John, murdered an Englishman called Henry Milne in 1515, and the following year Jock and Henry Tait, along with another 200 Teviotdale riders, burnt Chillingham in Northumberland and robbed a load of cattle and goods, while Edward Tait, Ralph Tait, known as 'Hareshard' and Adam Tait along with the Youngs, Davisons and others robbed Newton.

Five years later a Willie Tait was one of the leaders of a gang a hundred strong that raided Wark Castle, and in 1523 a number of the family were accused of trespassing and pasturing sheep in England.

Adam Tait of Town Yetholm, Dand Tait of Yetholm, the mou of Kelso, Roger and Ralph Tait of Town Yetholm, Sir Patrick Tait and George and Henry Tait were also accused of entering the English Middle and East Marches.

Andrew Tait received a remission for associating with the outlaw Andrew Armstrong in 1535; possibly the same Dand Tait that was one of the six Scotsmen appearing as the jury at truce days at Reddenburn between 1536 and 1538. He also appeared in numerous bills of complaint, along with Sir Patrick Tait and Will Tait.

When Robert Tait, brother of David Tait, received lands at Lyton from Hugh, Lord Somerwell, in 1540, the deal was witnessed by some of the Kerrs and Youngs and Andrew Storey was murdered by Dand Tait and his sons in 1541.

A year later around 2,000 English invaders planned specifically 'to put to the fire and sword' Cherrytrees, a stead of Henry Taits, in an invasion of the Bowmont valley and although the Teviotdale families were tipped off of the raid in advance, their corn was burned. It would have been worse, but the dank November weather left everything sodden, while Cherrytrees, Stankford, the Bogg and their pele tower, called Barearse, were also fired.

That event was probably a deciding factor in Dand Tait of the Stankford's decision to sign a document along with several other minor Scottish lairds to serve the King of England in 1544. His pledge was Davie Tait. King Henry VIII sent for the chief men of the Taits, along with the Davisons, Pringles, Youngs, Turnbulls, Robsons and Rutherfords as he attempted to subdue the Border by making them 'assured men.'

Five years later William Tait in Yetholm was a witness to Andrew Kerr gaining lands, and in 1571 the Taits of Teviotdale burned two houses in Downham and took away goods and cattle. Three years later William Tait in Stankford and his sons (blank) Tait and George Tait were outlawed 'at the horn' and their goods gifted to William Kerr of Cessford. That William Tait may have been the 'servitor' to William Kerr, younger of Cessford, who was part of a gang that included Walter and James Kerr, Robert Hoppringle and William Grymmislaw, who were fined £333 for hanging a thief called Geordie Young without an assize.

His son George was also in bother, with Andrew alias Dand called the Baillie, for resetting and intercommuning with John Ker in Kerchesteris. In that decade some of the Tait reivers included Edward and Henry Tait in Cessford, William and Dand Tait in Cessford Mains and William and Robert Tait in Cessford Burn, with the bulk residing around Yetholm; William of Stankford and his sons David called 'Borgwell,' Robert, George and William, who killed the minister at Kirk Yetholm, ironically another of the family, William Tait called Priest's Will, in 1579. They were fined £133 6s 8d for the crime. Priest's Will's three-year tenure at the kirk, from 1576, is still recorded in the building, though his demise is not. Dand Tait lived in the pele tower Barearse, with his son George, and in 1574 he was receiving money from the Scottish crown, as was William Tait in Stankford.

There were a number of Taits in Town Yetholm itself. Humphrey, Stephen, called 'the Good Man', Patrick, Gilbert, Andrew alias Dand the Burgess and Dand the Baillie; there were Thomas, David, Robert, Steven and William Tait at a farm called the Hole and Henry and George Tait at the Bogg; there was also Thomas Tait, called 'the Tailor', while William Tait lived at Cherrytrees with his father John – they first appear in the records in 1576 with a £3 fine each for intercommuning with rebels. That same year Will Tait in Yetholm, Dand Tait in Yetholm, Dand Tait in Barearse, George Tait, his son, Dand Tait in Dowknow (the son of William Tait in Stankford), and Stephen and Humphrey Tait in Yetholm were among the signatories on a Band of the Clans of East Teviotdale in a Bond of Manrent to serve Archibald, 8th Earl of Douglas.

Two years later, Willie Tait of Cessford Burn, known as 'a fierce man of Teviotdale' and a follower of the Cessford Kerr's in the Earl of Morton's ranks at Falkirk, rode out in front of the Earl of Angus's assembled army as they faced each other and challenged his men to a duel 'to break a spear for his lady's sake.' He fought a James Johnstone on horseback with spears as both armies watched on from either side of the riverbank. Tait was unseated and killed while Johnstone was left with terrible injuries as the lance went clear through his thigh, shattering bone and tearing flesh.

In 1583 a note appeared from the English stating that Sir Thomas

Grey's horsemen of Wark and one or two bands of the garrison at Berwick were able to keep the peace whenever the 'Youngs, Taits, Pringles and other Teviotdales begin to radge, and drive them to forsake their houses and whole towns of both Yetholms, Hayhope and Cherrytrees.' However, in 1587 Will Tait of the Burnfoot was part of a crew made up primarily of Youngs, Burns and Davisons, with 30 others, who reived 30 kye and oxen, six horses and mares, insight, silver and gold, coined and uncoined, from Sir Cuthbert Collingwood's tenants at Branxton.

Henry Carey, Lord Hunsdon, was warden of the Eastern March and had strategically placed George Tait on the Grey's land at Shotton, just over the Border in England, in the 1570s on a 40s tenant farm and Ralph Grey claimed that 'the country knows that Tait has spent his blood rescuing Englishman's goods.' That same year saw Andrew Tait in Dowknow, son of William Tait in Stankford, witness a land deal between Robert Frissell of Overton and William Aynsley of Fawlaw. The Dowknow Taits and the Frisells of Overton were long-time raiding companions and John Tait, called Chief, of the Dowknow was caught lifting sheep with William Frissell at Kilham in 1604. He was also up at Jedburgh Assizes as late as 1622 accused of stealing sheep from Willie Waulds in Auld Graden and the Laird of Greenhead himself, as well as other raids with John and Thomas Frissell, sons of the Laird of Overton. John Tait, 'Chief' got off on a large bond with Robert Frissell (the former pledge) and George Tait in Shotton acting as surety. The Frissell boys weren't as lucky and were hanged. The links between the two families ran deep and Dand Tait, younger of Dowknow, put up 500 merks each for the release of George, James and Thomas Frissell, brothers to 'Quarrelbus' at a Jedburgh Assizes in 1611. In October that year Andrew Tait and Thomas Tait were absent from a Jedburgh court hearing along with a long list of others who must have felt that the Jeddart Justice being doled out at the time was best avoided by just not bothering to show up.

Dand Tait at Barearse was prominent in 1595; in a complaint of Sir Robert Kerr's to the English, he'd been made prisoner in his own home and robbed of gold and silver rings then taken to Berwick, but the Border Commissioners said it must have been an old story. His son George of Barearse also had a complaint in against William Wilkinson of Chatton for stealing six cows and oxen in daylight.

The Taits were involved in a daytime raid at Hethpool with the Kerrs and Youngs where they lifted 46 head, shot John Grey and hurt one of the Brewhouses following and took his horse, and the Taits raided William Davison in Gamma Mylles. George of Barearse is also recorded that year for raiding John Fyueh of Twysell House, gentleman, with David Tait, his son, and William Tait, his brother.

In 1597 the chief men of the Taits are listed as Will Tait in Stankford, David Tait in Cherrytrees, David Tait in Bare Arse and Will Tait in Yetholm, all within a mile or so of each other, suggesting that they are all family and related in some way. David is often misread in the records and is usually in fact Dand. That is certainly the case here.

By 1598 'very many' of the East Teviotdale Taits were filed in a 'great number' of English Bills that began with Henry Tait of the Bogg filed in a bill of Thomas Routledge of Kilham, and Steven and William Tait in the Hole were filed in a bill of Wattie Jackson's of Hedden. Henry Tait of the Bogg and his sons Robin and William were fugitives and declared outlaws after avoiding a Justice Court in Jedburgh during the pacification of the Borders in 1605, as was John Tait of Dowknow's associate Will Fraser of Overton and his brother John. Henry had been in bother in 1586, along with his brother Dand, Jamie Tait in Kirk Yetholm and Jock Tait in the town of Halroude, when they appeared in a list of names issued by Jedburgh Justice Courts as 'especially complained upon.'

It was for those 1598 bills, and other previous offences, that William Tait of Cherrytress would stand as a pledge for the family. The Taits apparently rented Cherrytrees from the Rutherfords of Hundalee, as well as Shotton and lands in Kirk Yetholm, while Stankford was reputedly rented from the Cessford Kerrs. Will was a disreputable associate and henchman of the Middle March Warden Sir Robert Kerr and was described in a note by the jailers as 'a man of wealth but small action.'

William Tait of Cherrytrees was one of the prisoners that leapt from the walls at York during the escape attempt and put his signature (a cross, as he couldn't write) on the letter in 1600 along with Robert Frissell, Richard Rutherford and Thomas Aynsley, offering to satisfy the bills that they stood for, by payment or the delivery of the men in the bills to their value, which was denied. However, in 1602, the four went sent to Alnwick guarded by 100 horsemen, then taken on to Berwick where they were thrown in the 'loathsome prison' called Haddock's Hole.

William Tait was described as 'very sick with an ague and the dropsy ever since he came and like to die' by Sir John Carey, which probably went some way as to explaining why, although the friends of all four were making offers for their release, he felt that three would quickly relieve bills to free themselves. Tait being the one that he feared would 'stick long on his hands, as he saw none of his friends doing anything.'

He survived, but it proved an expensive business being a prisoner – Tait's costs during the time of his detention from 29 May 1598 to 15 April 1603 ran to a total of £3229 in Scottish money. The commissioners of Scotland ordained that all of the clan should contribute to his costs, but they refused. The in-fighting over money rumbled on and in July 1605 William's son James was killed at the green at Cherrytrees, with James Tait of Kelso being accused by his father and brother John of the murder, but he was acquitted as innocent. James was a brother of George Tait in Barearse.

A month later, Sir John Kerr of Hirsale appeared for the leading members of the clan that agreed to pay any such sums over the 10 merks due from each of them for William's weekly expenses while he remained a pledge in England. Dand Tait of the Dowknow, George Tait in Barearse and William Tait his brother, Thomas Tait, called of the Holes, in Yetholm, Robert Tait in Stankford, George Tait in Stankford, Jock Tait in Yetholm, James Tait, called James the Bailie, in Yetholm, Ralph Tait in Yetholm, and Thomas Tait in Yetholm, called Tom the Bailie, all subscribed.

But by 1608 William Tait of Cherrytrees was bitterly complaining that he was still owed 10 merks to cover his weekly expenses incurred during his time in captivity in England from some of the family, namely, Robert Tait in Stitchill, called of Barearse, Steven and William Tait, sons of George Tait in Barearse, Thomas Tait called the Tailor, David Tait, his brother, David and Robert Tait, brothers of Thomas

Tait of the Hole, George Tait called of the Bogg, Gilbert Tait of Yetholm, Steven Tait called The Good Man and David Tait called Borgwell.

By 1612 William Tait was no longer at Cherrytrees, his estate being described as 'distressed.' His links with Sir Robert Kerr did at least provide some relief as he was granted a pension of 100 merks for the rest of his life by King James VI in a letter to Edinburgh from London.

Three years earlier a man named William Hogg was ploughing a field in Yetholm when he was attacked and left for dead with a number of the clan standing accused of the vicious assault. George Tait in Stankford, George and Thomas his sons, Gilbert Tait in Yetholm, Dand Tait in the Dowknow, William Tait his son, Thomas Tait in Yetholm called of the Hole, accompanied by David Tait in Yetholm, Andrew Tait called 'Dand above the Gate', and others, 'armed with swords, gauntlets, platesleeves, lances, spears and halberts' had set upon him.

George Tait of Stankford, the father of George and Thomas Tait who were identified as the main culprits, along with Gilbert Tait in Yetholm, was locked up in the Tollbooth in Edinburgh for his boys on a 500 merks bond not to hurt William Hogg or his father John, who was the portioner of Old Roxburgh.

The Hoggs wouldn't let the matter lie and got a summons for the bulk of the clan to appear. George Tait of Barearse, Dand Tait of Dowknow, Thomas, Humphrey, Steven and David Tait in Yetholm, George Tait of Shotton, Stephen Burn of the Bog, William Tait, brother's son of Gilbert Tait in Yetholm, Henry Tait in Bog, Robert Tait his son, George Tait in Stankford, William, Gilbert and David Tait in Yetholm, David, William, Robert and George Tait, sons of the said Dand called of the Dowknow, William Tait oy to the said Dand, John Tait in Shotton, William Young of Feltershaws, William Young his son, and William Burn, son to Stephen Burn of Both, were all implicated in the matter.

Intriguingly, Thomas and John Tait of Yetholm were called before a secret meeting in 1608 alongside Gilbert Kerr and William Rutherford after they'd be cited to appear before King James and the Privy Council of England to answer charges under the pain of £100 sterling; they sought the advice of the Scottish Privy Council, who read the charges, 'written in parchment and sealed with wax', and found that 'such a form of summons was a novelty of a dangerous preparative, importing prejudice to the whole estate.' They were advised not to obey the charge and that the council would write to the King and ask him that 'no more of such citations should be directed against the subjects of Scotland.'

During the last few kicks of the Reiver period, Robert Tait of the Dowknow was denounced a rebel for not appearing to answer charges of intimidating a Robert Scott of Hartwoodmyris with the Kerrs in 1612, and George Tait of Dowknow was declared one of the last outlaws in 1618.

Some of the family slipped over the line into Northumberland and John Tait, alias Jock Tait 'Scottishman' of Burradon along with two Englishmen named Arthur Ogle of Trewhitt, gentleman, and George Reed of Burradon, gentleman, stole six ewes each from Martin Ogle at Tritlington in 1600, while in 1610 Lancelot Tait, a labourer from Shotton, and Robert Young of Awtonburn, stole a yellow ox and a 'sad branded cow' from David Story of Resden.

In 1622 David Tait, bailie in Yetholm, and Thomas Tait, were charged with impeding a law officer in the discharge of his duty; once again, with the Kerrs. Robert, Earl of Lothian, was angry with Sir John Kerr of Jedburgh, knight, after becoming a cautioner in various sums for him – basically putting up bail. He got wind that Sir John and Gilbert Kerr were at Lochtour and sent a gang to apprehend them, but the Taits and a number of Kerrs and Scotts turned up armed to try and spirit Sir John away. They violently rushed the house, blew out the candles and, in the darkness, grabbed the officer and his men and threatened to kill them. They all ended up getting locked up in the tollbooth in Edinburgh.

Hob Tait in Cessford Mains entered Will Tait as a pledge and was dismissed and put to liberty by King James's Border Commissioners the following year. It was a better result than drowning, swinging from gallows, being deported, or losing your entire estate.

Dand Pringle of Hownam

In 1588 Dand Pringle of Hownam, with his illegitimate son, Wattie Pringle, Hob Pringle of Kelso, and William Pringle of Chatto stole a horse from Thomas Dixon of Whitton. Hob Pringle of Clifton was part of a raiding party including Burns, Davisons, Kerrs, and 40 others, that reived 120 kye and oxen, 6 horses and mares and took insight worth £30 sterling from Cuthbert Collingwood of Titlington around the same time.

The Pringles (originally Hoppringle) were raiding far and wide; Wattie Pringle, younger, of Over Chatton, with Robert Pringle of Kelso and William Trewhitt stole 14 kye and oxen from James Burn of Warkworth and they hit Alnwick fair to take 11 oxen. Davie Pringle of Over Chatto, Dand Pringle's bastard son Wattie and a Rutherford were the named as the guilty parties in that one.

Davie Pringle of Chatto was raiding Alnwick again in 1589 with Ralph Mow, Tom Marshall of Mow, John Young of Kelso, and George Brewis to take seven cows and a 'stott' from Roland Glenn and Ralph Swan.

When Lord Russell was shot and killed at a Day of Truce in 1585 (reputedly by William Kerr of Ancrum's brother), Andrew and George Pringle were present and signed a statement prepared by Sir John Forster on the incident, though it appears that these were English gentlemen. Andrew complained in 1587 that he'd been robbed of three oxen by a man named Cowart, one of Wattie Pringle of Clifton's foot soldiers, and Jock Storey of Awtonburn, a member of James Young of the Cove's crew.

The Pringles were another family that lived on both sides of the invisible line, though they were more prevalent in Scotland. Their tower at Smailholm was burned by an English invasion party of around 1,000 led by Dacre's brother Philip, Sir Ralph Fenwick, Leonard Musgrave, and others, in 1524 but as they drove away cattle and plunder they had the misfortune of bumping into around 2,000 Teviotdale riders and 'marshmen' who were preparing to raid in the other direction. Both sides got off their horses and got stuck into each other; the English killed around 30 and took 300 prisoners and three standards. But the Scots weren't daft; when they had split, some of their men came in behind the English and killed the infamous John Heron the Bastard, the anti-hero of Flodden Field some 11 years earlier, who was involved in a blood feud with the Kerrs and Taits. Six more were killed and Fenwick and Musgrave were taken prisoner with 20 others and some of the Scottish prisoners rescued. The English force turned and chased the rest of the Scots from the field with Andrew Kerr, the Scottish Middle March warden, and his uncle Mark being so badly injured during the fight that it was thought that they couldn't live.

Andrew Kerr did, however, survive, though the battle-scarred Laird of Cessford was killed just two years later by men of Sir Walter Scott of Buccleuch in their attempt to free the young King James V from the clutches of Douglas at the Battle of Melrose. Six of the Pringles were implicated in the killing; Alexander Pringle in Torsonse, his sons John, James, George and Adam and his nephew James were served a warrant. Those same Pringles were involved in another murder earlier that year when they slaughtered William Thomson.

James Pringle was a servant to the King of Scots and at a Truce Day at the Lochmaben Stone in April 1538 he had told the English official Edward Aglionby, who was meeting with Scottish West March warden Lord Maxwell, that himself and 20 other Pringles were to join a Scottish force into Ireland when 'John Charters returned from France.' Maxwell said that he was going across the water with 'the master of Kilmaurs, the earl of Glencairn's son, two or three knights, and about 300 men of the best they can try in all Scotland.' His son reckoned 800 men, but Aglionby was more inclined to believe his father. It was an amicable meeting; the English were pleased that they had killed a Scots reiver called Edward Irving (Gib's Edward) and captured another called Willie Richardson, 'two of the notabest Scotch offenders since Dick of Woodfoot and George Twine died', while taking cattle at Greystock. Richardson had badly sliced up the face of the man that killed Irving but was taken and locked up in Carlisle Castle and Aglionby felt that 'the Borders were in as good stay as ever he saw them.'

It wouldn't last and in 1548 George Pringle of Torwoodlee was accused of treasonably 'assisting the Ancient enemies of England' and giving and taking assurance from them. These offences stemmed from the 1540s rough wooing period as the Pringles had signed up as 'assured Englishmen' and were at the Battle of Ancrum Moor when they swapped sides half way through with their neighbours. Jock Pringle of Clifton was their signatory on the document binding them to Henry VIII, if only for a short while, giving them licence and pay to raid and harry their neighbours that hadn't signed up.

George Pringle had been taken as a Pledge into England following the Battle of Solway Moss in 1542 along with such luminaries as James Ormeston of Ormeston; the laird of Grenhead (Kerr); the Davisons of Marchloughe; the laird of Lynton (Kerr); the laird of Makerston (Macdowell); Robert Elliot of Hassenden; the laird of Ryddell (Ryddell); the laird of Bon Jedburgh (Douglas); the sheriff of Tevidale (Douglas); the Halls; the Olivers; and the Crosers. Pringle was held at a man called the Parson Ogle's and was freed in exchange for him in 1545. The others were held by Northumbrian gentlemen such as Sir John Widdrington, Lord Ogle, Sir John Delaval, Percival Selby, John Ogle of Twissill, Robert Collingwood of Eslington, Thomas Collingwood of Reyall, Ralph Collingwood of Tytlyngton, Edward Gallon of Trewhit, Thomas Clavering, John Rothom, George Fenwick of Brinkburn, Thomas Foster of Ederston, George Carr of Lesbury and John Hall of Otterburn.

And in 1543 Robert Pringle and twelve of his servants, including Adam Pringle, had to deliver oxen, eight kine, 300 sheep, and eight labouring horses and geldings to the Captain of Norham in what looks like a compensation payment. That same year a James Pringle was sent down a prisoner to Carlisle Castle in the aftermath of Solway Moss while a Sandy Pringle had left Scotland for Newcastle and was taken on as a servant of the English King; his son Dandy remained in Scotland and was sent for by the English in 1565 to give information on Lord Bothwell, who was back from the continent and at Hermitage.

It wasn't all high espionage and in 1544 John Pringle of the Murrus, his son, and a brother of the laird of Thorndikes fired arrows into an English raiding party made up of Carrs, Swinhoes of Cornhill, Dixons, and the garrisons of Wark and Cornhill that had burned Glengelt and driven off sheep, cattle and prisoners. The laird of Thorndyke's brother was captured and although Pringle was knocked off his horse and hit the ground, he was rescued by some men of the Humes.

In 1555 Alexander Pringle of Craigleith and his son George left David Pringle of Trylieknows and his son Alex with terrible injuries when they assaulted them and took their cattle in a seemingly purely family fall-out. Alexander of Craigleith and his son were tough characters with a taste for violence and in 1563 they were in hot water again for mutilating John Scott's right arm and were ordered to appear at a Selkirk Justice Court.

When an Englishman named Ralph Gray filed a bill against a Pringle at a Truce Day in 1568, the Pringle threatened revenge 'openly amongst the whole assembly the deponent contrary to the law and truce,' which broke up the meeting as the Scots refused to hand Pringle over and it all threatened to get out of hand with a menacing atmosphere developing. The Pringles were certainly a handful and not to be messed with; two years later they were at feud with the Elliots and 300 of each side gathered after a number of murders and revenge slaughters had forced a day of law for a trial. Although swords were drawn, and a few pistols shot off, only a few were hurt, and the hearing was put back by the Earl of Morton for six months.

The Grays were a thorn in the side of the Pringles again in 1573 when Thomas Gray and his men lifted 1,000 of their sheep and other cattle that the Northumbrians claimed were feeding on English ground. It may have been a way of justifying their taking legitimately, but Gray reckoned that not only were they taken in England but were stolen anyway and for 'good neighbourhood' he'd given them back apart from 'twenty wedders in name of poundage.' An English official noted that 'it appears hereby, and by other froward dealing, the Borderers like not of the good amity between the realms.'

The Pringles remained involved at the top end of Scottish society and in 1589 a Thomas Pringle was captured by the English with letters from the Earl of Huntly to the Duke of Parma and the King of Spain, which were denied as forgeries and 'plotting done on the South of the Tweed.' He was sent as a prisoner to Berwick.

The family's earlier association with the English long held a black mark against them and as late as 1576 James Pringle in Hownam was fined £66 13s 4d for 'traitouously coming in company with the lieutenant and army of the English for the time and taking part with them in the burning of the town of Selkirk and the house of Newark 28 years ago or thereby.'

John Pringle in Bents picked up a fine for associating with Thomas Kerr of Ferniehurst at the time, so they just couldn't win. He was also charged, along with James Pringle of Hownam, and Walter Pringle in Clifton, of violence and the destruction of a house belonging to the laird of Hundalee in Grubet.

Robert Pringle in Halden was murdered in plain daylight on a trod to recover his own goods by Tom Ewart from Wark, John Johnstone in the 'Yet,' Alexander Clark of Wark, the Constable of Wark and many other inhabitants of the village who also left his father Thomas with horrendous injuries in 1596, while Dand Pringle of Hownam (the pledge's father) and Jamie Pringle in Clifton where reived of five score ewes and wedders by Roger Strother in Caldington and Jamie Strother in Buckton as the tit-for-tat continued. A year later the Pringles raided John Ord, the Mayor of Berwick, and took four score sheep from the Grotehaugh.

The pledge Dand Pringle of Hownam was described as a man of some living and action in the gaolers notes at York and he'd first appeared in the records in 1576 for appearing dressed in battle gear with Thomas Kerr, formerly of Ferniehurst, at Jedburgh. He was fined £20 with other members of the family such as his father James and his brothers James and Robert.

His brother Thomas and John Dalgliesh of Wideopen, with two others of that family, stole five geldings and a mare from Berwick bounds in 1596. One of the horses belonged to John Carey, which made them a grave enemy. Carey rode to Wideopen with 50 men and killed John, 'cutting him all in pieces.' Such was the justice that the Scots could expect from the English East March Warden, a respected and respectable official, so it's little wonder that the reivers constantly took matters into their own hands. Dand was imprisoned in York until being moved up to Berwick in September 1602 and straight into the hands of John Carey. He must have felt it was a case of out of the frying pan into the fire, but in 1611 Dand Pringle of Hownam appeared at Jedburgh as a cautioner for William Pringle of Hownam for £100 and James Pringle of the Gate for 400 merks, so he must have at least retained some of his cattle rustling fortune, unlike the York gaoler Redhead who had fed them for two years or more before being sacked. Thomas Burghley was concerned about Redhead's payment as his 'estates will be broken if it shall not please her majesty to have a princely consideration for them.'

The Pringles were still proving a handful and in Jedburgh during 1607, Alexander Pringle of Hownam, Dand Pringle, called little Dand (perhaps Dand the prisoner's son), and three of the Mows fell out with five of the Kerrs, from the Gateshaw and Hayhope branches, with 'hostile pursuit, invasion and some bloodshed' taking places during the ruction. They were all ordered to make mutual assurances.

And long after the Borderers had been subdued, in 1844 a James Pringle was found guilty on a charge in Northumberland and sentenced to seven years on Van Dieman's Land. He was transported out on a convict ship to Australia with 263 others. The times had changed but the lawless spirit remained.

John Robson of Chosenhope

The Scottish Robsons were every bit as active in reiving as their cousins across the Border in Tynedale.

In 1493 Walter Robson in Harden was 'denounced at the horn' for murdering the Laird of Eldmere and he was also intercommuning with an outlaw called Archibald Armstrong, while in 1516 James Hardy of New Cartington, an Englishman, was murdered on English ground by a gang consisting of Robin Robson, his brother Allan Robson, Ralph and Jock Robson, George Robson of Fawley, laird of the Wells, David Kirkton and others.

The following Robsons were Scottish rebels fugitive in England in 1540 - Watt Robson and his sons Willie, Jamie, and Lance; Adie Robson of Howston and Hob Robson of Ancrum, while John Robson, called Paulie's Jock, was hanged after being found guilty of common theft and reset of theft in 1556.

Harry Robson in Barehope was named in a long list of people 'specially complained upon' at the Justice Courts at Jedburgh in 1586, and Ralph Robson of Houston, James Hall of Newbiggin and Ralph Aynsley of Thickside had to appear for their boss, Andrew Kerr of

Ferniehurst, 'for the quietness of the Borders, under pain of rebellion' at Dalkeith in 1587. Ralph and his brother Ninian were notorious raiders who had hit John Davidson in Whitton near Rothbury around the same time and were again named as men of Ferniehursts.

A Thomas Kerr was held prisoner by the English in 1569 after being caught delivering secret letters. His guide into England was an ostensibly English Robson who lived 15 miles from Berwick, under Cheviot, just a mile from the Border, so whether he felt more kinship with the Teviotdalers or Tynedalers of his name is up for debate; but that is the nature of the Border. The English don't want us, and the Scottish won't have us is an old saying and very apt in this instance.

John Robson of Hownam took a white horse from William Collingwood in 1585, and in 1589 James Robson of the Burvens was riding with James Hall of Heavyside, younger, John Mow, and 20 other men to carry away cattle and horses from Thomas Reed of Burradon and his brother John Reed of Farnham. The Robsons and their gangland friends the Davisons, Mows, Aynsleys, and Halls continued to hammer Northumberland throughout the decade with Ralph Robson of Middleknowes and the Oxnam Robsons particularly active reivers.

Ralph and Rinion Robson of Oxnam were with Andrew Rutherford of Littleheugh, Andrew Frissell of Overton and James Hall of Heavyside to steal 28 cattle and a horse from Wharton in 1587, and Ralph was with James Davison of Burnrigg and others that took 60 cattle, three horses and 100 old sheep from Hugh Urpeth of the Newton.

The Robsons and their West Teviotdale associates were picking their way down through the valleys of upper Coquetdale again as James Robson of the Burvens, Rinion Robson the younger of Middleknowes, Jamie Hall of Heavyside, elder, with his brother Robert and Jamie Hall of Capupp reived 24 kye and oxen, six young nolte and four calves from Jenkin Humble of Wharton.

Ralph Robson of Middleknowes hit Thomas Hall of Stitchellheugh with Jock Hall of the Sykes, George Pile of Milnheugh, Davie Aynsley of Fala, William and Thomas Hall and Roger Aynsley of Cleethaugh in a raid that saw them drive off 12 cattle and a mare, while Hob Robson of Barehope, with Mungo and Giles Douglas, took six kye and oxen from Thomas Gray at Alnwick West Park. Charles Robson of the Wells, Rinion and Ralph Robson, Jamie Hall of Newbiggin and Peter Hall of Capupp robbed 20 ewes and wedders, a horse and a mare and £10 insight out of the Laird of Trewhitt.

Raiding parties were well organised, tight-knit and went out with people that they knew and trusted. They comprised of family gangs and those they had grown up with together. The reivers obviously had to know that the people they were with could be relied upon to handle themselves if the victims got together to run a hot trod on them, and they knew that a counter-raid would more often than not be coming in retribution.

How much of a green light the likes of the Robsons would have to get from the boss, in their case Ferniehurst, is unclear, but the bosses did take a cut from the spoils so must have had some idea of who was doing what and to whom. It was all a racket, and everyone had their hands out for a piece of the action. Ralph, Rinion and Jock Robson were out in the moonlight again with Will and Tom Hall of Middleknowes, and Jock Hall of the Sykes, to drive away six oxen and a mare from widow Stamper at Thorton, and Matthew Robson, John Robson called 'the Pudge' and Jock Hall of the Sykes took John Hall of Otterburn and Jenkin Brown of Carisheugh for 18 kye and oxen and a mare in 1589.

James Robson of the Burvens rode with his mates James Hall of Heavyside, John Mow, and 20 foot-soldiers, to target Redesdale and the Reeds, lifting 24 cattle and a horse, while Rinion Robson of the Wells took 50 cattle, a horse and a pair of plough irons from the Hedleys at Garretshiels with Robin Learmonth of the White Cross, Davie Pile, Ralph and Roger Aynsley of Cleethaugh and John Hall of the Sykes. Then Ralph Robson of Middleknowes, Davie Aynsley and George Pile were back to take 12 cattle and a mare from Thomas Hall of Stitchellheugh again.

The Robsons of Chatto and Barehope took six oxen from George Ord of Tweedmouth while Jock Robson of Crailinghall, Jock Robson 'the Flesher,' and Andrew 'Shortneck' Robson raided William Fenwick of Wallington, and in 1596 John Robson of Over Crawlinghall and Thomas Davison of Burnrigg stole 13 cows and oxen from Ralph Grey.

During the early 1590s Thomas Robson was convicted of March treason with the other Scotsmen Stephen, George, and Thomas Douglas, William Hall and Percival Harris, and in 1600 the Teviotdale Robsons were in hot water with the former Scottish East March warden Sir Alexander Home of the Snook after they'd raided Roger Selby of Graden. Robert Kerr of Newton, who had since died, and John Home stood the £30 to satisfy the bill. Home had paid his £15 share but since Kerr had died, the Homes wanted Kerr's widow and son to pay their half for their crew's damage.

There seems to have been some confusion of the pledge delivered by the Scottish Robsons at the West Ford; Jock Robson of Oxnam was originally desired by the English on the first couple of lists issued, but it was a 'George Robson' that was delivered by Cessford. In subsequent lists it is John Robson of Chosenhope that is named as one of the men of very small action and obscure men on the jailer's sheet and he wasn't part of the Whitehaugh escape attempt. The wily Robson – whoever he really was – had the last laugh though as he himself escaped out of York castle on his own into Scotland and was freed of the bills he was stood for before April 1600. It must have been a major embarrassment for the English officials as further details of his escape have proved difficult to track down.

Richard Young of Feltershaws and James Young of the Cove

Sir Robert Kerr 'loved the surname (Young) best in Scotland,' according to Sir John Carey. James Young of the Cove was 'near and dear' to the Scottish Middle March warden, and obviously one of his most trusted capos.

James was listed as a man of wealth but of small action by the jailers at York when they received him, but he had been heavily involved in loads of disorder which beings into question the validity of the information that they had been given; in 1575 he was remitted and discharged on a £40 precept from a justice court of Roxburgh along with his servant Jock Clark, James Pringle in Hownam's son Dand Pringle, and his servant James Aitchison.

A year later James' brother Robert got off Scot-free for coming arrayed in battle gear with Thomas Kerr, formerly of Ferniehurst, when he had gathered the East Teviotdale clans and intended to burn the burgh of Jedburgh in 1572, while Richard Young, John Young of the Nyuek, Thomas Young, officer in Lempitlaw and David Tait in Eckford were fined £4 for their part in the affair.

Others of the clan received heftier fines. Andrew alias Dand Young, called Comber, and his brother Thomas, called Knackers, sons of George Young, called The Gun, and John Young in Blackhall clocked up totals of over £26.

That same year Andrew, alias Dand Young in Cessford, along with William Young in Otterburn and a number of Kerrs, Davisons and Pringles were fined over £6 each for intercommuning with rebels, and Mark Young in Spittalland was fined £10 for the murder of James Kerr in Caverton three years earlier.

James Young of the Cove led a raid on John Reay of Hadston in 1589 when he, along with his brother Mark, Tom Young, Jock Young 'Blackhall,' Tom Burn of Elisheugh and his brother Mark, and the Laird of Corbett's sons John and James Kerr, took three mares and insight.

Richard Young of Feltershaws was part of a gang that stole 11 oxen from Thomas Collingwood of Little Ryle at Hedgeley in 1589; the other riders included one of the other pledges, namely Ralph Burn of the Cote, the son of John Burn, along with Ralph Burn, called 'Shortneck,' Charles and Mark Burn of Elisheugh, Jock Young of Awtonburn, known as 'Jock of Blackhall,' and Thomas Young 'Tom of Townhead.'

As it was his brother James that had initially been named as a pledge, it can only be assumed that Richard stepped up in his stead. James of Feltershaws, and another brother, Dand, with Tom Young of Awtonburn, Jock Young 'Blackhall,' John Pringle of Clifton and John of Kelso, George Kerr in Primside Mills, Robert Davison of Easter Fowmerdon, and Watt Pringle of Clifton had taken 18 kye and oxen from Edmond Crawster and Nicholas Forster.

The Youngs raided primarily with the Burns and Taits under the protection of the Kerrs, who undoubtedly took a piece of the action in tributes, so it was unsurprising that when they were locked up at York Richard was in a room with William Tait and Ralph Burn, along with the youngster William Elliot, while James Young of the Cove was interred in a chamber with William Hall, his mate Dand Pringle and Richard Rutherford. Richard Young of Feltershaws was under the 'men of very small action and obscure men' description handed to the jailers.

The Youngs were constantly raiding throughout the 1580s and 90s. They had been noted in a 1583 list on the loose men of the Borders alongside the Davisons, Burns and Pringles as the worst East Teviotdale offenders, and in 1596 Sir Robert Carey wrote that Northumberland didn't dare rise upon those familes, plus the Halls and 'any they make accompt of' for fear of deadly repercussions; they would 'have his life, or two or three of his nearest kinsmen in revenge.'

Dand Young of Clifton, the son of a man known as 'Crooked Pledge,' lifted 44 sheep from Michael Hebburn of Hebburn with William Hall of Hownam Kirk and Jock Hall 'Ostler' in 1587. Dand Young of Woodside along with Dand Hall of Awton Burn, Dand Glenhome of Mow and Will Hall of Woodside End took nine cows and oxen in another raid.

The Kerrs, Youngs, Burns, etc raided Adam Smith of the Briggemylle at night taking 20 neat and 5 horses and mares, and the same crew cut up Gilbert Wright's doors with axes in Cowpland during an assault. The Youngs were smashing up doors again at Haggerston with the Halls, Piles, and Aynsleys, lifting 30 neat, five nags and leaving four men for dead. They also smashed up Ralph Selby's tower at Westwood and took three geldings, then were at William Cowert's of South Charlton to steal two nags. The Youngs were also with James Davison of Burnrigg at Wark-on-Tweed lifting six kye as they terrorised north Northumberland with successive and repeated reiving.

The Youngs, Davisons, and Burns, took 40 kye and oxen from Hethpool in daylight and in a night raid of their own lifted 30 kye and oxen from Thomas Routledge of Kilham. As well as the Cove and Feltershaws on the Bowmont, the Youngs had steads at places such as Linton, Blackhall, Aikwood, Braidley, and Ormston.

In 1575 William Young was a Warden Officer of the Middle Marches and was paid £14 6s14d for the role. The Youngs had long carried much influence in the area; in 1493 Simon Young in Rouchlee was charged with treasonably bringing the Englishmen of Tynedale to Hundalee, with Andrew Ker of Ferniehurst standing as surety, and five years later the mighty Walter Scott of Buccleuch stood as a pledge for George Young after he'd been taken by Rinzeane Rutherford and Hugh Douglas at Minto. Buccleuch had to present Young at the next session of the Justice Courts of Jedburgh or face a fine. A Roger Young was held by the English for offences and released from Berwick as far back as 1335, while Jock Young of Otterburn, Jock Young of Cessford, and Will Young of the Spittal were implicated with others in a 1516 murder of Englishman Ralph Strowther. In 1521 Dand Young and Jock Young of Cessford were among the leaders of 400 men that met at Hoselawlough and raided the castle at Wark-on-Tweed.

Two years later John Young of Yetholm, James Young called 'The Good,' Dand Young of the Woodside, Robin Young, and Richard Young of Clyston were among the list of Teviotdale men accused of trespassing and pasturing sheep in Northumberland, and John Young of Otterburn and Dand Young of the Woodside both appeared as one of the six Teviotdale jurors hearing bills at the Reddenburn between 1536 and 1538.

In 1543 George Young was named as a 'chief setter on all spoils' with Will Davison, 'a great thief', and one of the Pringles following a raid on an English village. The Youngs farmsteads on the south bank of the Bowmont burn, by the rise of the Cheviot hills, were burnt by Hertford in the infamous English raid. Awton Burn, Cove, Woodside, Owsnopside and Feltershaws were all left smoking and smouldering. So, in 1544, James Young, Dand Young of Oxenside, Tom Young 'the Gown,' Jock Young of Yetholm, and Young of the Woodside, all signed a document to become 'assured' Englishmen with the rest of the East Teviotdale gangs. James Young stood as pledge for the Youngs. However, there were repercussions following their 'turncoat' behaviour at the battle of Ancrum Moor. On 29 May 1545 John Foster's garrison of Fenton, John Selby of Twisell, James Selby of Tillmouth, and William Swinhoe of Cornhill, rode into Linton Lough and the Bowmont and slew Dand Young of Felthershaws.

The following members of the family were signatories on the 1576 Bond of Manrent to Archibald, 8th Earl of Angus: Will Young, James Young, John Young in Linton, Richard Young in Yetholm and William Young of Feltershaws. The Youngs, Burns and Kerrs under Sir Robert Kerr were causing considerable damage on the English Middle March, and a list of raids that they'd carried out and not been charged for was released in the 1580s as the victims sought justice in vain.

John Shotton had been raided and, to rub salt into the wounds, was wrongfully delivered by Sir John Forster to Dave Burn of the Bought for a bill that he'd already paid for; the widow Taylor was robbed of four cows, William Davison of a mare and 10 sheep, Thomas Neilson 20 cows and oxen, Robert Harrowgate of 30 cows and oxen and two horses, Edward Anderson of 30 oxen and cows and three horses, John Harrowgate of 24 sheep, 11 pigs and a horse while Edward Michell lost twenty cows and oxen and a horse. The long list of unsettled bills continued with Edward Shotton losing a horse, two oxen and 16 sheep, Edward Crisp being robbed of 40 sheep, 3 oxen and ten pigs; Thomas Whitehead was taken for 36 oxen, a cow, a mare and insight, William Nicholson of 15 cows and oxen, one mare and seven sheep, William Archer of 11 oxen, John Crisp of a cow and 32 sheep, John Harrogate of 40 sheep, James Crisp of two oxen and a cow, Richard Crisp of 12 oxen and a mare, the widow Crisp lost 13 sheep and two cows and John Crisp 20 oxen and cows and insight. William Gibson was raided and lost 13 oxen, Andrew Gibson ten sheep, John Gibson 10 oxen and cow, one mare and £20 insight while the widow Gibson had two cows stolen by the gangs. This was from just one small area of Northumberland and gives some idea of the constant raiding being carried out by the East Teviotdale men and the confidence that they had in avoiding answering for their crimes.

This was displayed again as shortly after Sir Robert Kerr had sprung James Young of the Cove from his detention at Swinburne Castle in 1597, he was named as the chief rider in an assault on Kilham. Young was described as Cessford's 'chief instrument' in raiding and when four Teviotdale riders broke a man's door and took his cattle, the village of Kilham pursued them in a lawful trod, hurt three of the reivers and took them prisoner in retaking the stock. The fourth rider made it away and raised East Teviotdale to come to their assistance. As the dawn broke, 40 Scottish riders descended on Kilham but were fought off and another two were taken prisoner. This proved too much of an affront and by seven in the morning 160 riders, led by Young, swept in and rescued the prisoners, killed one of the villagers, left seven for dead, and many others maimed and injured.

But the times were changing, and so was Sir Robert Kerr. The English officials were surprised, but pleased, when in Cessford had George Young hanged in 1602 in what was described by Sir John Carey as a 'rare piece of justice.'

Young wasn't happy when he was delivered at a Truce Day at Redding Burn and he punched the man that had filed a bill against him then, swearing and cursing in a fit of temper, threatened to stab the English Deputy Warden.

Kerr himself was angry when he heard that his own deputy had not delivered a different man and promised to bring one 'fitter for the bill' at the next meeting. Young was brought back and hung on a gallows that Cessford built, then stripped and his body hung in chains as an example. It was noted that nobody dared take the body down, nor even speak of the incident.

Kerr might have been seduced by the trappings of court and royalty, but James Young of the Cove wasn't. He was either the pledge delivered to Sir Robert Carey and taken to Berwick in July 1602 or one of the men that were still being held captive. John Carey noted that the ones who were left were all from families that had committed murders in the East March, naming the Youngs, Burns and Pringles, and were finally sent away to Newcastle-upon-Tyne to be met by Carey for transport to Berwick on 2 September 1602. The years inside didn't put an end to James Young of the Cove's reiving ways and in 1605 he was up on a charge at the Northumberland Assizes with Lancelot Kerr of Sheilestockbraes and James Young of Blagdon, alias James Young of Knowe, when at around 11 o'clock in the evening they stole 20 ewes and eight hogs from Thomas Wilson at Wooler. All three were declared fugitives from the justice court held at Jedburgh on 14 April 1606.

9. THE BEGINNING OF THE END

SIR JOHN CARMICHAEL was described by the Bishop of Durham as Sir Robert Kerr's 'greatest friend and favourer, on whom he chiefly depends' in 1596, and as 'the most expert borderer' by the churchman a year later. On 17 June 1600 Carmichael was gunned down and murdered on his way from Annan to Langholm in a gangland execution carried out by the shooter Ringan's Tom Armstrong. A gang of 16 Scotsmen, and two English, had waited in an ambush for the man who had been appointed the West March warden in October 1599 smack bang in the middle of a feud between the Maxwells and Johnstones. The Johnstones had forcibly taken back Lochmaben castle and slaughtered and spoiled a number of 'worthy persons' while their chief, the Laird Johnstone, was being held in ward. After robbing Carmichael's body, Willie 'Kang' Irving draped it over his horse and carried it to Lochmaben. The crew that carried out the hit had met at a football match to plan the murder and were named as Sandy's Ringan Armstrong and his sons Tom, Lancie, Hugh, Archie and Watt; Sim and Lancie Armstrong of the Side, Rob's Sandy, Rob Scott, Tom Taylor, William Forrester and William Graham of the Braid.

Lord Scrope felt that Carmichael had been killed for his good service and for agreeing with him to keep the West March riders in order 'and thus they are broken loose.' The following month the principal murderers (the Hollows Armstrongs and the Kang Irvings) were reported by Scrope to have raided Burgh, then Stanwix while the lord Bishop of Carlisle was preaching there. They had taken all the horses before moving on to Linstock and taking cattle; most troublingly, they had stolen all of the lord Bishop's brother Adam's beasts and beaten his wife, 'wounding her piteously.' A storm was brewing over the Borders and King James was urging Scrope and Richard Lowther to apprehend the killers – 'Sandy's Ringan's sons, certain others of the Armstrongs and their associates…thieves and limmers, and evil professed enemies to the peace and good rule of the countries' – should they cross into England seeking sanctuary.

Carmichael had long served the Scottish Crown in a number of important roles including warden and as an ambassador to Denmark and England. In 1592 he almost lost his sight due to an old injury in one eye and 'a thick film or skin lately grown on the other that he looks to be utterly blind within short time, whereby he purposes to retire from Court and live quietly at home,' but he recovered sufficiently enough to carry on with duties though he must have wished he'd just retired from the action then.

The Scottish West March problems had a lot to do with the Laird of Johnstone's failure to deliver his pledges at the West Ford meeting. Both he and Buccleuch were locked up in Edinburgh tower for not bringing them in July 1597. John Carey claimed that Johnstone hadn't brought them as he was at feud with the Maxwells and 'did not dare diminish his strength by delivering his friends.'

By the September he'd been kicked out of the Warden's job and the Douglas Laird of Drumlanrig wanted to take over as he 'expected some of the pledges who refused to enter to Johnstone would submit to himself.' Douglas said that if he couldn't gather the pledges, then he would deliver Johnstone, who was still imprisoned in Edinburgh castle, in their place. He didn't, of course, and the two families were reaching something of a compromise by June 1599 by agreeing to 'marry together' but both of them were imprisoned again by the King in August and he turned to his trusted friend Carmichael to sort things out soon after.

At that time the Armstrongs seemed to be conscious of the fact that they could be targeted and persecuted as those of the clan living on Lord Maxwell's lands made offers of pledges 'as they could have or get' to the Earl of Angus, lieutenant of the Marches, for both English and Scottish complaints while also wanting to make redress with England and 'conform to the laws of the Marches, providing the like order be observed by both countries to others.'

But just six months after Sim Armstrong of Whitehaugh's escape from York, in April 1601, Buccleuch and his deputies refused to answer for his bothers Andrew, Francis and John Armstrong or his sons Sim of the Rone, Archie and Sandy, nor Archie 'Whitehead' Armstrong and his brothers John and Sim, Alexander's Archie and his brother (all of the House of Whitehaugh) and Sim Armstrong of Caffield, 'his man' Tom Rannik, Andrew Taylor, John of the Whisgills, John 'The Lord's Geordie' Hill, John Armstrong of the Side, Sim's Archie and Robert Scott of Haining and King James demanded they be given up to Lord Scrope and Robert Carey. Those implicated in the Carmichael murder were also to be handed over, being named further as Ninian (Sandy's Ringan) Armstrong in Auchenbedrigg and his sons Tom, Hugh, Lantie, Walter, Archie and Dand; Sim and Lantie Armstrong of the Side, Rob's Sandy Armstrong, a Nixon, 'Lang Sandy' Armstrong in Rowanburn and Rob Scott; Tom 'the Laird' Taylor, Will Graham and Will Foster – 'all Englishmen' – and Jock and Humphrey Bell.

Although it appears that his assassination order came from the Johnstones, the Laird Johnstone was back in power and had met with Scrope's deputy Richard Lowther at the Annan Dyke where they proclaimed and denounced all the above as outlaws. By September 1601 Johnstone had apprehended one of Carmichael's murderers and, according to Scrope, had 'gone with him in great triumph to the King, where doubtless he shall be executed.' Tom Armstrong had his right hand cut off before being hanged at the mercat cross in Edinburgh alongside Adam 'the Peck' Scott – 'one of the most notable thieves that ever raided.' The Peck was charged with murdering Harry Ranald, Andrew Smith and Roger Shaw, assaulting others, and lifting hundreds of cattle and sheep. He'd also taken prisoner the minister of Lynes House, John Kerr, while burgling his home.

Armstrong's body was hung in chains at the Borrowmuir after, the first example of this happening in Scotland. The Armstrongs must have felt aggrieved and betrayed by Johnstone. Not only had they carried out the killing most likely on his behalf, but they had backed the Johnstones and fought for them against the Maxwells during the infamous battle of Dryfe Sands in 1593 alongside Buccleuch's Scotts, the Elliots and Grahams. However, they had also taken the side of the Maxwells in 1584 when they had released one of Kinmont's sons from the pledge chamber in Dumfries after he'd been locked up by the Johnstones, so their loyalties were ever changing.

The King headed south to the border in March 1602 and

'prevented an imminent disorder' by pacifying 'a great trouble between the Lord Maxwell and the laird of Johnstone' where all men submitted themselves to him – except the Armstrongs - 'the slayers of Carmichael.' Lord Maxwell would not come into the West Wardenry, the master of Herries was imprisoned in Newbottle and young Lochinvar in Edinburgh castle as the sovereign attempted gamely to put an end to the chaos. By the August of that year Johnstone was at Langholm seeking revenge for Carmichael's murder (he was killed himself in 1608 by Lord John Maxwell, who fled to France but was beheaded 5 years later) and Lord Scrope had burned out the houses of the men in Bewcastle that had sheltered the fugitives, reputed to be William Graham of Mote and Geordie's Sandy Graham.

In January 1603 the noose was starting to tighten further as the English Warden had broken into his old adversary Kinmont Willie Armstrong's house and found a Johnstone and Sandy's Ringan Armstrong there – both of whom were implicated in the killing. He sarcastically wrote to Cecil that by finding them he 'thought to do a favour rather than deserve complaint.' But the matter seemed a little more complex than just that. Scrope had ridden another raid on Kinmont and justified it by saying that Armstrong had spoiled the two towns of Heskett since his release from jail in the capital and that he was seeking to apprehend the Irving's and two of Kinmont's men, described as 'nightly spoilers,' that had been agreed upon with the Laird of Johnstone as outlaws.

Kinmont had been locked up in the tollbooth in Edinburgh in November 1602 and Watt Scott of Harden and Gilbert Elliot of Horsleyhill were placed on a £2000 bond that on his release he would remain within the burgh of Edinburgh until pledges for the 'gang of Kinmont' – any two of Geordie, Geordie's son Christie, or his brother Sandy Armstrong - were received on January 1 1603. A perplexed Scottish court official, no doubt as confused by all the complicated inter-family relationships as everyone else, erroneously recorded his name as William *Elliot* of Kinmont.

With the benefit of time and distance, it seemed as if the slippery Scrope was hoping to implicate Kinmont himself and get him to the gallows after all the embarrassment caused when Buccleuch had broken him out of Carlisle. He was also passing the buck to Johnstone with King James, who was in a rage and almost removed him from office, but for the intervention of the Earl of Mar, though the monarch did say that he would 'believe him no more.'

Tellingly, in February 1603, Francie Armstrong of Kinmont signed a bond to serve Johnstone 'against all men except the King' with the Warden similarly tied to Francie to maintain him in his lawful affairs. The document was important enough to be witnessed by the likes of Walter Scott of Tushielaw, Patrick Porteous of Halschaw, Mungo Johnstone of Lockerbie's son William, and others.

In April 1605 the Kinmont Armstrongs were the principal prisoners being held at Carlisle castle when 29 out of 33 being held bust out and on their escape fled back across into Scotland, while in May 1606 William Armstrong, the son of John of Kinmont, who had been one of the condemned men that broke out of Carlisle, went on the run in Scotland with six of the Grahams.

The Eastern and Middle Marches had been somewhat subdued by the taking of their pledges and the West was causing the biggest headache by far on both sides of the Border at the time. The Grahams, as well as being heavily involved with the Carmichael killers, stood accused variously of making up their own laws, being insolent and disrespectful to Buccleuch as he rode through a large gang of them at a meeting with Scrope at Rockcliffe, of riding with the Earl of Angus to burn the Johnstones at Lochmaben, bringing in Scottish raiders and levying blackmail and committing murders around Carlisle, to name but a few. Scrope worried that the Grahams and the Carletons were plotting to murder him. In September 1600 their many misdemeanours included attempting to kill John Musgrave at Brampton by firing thirty guns at him and trying to burn him in his house, breaking Jock of the Peartrees out of jail in Carlisle, kidnapping the 8 year old son of Mr. Salkeld of Corbie to exchange for the imprisoned thief Wattie Graham, taking protection money and robbing anyone that refused to pay, burning Hutcheon Hetherington's house to force him out and then cutting him to pieces, burning out Richard Brown, who had killed a Graham red-handed, and forcing him to pay 'to buy his peace.' They also hurt Thomas Middleton, the son of a justice of the peace who had condemned Richard Graham for horse theft, and likewise made him pay up. The Graham mob were threatening and assaulting anyone that dared pursue a trod, murdering anyone that gave evidence against offenders, resisting arrest and saying that Lord Scrope was nothing to do with them, and maintaining a gang of common fugitives such as one called Stoddart, Henry and William Wilson, Robert Scott, Jock the Trotter, Fergie of the Redkirk, Jock Richardson, Robert Saundie, Thomas and Gifford Carleton, Thomas Taylor, Davie's Willie, William Lamb, Roland Beattie, Hector Rich, his son young Hector and others.

They had committed robberies and murders throughout North Cumbria and guided the Scots in others while 60 of the Grahams were outlawed at the time for murders, burglaries etc. and they'd forced out 'men of good service' such as the Storeys and Taylors and replaced them with 'Scots and other bad people' that shared in the profits of their organised crime empire.

The Grahams, like the Armstrongs, could sense that trouble was brewing and they sent a petition to Lord Scrope, signed by Walter Graham, J. Graham, Walter Graham of Mote, Richie Graham of Brackenhill, William Graham of Rosetrees, Alexander Graham of Kirkandrews, David Graham of Bankhead, Willie Graham of the Fauld and Hutcheon Graham, younger, offering to stand themselves bound to Scrope to underlie the laws, to become good subjects, to assist in trods and to seek revenge for Scottish offences on his behalf. They believed that the Cumbrian gentry, such as the Lowthers, were seeking their destruction and 'would cut their throats with their hands if they dared.'

They weren't wrong; the gentlemen of Cumberland and Westmorland themselves were petitioning young Lord Scrope to deal with the Grahams, Hetheringtons and Taylors with executions and imprisonments in early October 1602 and they were again bound to Scrope for the behaviour of themselves and their clans.

Walter Graham, the Goodman of Netherby, stood for himself and his sons Richie and Arthur, his brothers William, Richie, Dick, Thomas, Arthur and Andrew and their henchmen Thomas Tait, Alexander Graham, John Gibson, Richard Graham, Richie Armstrong, Herbert Johnstone, Willie Baillie, Andrew Little,

Christopher Calvert, John Beattie, John Armstrong and another John Gibson. John Graham of Anghousewell was answerable for himself, his sons Richie and Walter and brothers Geordie, William and Arthur with a gang including Willie Graham, Henry Graham of Scaleby, the miller William Blacklock, Reyne Graham, Cuddie Glesby and 25 others, while Fergus Graham of Sowport was responsible for himself and his sons Willie and Jamie and his gang including John Wilson, Lewis Thomson and others. Davie Graham of the Millens, the Grahams of the Peartrees and the Goodman of Mote and Brackenhill also stood. Young Hutcheon Graham's 'clan and gang' were John Little, Geordie Edgar, William Little, Andrew Elliot and Jock Anderson, and so on, the whole total of the Grahams and their associates standing at a formidable crew of 439 men.

So matters were already coming to a head when Queen Elizabeth I of England died in March 1603 and it all kicked off with an 'Ill' or 'Busy' week of ten days of intensive raiding by the Grahams and other crime families as King James travelled south to claim the English crown.

Sir Robert Carey had brought the news of the Queen's death to Edinburgh in a ride that left him bloodied and bruised after several falls, such was his haste to be first to bring the news to King James. He recorded in his memoirs that the West Marches broke out in 'great unruliness' but he was too shattered after his long ride from London to deal with it so offered to send his two deputies to sort things out and Sir William Selby, Henry Widdrington and William Fenwick were dispatched with a garrison from Berwick to put the rebellion down.

130 bills of complaint were lodged against 200-300 men of the Armstrongs and Grahams that stole livestock and goods, burned and robbed, and killed around seven people in a rampage that went as far south as Penrith. Richard Graham of the Redkirk, with his sons George and John, brothers Fergus, Walter and George, and illegitimate brothers Christie 'Wittye' Graham, George 'Boydes' Graham, Richard 'Corrie's Richie' Graham and Andrew Graham were noted as 'thieves all' and particularly active in the 'outrages, incursions, forays, burnings, murders, mutilations and taking of prisoners.' At Hexham in 1606 it was recorded that Fergus Graham,

now of Wall, in Northumberland, had his execution for crimes committed during 'Ill Week' stayed after he 'in great part made satisfaction,' so he must have coughed up to pay back the people that he had plundered during the mayhem. Others weren't as lucky.

The death of the Queen didn't just lead to an outbreak of thefts and lawlessness by common gangsters, however; Sir John Carey handed over Berwick to John Bothwell, the Bishop of Holyroodhouse, and King James knighted over 300 noblemen on his two-month journey down to London accompanied by Sir Robert Kerr, who had been named Lord Roxburghe in 1600 and was created the 1st Earl Roxburgh in 1616. Sir Walter Scott got his great wish and was named Lord Scott of Buccleuch in 1606 as those close to the Regent were rewarded. Mark Kerr of Ferniehurst was made Earl of Lothian in 1606 while George Home was named Lord Hume of Berwick in 1604 as the leaders of the Border families quickly turned on their own unruly followers.

There were more immediate matters of retribution in hand and on December 4 1603 King James made a proclamation from Wilton condemning the 'spoils and outrages done upon them at our first entry into this kingdom, by divers borderers, but specially by the Grahams, (who) cannot be ignorant what care we have had, that punishment should be done upon the offenders, having for that purpose to our charge maintained our forces to apprehend them and commissioners to try them according to the law.'

The King went on to state that all of the offenders, especially the Grahams, were persons not fit to live in the Border countries and claimed that they had 'humbly besought us that they might be removed to some other parts where with our gracious favour they hope to live and become new men and to deserve our mercy.'

James seemed dubious that the people would be pleased with such an action (transplantation) instead of just killing the Grahams. He pacified the local population that had suffered under their reign of organised crime by stating that: 'their lands may be inhabited by others of good and honest conversation' in a long and vicious document.

It had been decided – the Grahams had to go.

10. AFTERMATH

ARTHUR GRAHAM of Mote left a lasting legacy before his deportation to Ireland in 1607 when he chiselled his name into the stone of Carlisle castle. He had been held there with others of the family before being taken to boats at Workington and his name is still visible today, neglected and forgotten but defiant in the sandstone opposite a window jamb at the top of a stairwell. Carlisle castle has more famous 'prisoner carvings' of beautiful cut animals and crests that remain protected behind Perspex and celebrated, but Arthur's mark has only been revealed after plaster was taken off, light key marks over his name, a very real and poignant monument to the Grahams of Esk and what followed.

King James VI was now titled the First of England, Scotland and Ireland and he quickly set about sorting out the troubles in the Borders by renaming them the Middle Shires, dismantling the pele towers, beating their iron gates into agricultural ploughs and setting up a commission to handle the dirty work.

His Commissioners for the Borders were named as Sir William Selby of Branxton, Sir Robert Delaval, Sir Wilfred Lawson, Sir William Seton, Sir William Home, Joseph Pennington, Edward Grey of Morpeth, Partick Chirnside, Robert Charters and Gideon Murray of Elibank, who were sworn in at Westminster in February 1605.

They summed up the whole reiving period in a single sentence: 'one of the greatest causes of their offences is hope of impunity and the greatest motive of their hope is after murders, felonies, riots, routs, unlawful assemblies or other offences committed in either country to escape punishment by flying into the other,' so their solution was to simply remove the border, end the March Laws, and bring offenders to justice so that 'all our loyal and obedient subjects may live in peace and tranquility without fear of rapine and spoil and danger of their lives and that murderers, felons and other delinquents may be punished according to our laws respectively in that behalf.'

The commissioners received a complaint from London the

following year of heavy-handedness in their doling out of justice in Tynedale and Redesdale, citing the case of a man called Michael Davidson of Biddlestone who'd been apprehended for burglaries and felonies committed twelve years previously when he was just 12 years old. Although he was reprieved for being underage at the time of the crimes, his cousin John was hanged for the same offences. The Whitehall officials wrote that they could not help but 'be somewhat doubtful of your due observation of his Majesty's meaning'.

The Commissioners responded to the complaints by the inhabitants of Tynedale and Redesdale about their severity; pleading against the dropping of all offences committed during Elizabeth's reign, claiming that they had only gone after notorious offenders and that the Biddlestone Davidsons had resisted when they had gone to their house searching for Sir Thomas Percy.

The repercussions of Guy Fawkes' Gunpowder plot in November 1605, when he attempted to assassinate King James by blowing up the House of Lords during the State opening of Parliament, affected the Northumberland riders loyal to Percy, who had been implicated in the scheme. Robert Davidson of Alnwick was a servant of Percy 'the traitor' and was being held by William Hall of Hepple. The commission wanted security from him that he would not escape. Six people condemned at Newcastle were also followers of Percy. 17 men were executed at the Gallowgate at the time, four of whom were Scots riders.

The Northumbrians in the main escaped relatively lightly in the following purges, although a number were locked up in Newcastle, with its formidable oubliette, known as Heron's pit. By May 1607 the Commissioners for Northumberland; the Bishop of Durham, Sir William Selby, Sir William Fenwick, Edward Gray and Edward Charleton; received an offer from the King to select 100 men from any of the outlaws of Redesdale and Tynedale (except the ringleaders) imprisoned for lighter crimes to be handed over to the Border Commissioners for service in Ireland. Any fugitives that wanted to enrol would also be allowed to do so. The King ordered the Border Commission to receive those troops and 'induce the remainder of the loose people to apply to honest ways of living, on pain of suffering the penalty of law.'

The Grahams, who were 'abhorred by the people of Cumberland,' had been similarly enlisted to fight in Brill and Flushing in the Netherlands in July 1605 with 100 being signed up to go, but only 72 turned up to be sent to Newcastle before sailing with their conductor William Breadman and Lieutenant William Nodder. The original intention was to send 50 to Brill and 100 to Flushing, but the Commission claimed that they had been hindered by Jock of the Peartree and Hutcheon Graham of Gards. Young Hutcheon had been discharged by the King two months earlier for his assistance in the taking of Sandy's Ringan Armstrong, providing he gave back stolen goods and security for his good behaviour, but the gangland culture was so deeply ingrained in him that the officials later claimed that Hutcheon and his followers were 'chief causers of the disobedience of the Grahams.' Buccleuch had taken 200 followers with him to do battle in Protestant Holland's scrap for independence from Catholic Spain the previous year and he would remain there as a Colonel in the Scotch Brigade until 1609.

Four of the leading Grahams; Richard Graham, the son of Walter of Netherby, David Graham of the Bankhead, Alexander Graham of Kirkandrews, alias 'Geordie's Sandie,' and Hutcheon Graham of Rockcliffe; had turned themselves in for military service, while three other denounced fugitives went on the run: young Hutcheon, William Graham of Medopp, and George Graham of Burnfoot. Two of their families were kicked out of their houses and had their roofs uncovered, though the Grahams had stripped many of their own homes before the men arrived.

Hutcheon believed that his pardon from the King for the taking of Sandy's Ringan still held and was keeping 16 more of the Grahams that were scheduled for service from coming in, such as Rob 'Rob's Robbie' Graham, the Scotsman Rob Graham of Langriggs, Jock of the Peartree, whose brother Watt had been hanged, and Richie of Randleton who eventually thought better of it and went to Flushing.

Hutcheon and Jock of the Peartree were causing the biggest headache and were described as 'two principal evil men' and the commission were starting to push for other surnames to be considered for military service, writing to London that 'there are many here besides the Grahams inured to blood and theft, more meet to serve his Majesty elsewhere than to remain here.' By the September of 1606 the Bishop of Carlisle was naming those families who he felt could be supplied to increase the 'decaying numbers at Brill and Flushing'. He stated that the Storeys, Armstrongs, Hetheringtons, Bells, Fosters, Nixons, Nobles and Routledges 'have been as offensive as the Grahams, though not so powerful' and urged a purge of the Scottish Border, chiefly in Annandale and Liddesdale, as the King 'had done on Esk and Leven.'

In October 1605 there was a jailbreak at the Sheriff's gaol in Carlisle and five escaped, with Sir Henry Leigh asking to be blameless as he 'kept the Castle, not the gaol' and a number of loose Grahams had returned to the area; by January 1606 more Grahams were on their way back and the tenants of the Earl of Cumberland promised to pay him their corn rents 'notwithstanding that they have paid the same to the Grahams, who have broken out as open outlaws, and are the sole hindrance to the peace of the county.' The Grahams had reverted to type and were back demanding blackmail and menacing the countryside and although there were executions following gaol deliveries at Carlisle and Newcastle, it was reported that the Grahams were hopeful of a general pardon. Sir Henry Leigh and Sir William Cranston were ordered to arrest them; Leigh again came up with an excuse, saying that the chief obstacle to apprehending them was that they had been received in Scotland.

But gradually the successes came and by April Jock of the Peartree and Jock's Ritchie Graham had been captured and taken to London for trial. By the June it was agreed that they should be transplanted to Ireland, while some unmarried men were to be scattered and sent to 'cautionary' towns in the Low Countries (Netherlands). William Selby and Wilfred Lawson led a search party for members of the family under the disguise of a hunt, which got lost in the fog. They also searched the house of Sir Richard Lowther for Grahams and caught up with ten.

The Cumbrian gentry and landowners happily handed over £408 19s 9d to send the Grahams over the water to Roscommon – though Sir Ralph Sidley managed to do it for £300 and appears to have pocketed the rest – and on 30 August the Grahams 'all principal men of their rank or principal offenders in action', were deported.

Those first Grahams to go were Walter of Netherby, his son John and daughter Margaret; Richard of Bakey with his wife Mary and children Richard, Edward and Jane; John of Sandhills, with his wife and eight kids, Richard 'Jock's Richie' and his wife, Jock his brother, and his children and servants; William of Aikshawhill with Elizabeth Graham and Janet Hetherington; Robert 'Christie's Robb' his wife Jane and two young daughters; Richard Graham of Slelands and his family; Robert of Aikshawhill, John of Lake, Hutcheon of Cargo, with a Thomas Armstrong, George alias 'Beds', Robert of Lake, Richie's Geordie, Richard of Randlinton, William of Carlisle, William of Micklewille and William and Robert of Medhope; George and Robert of Mill Hill, John of the Peartree, George of Sandhills, George of Longtown and 'Long Henry' Graham, along with servants and family.

Other surnames that were shipped across were George Hetherington of the Bussie and his wife Janet, Robert Foster of Baxwigill, George Little with his wife and five children to follow, a saddler called John Maginn, George Briars and Patrick Beattie with his wife and three kids. George Irving, William 'Flangtail' Graham, Watty Murray, Alex Byers and Andrew Graham of the Mill were sent with no allowance.

It wasn't a great success and within a year most of them were back on the Border. It wasn't just the Grahams that were being put under increasing pressure, however, and a Border Commissioner's report on the first year of the Pacification of the Borders during 1605 noted that 32 men had been hanged and 15 banished from Scotland at Justice Courts in Hawick, Peebles, Jedburgh and Dumfries.

The first victims of the virtual genocide that followed were Will Harkness, William Little, Edward Johnstone, John Scott, Tom Turnbull of Harecton, Andrew Little in Tailend, Sim Glendinning, Jock with the Ruffs, Will Elliot called 'The Guide', Will Oliver of Barmkin, Tom Little called Jeanette's Tom, George Patterson in Moling, Andrew Armstrong called 'Collie', Archie Crosier in Cleuchheid, Adie Armstrong in Whitetails, William Patterson, Archie Milburn called 'Cold Archie', Davie Johnstone called 'Blue Cloak', Davie Johnstone called 'Chump's Davie', Hob Armstrong of the Binks, John Sim in Crookham, Richie Elliot of Heuchhouse, John

Beattie called 'Bid on him Jock', John Beattie of the Shiel, John Gilchrist, Jock Armstrong, Will Patterson and Jock Frissell. Sandy Armstrong, called 'Ringan's Sandy', was executed for the murder of Sir John Carmichael, and an Englishman called George Wallace was also killed. Notable thieves among those first executions included John Elliot in Hillend, who was one of the gang of Elliots and Crosiers that had taken eight Redesdale men prisoner and stolen their horses at the Kirk Ford as far back as 1589, and John 'the Grip' Noble who in 1595 signed up to Sir John Forster's 'appeal to Christian people' to put an end to the feuds between the families; he was a heavy player to appear on the document alongside some of the leading Elliots, Armstongs, Nixons, Forsters, Hendersons and Edward and Gilbert Loraine.

Those that were first banished were named as Gavin Johnstone of Riggshaw, Willie Irving called 'Rostie's Willie', Tom Armstrong of the Craig, Davie Irving of the Holme, Tom Martin, Gib Elliot called 'Dandie's Gib', Willie Armstrong of Arkleton, John Irving of Steelhill, Robert Elliot of Glenvorane, Francis Graham, son to Christie's Watty, Hob Elliot of Hill, John Elliot called 'Christian's Johnny', Willie Elliot called 'Great Lays', Archie Scott of Glenrauchane and John Falayis.

Two of the Grahams that had been deported were back within a month, and another from a 'cautionary' town; the Bishop of Carlisle despaired that they were 'hearing rumours that many of the most offensive persons of them are already back in Scotland,' and explained that one of the Grahams that they had in prison said that they were coming back as they couldn't get any of the money given for their relief out of Sir Ralph Sidley, so it appeared that he had appropriated a great deal more than the original £100 and he was demanded to appear at Court.

Later in November 1606 a list of the Grahams and other fugitives was issued and included Richard and Arthur Graham of Netherby, Thomas, Dick's Davie, young Davie, Will's Wattie, Geordie's Sandy and his brother Francis, Francis of Logan, David of Bankhead, Will 'Cockplay,' Will of Longtown, Fergus, Richard, Robert of Howend, George of Carlisle and his son Andrew, Archie and Fergus of Millhill, Will's Arthur and Will's Fergie, Robert, James, Richard of Riggheads,

Thomas of Randleton, John of the Bailiff, George of Rulespiel, Bell's Sandy and his brother Reynold, Arthur of the Lake, John of the Neak, Florry of Browfoot, Will's Geordie, Jock of Galloway, Patrick 'Mark's Tom's Patty,' William 'Flangtail,' who was fugitive from Ireland, John 'Pout,' Plump's Fergie, Fergie of Bailiff and Richard Purtham, George Storey of the Holme, John 'Plowey' Irving, Bartholomew Warwick of Newby, Will Graham, the son of Watt of the Bray. The notorious Willgavy crew were also fugitives: Anton's Edward Armstrong, Thomas 'Geordie's Tom' of Willgavy, Andrew 'Ingram's Andrew' Richard, Thomas (Anton Edward's son), Jock Stowluggs, and the Fosters Andrew's Johnny of Stonegarthside, Red Johnny, William and Quentin of Crakethope.

Some very serious villains were starting to fall victim to the purges and in January 1607 it was reported from Carlisle by the English commissioners that Jock Stowlugs Armstrong, Edward's Tom Armstrong, Christopher Irving alias 'Gifford Carleton,' Robert Graham and William 'Flangtail' Graham had been tried and executed. Irving was part of the Willgavy gang that had had been sent to Brill while Flangtail was an infamous murderer who had returned from Ireland along with William Graham of the Lake, who was also hanged, while on February 23 1607 The Earl of Dunbar wrote from Berwick that Mangerton, Whitehaugh, William Elliot, Andrew Armstrong and Martin Elliot had been executed for 'very odious and criminal causes' with fourteen others hanged for 'stealth and other punishable courses,' most likely at Newcastle.

Two months later 10 more were executed on Tyneside, including John Pott, a man who the Bishop of Carlisle noted as 'convicted of burglary and for horsestealing, who being a person of evil note was not thought fit to be reprieved.' Robert Hall did, however, receive forty days reprieve and Sir William Selby stated that 'the people of Tynedale and Redesdale made full appearance, and showed greater obedience than at any time since the Commissioners began.'

While there was some success in subduing the Eastern Marches, in the West a second deportation to Ireland happened on April 22 1607 with Richard Graham of Netherby and a child, Arthur Graham of Mote, David 'old Davie' Graham with 'young Davie' and a child, Will's Wattie, Will 'Cockplay' his wife, three children and two servants, young Davie Graham of Bankhead, Will Graham of Longtown, John of the Nook and his wife Margaret, Richard of Nowtheard, Francis 'Hugh's Francie,' George of Meddop, Walter of Milne, William of Blackford, George of Ruleshiel, Anton's Edward Armstrong, Richard Sherdon, Thomas Irving, Stephen Blackburn, Quintin and John Foster and George Graham's wife with two children put on a boat and taken across the Irish Sea.

Hutcheon Graham, John Graham of the Lake and George Graham of Mill Hill were back by July with letters from the Lord Deputy of Ireland giving them licence to collect debts and other cash, but the officials were fearful that they would join with the 'greatly increased number of fugitives' who were lurking in the woods on the Scottish side and they were warned not to 'wander about in night time' or 'inhabit any of their former places.' They were sent back when a third and final deportation order was carried out on 14 September 1607.

Florrie Storey, who was charged with horse stealing during 'Ill week' and breaking prison, was kicked out along with Hutcheon, Richie Graham of the Braes, Thomas Beattie, Arthur of the Lake, William of Hethersgill, Peter Graham, Thomas Sanderson, Thomas Graham of Logan, Fergus Graham of Longtown and the wives of William Graham of Meddop, young Wetherby, Walter of Carlisle and William of Longtown. Cash sums were also sent over the water with them for William and Arthur Graham of Mote, Richie Graham (Brackenhill's son), John Graham of Whole Shields and Edward Graham of Mills, no doubt hoping to keep them there.

The Grahams were probably better off taking their chances across in Ireland anyway as the executions and banishments continued at home and the lists of fugitives greatly increased as the Borderers attempted to avoid justice. Others crossed into Ulster of their own volition during the Plantation, which handed 'English-speaking Protestants loyal to the King' the chance to start a new life on plots of land allotted to them, such as the Northumbrian gentleman John Heron, who was given lands with a total rental of £10 13s 4 d in Ulster in 1610.

In October 1606 19 more had been on the run from the Jedburgh Courts – Adam 'Sonsie' Scott, George Beattie, Archie 'the Gunner'

Armstrong, Andrew 'Bath' Armstrong, John, Eckie, Willie and Abie Armstrong, William and Thomas Aynsley, George and William Allen, Jock 'Jenkin's Jock' Nixon, Gavin Nixon in Burnfoot, Willie Henderson, Archie, Andrew and Simmy 'of the Side' Armstrong and Charlie Little. The Dumfries courts were similarly evaded at that time by the likes of Andrew 'Braid's Andrew' Scott, Tom Armstrong, Robin and Hob Elliot, Ebbie Armstrong, Tom Little, Archie Scott, George Armstrong, Arthur Graham in Langriggs, Watt and Davie Graham, Rob Carlyle and Geordie Bell in Annan's man Richie Tyreding as the numbers started to rise into the hundreds.

The process was ongoing and in 1611 another 58 were fugitives from Jedburgh and 120 from Dumfries. The following were hanged or drowned at Jedburgh that year: Tom 'Midrie' Aynsley, Hob Armstrong of Whitehaugh, David Clark of Hownamkirk, Hob Eccles, Mark Elliot of the Hill, Willie Graham of Hardwell, Wattie 'Cleckmay' Hislop, Tom Irving in Dowglen, Will Laidlaw, Richie Lawson, Andrew 'Boots' Little, Hob Moscrop, John Nixon in Larriston, George Oliver, Archie and David Roger and Hob Turnbull.

Dumfries handed out death sentences to Geordie Armstrong of Kinmont, Jamie Armstrong of Capplegill, Jamie Baillie, a man of the Johnstones, John Bell, Gavin and Sim Brydon, Archie Graham in Mill Hill, George Hill in Cummertrees, George 'of Bonshaw' Irving of Woodhouse, Tom, Watt and Willie 'of Ireland' Irving, Jeffrey's Willie Irving, Nichol Jardine, John and Will Johnstone, John Little and Cuddie and Jamie Moffat. Roland Yarrow, of Yarrow in Tynedale, complained that year that he'd been assaulted in Jedburgh in revenge for him going to inform on the Armstrongs and Elliots that had murdered Lionel Robson and others in the assault at Leaplish. Despite the apparent enmity between Tyne and Liddel, Roland Milburn of the Comb and Simon Elliot of the Binks stole an ox from Thomas Middleton of West Harle soon after.

Executions were also happening at Newcastle, and the following were buried in the graveyard at St. John's after facing the death sentence. Alexander Davison, Anthony Stokoe, Reynold Charlton, Henry Dodds, Arthur Robson and Archie Rogers in 1605; John Hall, Archie and Thomas Armstrong, and Cuthbert and William Charlton in 1606, and John Pott, Simmy Armstrong and George Reed followed in 1607. George Nixon, Bartram Potts and William Elliot were buried there in 1611, and Archie Reed, John Robson and William Armstrong in 1613. Gawen Reed and John Gibson were buried in the churchyard of St. Andrew's in the town following their executions in 1607.

By 1614 the King had to issue another proclamation for apprehending the Grahams that were again returning from banishment. He seems to have had a particular hatred for the family and was infuriated that they had come back from Ireland in such numbers, labelling them 'the principal and most violent disturbers of the peace and quiet of the middle shire' and 'hereby strictly forbid that none of the said Grahams hereafter do presume to return into our realms of England or Scotland out of Ireland or the cautionary towns of the Low Countries whereunto some of them are sent.'

Around the same time another bill was issued for settling the peace on the Borders that 'all inhabiting within Tynedale and Redesdale in Northumberland, Bewcastledale, Willgavy, the north part of Gilsland, Eskdale, Ewesdale and Annandale in Scotland, saving noblemen and gentlemen unsuspected of felony and theft and not being of broken clans and their household servants dwelling within those several places before recited shall put away all armour and weapons as well offensive as defensive as jacks, spears, casts, swords, daggers, steelcaps, hagbuts, pistols, plate sleeves and such like and shall not keep any horse gelding or mare above the price of fifty shillings sterling or thirty pounds Scots upon like pain of imprisonment.' They were also forbidden to carry or bear any weapons of any sort 'but in His Majesty's service.'

A list of the remaining Border Fugitives was issued by the Commissioners of the Middle Shires in 1618. They had been selected out of the fugitive rolls as the rest were 'known to be dead or out of the country, some in Ireland, and some in England, and frequently to come quietly in and out of this Kingdom' (Scotland). They lined up: Fergie Bell, called 'the Crow,' Sim Hall, son to John Hall in Sikes, Wattie Graham in Mossop, William Johnstone in Minehead, along with his sons Geordie, Andrew and Robbie; Jamie Johnstone, called Martin's Jamie in Priestdykes, Geordie and Davie Johnstone, brothers of Redhall, Hugh Corsbie in Dalruskane, William and Andrew

Beattie, sons of Archie of the Skoir, Gibbie Johnstone, son of Symie of Furglen, Davie Turnbull in West Leys, Will Kirkpatrick, son of Tom Kirkpatrick in Woodhead, 'Dun Willie' Elliot in Ailtour, James Scott in Chapelhill, Geordie Scott in Castlehill, Kirstie Elliot, called Hob's Kirstie, William Rutherford, the brother of Thomas Rutherford in Tofts, Andrew Johnstone in Mylnebank, called 'Kirstie's Andrew,' Matthew Bell in Auchenrivock, Johnny Beattie, called 'Johnny Idle,' Jamie Armstrong in Capplegill, Andrew Charters in Bus, George Turnbull, son of the Laird of Bedrule, George Tait in Dowknow, William Carruthers of Danebie and his son John, John Johnston called 'of the Gate' and Ebbie Armstrong in Kirktown.

The following year Sir William Howard issued a list of 'notorious thieves in Northumberland and Cumberland' who he desired to be arrested by Sir John Fenwick and Sir William Hutton, while in 1623 Lord Clifford noted that 'Tynedale and Redesdale men are the most cunning thieves; but many thieves stole from hunger.' He also complained that Newcastle gaol was so weak that many were escaping from it and was so 'noisome and infectious that many prisoners die.' Clifford sent eight men to Scotland for trial at Lord Buccleuch's request.

But the days of the Border crime families were far from over. They had been hanged, drowned and exiled but still they remained. In 1618 John Scott in Newark complained that Will Elliot of Hartsgarth (the former pledge), Will Elliot of Prikenhaugh, Will Elliot of the Park, Robert Elliot of Redhaugh, Archibald Elliot of Langhaugh and Quentin 'the Doo' Nixon had met with 100 'of all the disordered clans of the late marches' and launched a dawn assault on Netherfields looking for people to murder in their beds. When they found none, they said that if anyone gave their names they'd be back and 'would not only have their lives but would burn, destroy and slaughter whatever they had upon the ground.' A number of the complaints were of a much pettier nature and James and William Scott, the sons of the Goodman of Aikwood, with a number of their friends named Scott, Kerr, and Dalgliesh were all fined for carrying pistols under the pretense that they were for shooting hares and wildfowl as just one example of many for not giving up weapons.

Four years later they were still hanging borderers at the Jedburgh

Assizes for offences committed many years previously and John and Thomas Frissell, sons of the laird of Overton, Jock Wigham, Archibald Little, James White, Geordie 'Ower the Burn' Morton, Gilbert Irving, John Roddin, Robert Latimer, 'Din Jamie' Beattie, Geordie Turnbull, an Englishman called Tom Little, Archie Noble, Watt Nixon, Lancy Turnbull, Sandy Hamilton, Tom Armstrong, Nikky Moffat, John Johnstone in Hillhouse, Francie Elliot of Copshaw, Andrew Gibson in Softlaw and Archie 'Watschode' Henderson were all strung up by the neck and dropped.

Robert Johnstone, Tom Bell, Francie Hutchison, Jock and Willie Graham, John 'Richie's Jockie' Irving, Tom Taggart, Geordie Johnstone, Adam Hall, Christie Milliken, Bessie Parker, Tom Kerr, Alexander and John Johnstone, Andrew Murray, Jock Gillespie, Will Dodds, Andrew Young, John Beattie, Geordie Johnstone, Andrew Davidson, Adie Johnstone and Robert Forsyth were all declared fugitives while a number more were acquitted on bail with Francie Armstrong of Kinmont somewhat amazingly sitting as one of the officials on that assize. How those sentenced to death must have shook their heads at the irony of that.

As well as hanging, beheading or drowning in the rivers Jed or Nith, offenders were also sentenced to be branded on the cheek 'with the common burning iron,' a punishment passed down on the likes of Andrew Armstrong of Whitehaugh, John 'Catgill' Armstrong, Adam Robson in Old Jedburgh and Robert Little in Craighouse, among others, for theft and reset of theft in 1623.

The authorities had spent 20 years trying to break the stranglehold of the Border mafia, and although the days of large-scale raiding had been ended, the tradition of sheep stealing continued long on the Borders; it was no real surprise as characters such as Fergie 'the Crow' Bell who had been a fugitive for years was dismissed from the bar at Jedburgh that year alongside other notable rogues such as Will 'Rakkas' Armstrong of Liddesdale.

19 more were hanged, including Robert 'Scabbed Hob' Nixon, who had stolen just six ewes and eight sheep from Rosie Armstrong in Mangerton, and Abie Armstrong in Greens who had robbed a blind man called John Elliot of his purse with £4 in it then murdered him by chucking him over the Ancrum bridge. The others were John

Hall 'Chief' and Lancie Hall in Newbiggin, Tom Carruthers in Murthum, Tom Halliday in Molein, Rowie Foster 'Ower the Moss,' Sim 'the Guide' Elliot, Ally Armstrong in Side, William Wilson from Carlisle, John Mitchelson in Catcleugh, Watty 'Oswald's Watty' Bell, George Thomson in Bowholme, Mitchell Birney in Fairnylees, Pat Murray in Swineside, David 'the Smith' Beattie, George Johnstone in Essinside, Will Elliot, the son of Tom of Fawside, and Robert Rutherford, the son of Thomas of Tofts.

Others escaped death by going to the Low Countries under the charge of the knight Sir John Murray of Philliphaugh. The brothers Francie and Alexander Johnstone of Kirkhill, Hobbie and Abie Foster of Foulshiels and Geordie Armstrong of Woodhouseleys took this option while John Elliot of Carlisle and Edward Irving, the son of Lang Will of Hoddom, chose to leave Scotland and never return upon pain of death. John Elliot probably just turned around and went back to Carlisle, sniggering all the way home.

King James died in March 1625, no doubt despising the Grahams to the bitter end, and a new era was ushered in as the outlaws and wilder elements among the riding families eventually became known as moss troopers. In 1629 his successor, King Charles I, prepared a pardon from Whitehall for Edward Armstrong of the Ash, in Northumberland, and the Scotsmen Edward alias Kinmont Armstrong, Hector alias Stubholme Armstrong, and John 'John-with-the-one-hand' Armstrong for 'all robberies committed upon the Borders of England and Scotland, on condition that they depart from said Kingdoms and do not return without license.'

The 'fugitive and notorious thief' John Charlton of the Bower was apprehended and locked up in the High Castle gaol in Newcastle that year for stealing three cows from Thomas Fenwick of Lesbury, a black mare and 13 sheep from Thomas Middleton at Little Swinburne, two oxen from Nicholas Errington and three young beasts from Richard Wilson of Houghton, as well as being 'suspected of many other felonies.' Others held in the prison with Charlton included Ellen of the Bower, very possibly his wife, who was implicated in the raid on Thomas Middleton, and Gerard 'the Hint' Coxson, who was still friendly with 'the great thief' Robert 'Hobb of Copshaw' Elliot. Also imprisoned were Cuthbert 'Cuddy of the

Leame' Milburn, Michael 'Cuze' Hall of Ottercops, John Turnbull of Yardhope, James Robson of Bayshill, Henry Robson, Edward Turnbull, Gawen Charlton, and Walter Ridley of the Mill Hills. Simon Armstrong and Gawen Crosier of Langleyshank were accused of stealing a young grey mare, and Richard Forster, George Tait, John Brewis, George Pott 'late of the Raw,' Roger Dodd 'late of the Shaw,' Michael Elsden of the Moat, Edward Armstrong of the Armitage Milne, Edward Hall of Blackheddon, George Burn, Roger Robson, and William Pott of Longhorsley were also charged with thefts of livestock. The following were named as felons by the Newcastle Assizes in 1629: Edward Thompson, Anthony Fenwick, John 'Clower's John' Forster, the Scotsman James Henderson, John Anderson, Richard Taylor, Francis Tait, George Wilkinson, Hugh 'Pundy' Hutchinson, George French, and Isabelle Milburn.

Reputedly around that time the Carnaby family had a commission to try and apprehend wanted criminals in Northumberland. When one was captured by a young Carnaby, he asked his father what to do with the notorious felon, who in his exasperation is said to have replied: 'Why, hang him!' When old Carnaby later sent for the offender, he was told that he'd been executed according to his instruction. The Carnabys were fined £4 per year for the offence of hanging without a trial and were said to have continued to pay it for many years after. The tale, however, may have more basis in legend than fact as identically the same story is told about Sir William Howard in Cumberland.

There was no fiction in the heavy hand displayed by John, Earl of Traquair, at a Jedburgh Justice Court in March 1637, however, as the executions continued. 30 were hanged, five burned on the hand and 15 banished. Those that faced the rope were named Richard 'Hector's Richie' Irving, James Johnstone of Kirk, John Beattie of Tannahill, Archibald Armstrong of Hollows, John Pollock, Fergus Linton, Richard Coulthard, James Forrester, Simon Elliot in Binks, David and Robert Scott of Hawick, Robert Graham in Beggaraw, Andrew Graham in Oldface, Arthur Haire, Andrew 'of Bent' Scott, Simon 'of Blackhead' Elliot, Simon 'Beattie's Sim' Armstrong, Thomas Hislop, Andrew 'Little Andrew' Scott, Alexander Henderson, William French, James Johnstone, Adam Gillespie, John 'the Peddar' Davidson, John

Elliot in Starrycleuch, James Taylor in Clifton, William Pringle in Hownam, Alexander Hall in Chatto, Walter Mow in Oldsheugh and Hercules Crosier.

The names of those declared fugitives after missing the court were also familiar and included the likes of Francis Armstrong, the son of old Francie of Kinmont, John 'of the Side' Armstrong, George 'Christie's Geordie' Graham, William Crosier, the son of John 'the Friday thief' Crosier and other Armstrongs, Elliots, Fosters and so on – the usual suspects. The Englishman Matthew Robson, alias Leaplish, was remanded to jail for thefts in Scotland committed by Robert Gibson and Lyle Milburn.

By 1642 the most notorious criminals and outlaws were named in a list of those wanted to be apprehended and brought to justice at Dumfries and Jedburgh; the names are important as they represent the last of the old reiving fraternity.

They were John Johnstone of Graitney, George 'Christie's Geordie' Graham, George Carruthers, Herbert Sharp, Thomas 'the Clegg' Johnstone, David 'of Craighouse' Bell, Christie Armstrong in Stubholme, Margaret Hunter in Dumfries, Thomas 'Shakefoot' Bell, John Henderson, James and Edward Johnstone in Earshag, James and George Johnstone in Broomhill, George Dowie, William Dickson, John Johnstone, John 'of the Side' Armstrong, Simmie 'Caffield' Armstrong, Francis Armstrong of Kinmont (younger), Hob 'Thorbishop' Elliot, Will Crosier, John Graham, John Armstrong in Wintropheid, John 'of Capilgill' Armstrong, William Foster, Sim 'Archie's Sim' Armstrong and John 'Unshank' Armstrong.

The list of villains continued with Jock 'a God's name' Elliot, Sim 'the Colt' Wilson, Robert Elliot, John Wigham, William 'the Chieftain' Stuart, James Clark, William 'Langside of the Gall' Johnstone, John Johnstone, Daniel Irving, John Jackson, William Blacklock, John Wightman, John 'of the Gall' Graham, Gavin Taggart of Bus and Ludovic Carruthers of Wormibie; Richard Irving and his brother James, John Taggart, Archibald Steel, William Halliday, Robert Johnstone of Butterqhuat, Andrew Pott, William and Archibald Johnstone, John Blacklock, Simon Curry, Martin Glendinning in Moffat, Francis Bell of Greengatehouse, William Hutchison in Guthheid, William Johnstone, William Johnstone of Bigmure, John 'of the Gall' Johnstone, Francie Armstrong of Kinmont's son Geordie, John 'Jock of the Raffles' Carruthers and John Dunwoodie.

Also included were Simon Johnstone in Moffat, John Graham of Ley, John Bell, John Graham of Kadmurehouse, Robert Gilmoreson, John 'Perknow' Kinmont and James of Kinmont, John 'John of Sark' of Kinmont and his brother William of Kinmont, Sim Armstrong of Whiteslieside, William Armstrong of Woodhead and his brother Francis, Percy Rayning, Gavin of Raggart, 'Tully's Eddie' Graham, Walter 'Watt of the Bus' Scott, John Armstrong, the son of Tom of Mangerton, William Armstrong of Canonbie, Lyle Crosier and his son, Robert 'Christie's Hob' Elliot, Robert Henderson and his brother, Francie Armstrong, brother to Whitehaugh, William 'of the Boulex' Elliot, Hutcheon Armstrong and an un-named Elliot who was 'sometime servant to Stitchell.'

The fugitives took to the hills and it was reported in 1647 that Northumberland was still plagued by 'old thieves, with plenty of new added, called Moss Troopers. They are of late better horsed and armed than formerly.' They stole many cattle from the fields belonging to the High Sheriff and persisted in the taking of blackmail, so Hexham gaol was 'almost filled with these 'birds of prey.'' Bills and Acts for the suppression of the mosstroopers had been heard that year and again in 1649, 1657 and 1662.

70 horsemen rode on Carlisle castle on a Sunday evening in March 1648 and scaled the walls with ladders to break the gaol, wound the gaoler and release all the mosstroopers being held there before fleeing towards Scotland.

Nine mosstroopers were executed on Newcastle's Town Moor in August 1650, including Simon, George and John Armstrong and an Elliot, alongside 14 alleged witches and a wizard, while an old moss trooper called James Kerr, the son of a minister, escaped from jail in 1652 after robbing a soldier then stealing a horse. He was apprehended and condemned to be hanged at Edinburgh. The Northumbrian labourers Cuthbert Robson and Allan Hedley were granted pardons for offences by the Judges of Assize on the Northern Circuit around that time.

Charles Howard offered to take a company of Cumbrian mosstroopers to Jamaica as a band of mercenary soldiers of fortune in 1655 and in 1659 a notorious moss trooper and murderer called Tony Elliot was hanged at Carlisle. In 1704 Nicholas Armstrong of Housesteads was throttled and kicking at the end of the rope and his three brothers fled to America.

It is unclear whether the crime traditions of the Border families went West with them, as those of Cosa Nostra did, although a number of people connected to the so-called Irish Mob in the States may in fact have family heritage stretching back to the Anglo-Scottish Borderlands, such as Danny Greene, for example. The Cleveland gangster and Longshoremen's official was notorious for car-bombing his Italian-American competitors in the 1970s, and although he was immensely proud of his Irish roots and operated out his Celtic club, the Greens were numerous in Northumberland during the Sixteenth century and may well have moved on through the Emerald Isle, though this is unproven.

Former *Westies* gang member Mickey Featherstone could have Northumbrian ancestry, while Howie Winter of Boston's Winter Hill Gang may also have had distant roots in the area going back to the Winters that ran with the criminal gypsy Faa gang in the 1700s, with some of them being transported to America around that time. William Winter's body was hung in chains on the moor above Elsdon after hanging in Newcastle for the murder of Margaret Crozier of the Raw in 1791. Robert Armstrong was another member of the Faa gang who was locked up in Morpeth gaol in 1752. He threatened to kill the gaoler, his wife and daughter unless they handed over the keys to their cell and was transported to South Carolina for seven years, but may have been one of the 14 members of the gang, 'incessantly shop-breaking and plundering,' that had returned to Northumberland within two years.

Anthony Tait from Alaska was a high-ranking member of the outlaw *Hells Angels* biker gang and an FBI informant in the 1980s and several mobsters of Scottish descent are said to have formed the oldest crime syndicate in Canada, including the noted bootlegger Ben Kerr in the 1920s, while the bank-robbing Johnston brothers were major players in Montreal's *West End* Gang. Most of the borderers that left, however, appear to have ended up in the rural American South and Appalachian Mountains. A list of 54 rebel prisoners to be transported on the ship the *Godspeed* to Virginia in 1716 included a David Graham, William Johnson, John Shaftoe, James Rutherford, James Dixon, William Simpson, Rowland Robson and George Hodgson.

The rebel Confederate 'Bushwhacker' gangs that stole cattle and horses and robbed trains and banks while brandishing six-shooters during, and in the aftermath, of the American Civil War were led by men such as William 'Bloody Bill' Anderson, Bill Reed and George M. Todd, who could all be possibly traced back to Border Reiving families. With men riding in their gangs such as John Graham, S. Graham and Frank Graym; the Halls John, Joseph, two Roberts and Thomas, and John, Nathan and William B. Kerr, it is not impossible that at least some of the wild men were from families that had left for the New World. Other raiders with them also bore Border names, such as Thomas Bell, W.C. Bell, two men named Richard Burns, and Thomas and William Carr. James, John T. and Thomas Little; Ambrose and Thomas F. Maxwell; Hiram, Levi and Martin Potts; John Pringle; James Reed; Allen, Fernando and Sidney Scott; William P. Tate; Bob, James, Oliver and Oscar Thompson; Corteze Thomson; Robert and Thomas Todd; Frank, A.M., Henry and Milton Turner; John Watson and Joseph and George W. Young.

Australia was similarly populated by descendants of the Border crime families with the likes of convicts John Young and Benjamin Little being transported on the ship the *Lord Eldon* in 1817; around 45 Armstrongs and a similar number of Grahams were deported between 1787 and 1867 while the Kerrs, Elliots, Johnstones and others all appear on the lists of convicts transported. Aaron 'AJ' Graham is the notorious leader of the New Zealand biker gang *The Rebels* and the infamous Melbourne hit-man and armed robber Mark 'Chopper' Read may have had an ancestral lineage back to the area. Earlier Australian mobsters such as Joe 'Squizzy' Taylor and Harold 'Bush' Thompson could have also shared this pedigree.

But there was no mass exodus from the borderlands and the vast bulk of the local families remained; in 1701 John Fenwick of Rock was executed for the murder of Ferdinand Foster of Bamburgh in Newcastle, with the notorious John Hall of Otterburn involved. Fenwick stabbed Foster in the back when he slipped and fell as both drew their swords. When Fenwick was hanged, worried officials closed all of the Town gates as they feared a rescue attempt by the 'people of the North, where the name of Fenwick was held in great veneration.'

John Charlton of Lee Hall led a disturbance at a cattle sale in Morpeth in 1721 and others of the riding families that didn't head to the New World also continued in the old ways. Among the executions carried out at Morpeth in Northumberland pre-1800 William Simpson and John Todd were hanged for horse and sheep theft in 1742. Two years earlier, John Graham was hanged at Carlisle for horse theft, and in 1748 Adam Graham was hanged in chains at Kingmoor for murder. Joseph Hall swung at Morpeth for highway robbery in 1765, while George Davidson was killed for raping Isabel Blair in 1774. William Graham and William Cockburn faced the noose for burglary in 1785; Thomas Young danced on the gibbet for highway robbery in 1789 and John Scott became one of the last to pay the ultimate price as late as 1801 when he was hanged at the Fairmoor for stealing 49 sheep from Simon Dodd at Elsdon. Robert Robison was also hanged at Jedburgh that year for horse theft, but these were mainly small-scale one offs outside the sphere of organised crime, and the reputed last leader of the moss trooping gangs was a 'bold and desperate outlaw' named William Brown who was hanged outside the West Gate at Newcastle in 1743 for returning from transportation.

The gypsy gangs persisted in the countryside, however, and in 1773 two men called John Smith, alias Young or Faa (Fall) and Donkin Wright, who were strongly suspected of being 'part of a gang of thieves who take shelter in or about Rothbury forest, and travel the country frequenting fairs, horse races etc,' were apprehended. They were taken to Newcastle and committed as 'rogues and vagabonds' but broke out of jail. Wright's wife Mary (nee Reid) and Elizabeth Ogilvie were also placed in custody, while another female member of the gang named Mary Gordon was imprisoned for pickpocketing and other offences in 1780. Walter Clark and Margaret Dunn, members of the Winter Gang, were hanged at the Fairmoor in Morpeth for burglary in 1793, while a Martha Elliot was sent to Morpeth gaol for stealing clothes from David Hedley and Ann Davidson at Otterburn.

The remnants of the gang were reputed to have fled to near Earlstown across the Border and taken on the name Wintrip in 1812, but they were soon banished back to Redesdale. The locals would not tolerate them anymore, so the Winters went by the head of the Tyne and were gone – 'I have little doubt they were all hanged,' penned a writer in the *Durham County Advertiser* some 15 years later.

By 1826 the men of the hills were moss troopers no more, but the 'lads of heather' or 'heather-bred boys.' The name most-likely came from the old Tynedale rallying shout of: *Tarset and Tarret Burn, hard and heather bred, yet! yet! yet!* which was still being bellowed out by a reputed descendant of Barty of the Comb, Muckle Jock Milburn of Bellingham, to clear local fairgrounds around the 1820s. Muckle Jock was a noted player of the Northumbrian small pipes and a celebrated cattle auctioneer.

The livestock and horse stealing had ended and crime in the area took on a more urban character, such as an 1892 poisoning case in Sunderland involving the habitual female criminals Elizabeth Armstrong, Isabella Scott, Elizabeth Welch and Ellen Greig who had loaded a coal miner called Samuel John Brewis with opium (he died the next day) and robbed him of a half sovereign. Scott was making her 60th court appearance, and Armstrong her 27th. On being sentenced to three months with hard labour, Armstrong told the judge: "Thank you, sir, you're a lenient fellow."

In rural areas the bad blood that had existed for centuries between the men of the Coquet and the Rede were played out in fighting that consistently broke out at mob football games arranged between the valleys in the 19th Century, with three brothers called Potts charged with keeping the peace. There was once a famous mass brawl following a cock fight at Harehaugh, which saw the Coquet lads routed by the Redesdalers led by Percival and Alexander Hall. Battles between families and rural villages in Northumberland continued right up until the 1990s with drink-fuelled brawls involving the likes of Alnwick, Hexham, Otterburn, Rothbury and surrounding farms at country shows and discos. The tribal mentality never really left, and all the names are still there, including the Grahams, all across the border. A sharp rise in house prices and rural depopulation in recent times have begun to change the character of the area but so long as the hills are standing, the spirits of those that rode in them shall remain.

The Scotts of Buccleuch did rather well out of the whole business and the current Duke is reputed to own around 240,000 acres of land worth between £800m to £1 billion; his near relation, the Duke of Northumberland, owns lands of around 130,000 acres worth roughly the same, as well as the country seats belonging to the two families at Boughton, Drumlanrig, Bowhill House and the castles at Alnwick, Warkworth and Prudhoe for a start. The line of the Ancram Kerrs is headed by the life peer Baron Kerr of Monteviot, the Marquis of Lothian, and the Cessfords by the Duke of Roxburghe, making them among the wealthiest, most powerful and aristocratic families in Britain today. The old reivers Sir Robert Kerr and Sir Walter Scott would no doubt have smiled wryly in approval.

THE RIDING FAMILIES OF THE ANGLO-SCOTTISH BORDERS

English West March
Graham, Armstrong, Little, Hodgson, Routledge, Forster, Noble, Croser, Nixon, Milburn, Bell, Musgrave, Salkeld, Carleton, Taylor, Storey, Ridley, Dacre, Lowther, Hetherington, Sawfeld, Curwen, Rome, Richardson, Harden.

Scottish West March
Johnstone, Maxwell, Irving, Bell, Little, Graham, Carlyle, Armstrong, Carruthers, Thomson, Glendenning, Moffat, Latimer, Kirkpatrick, Wigham.

English Middle March
Heron, Fenwick, Collingwood, Percy, Selby, Ogle, Ellerker, Carlisle, Carnaby, Radcliffe, Wilson, Wake, Huntley, Carr, Jameson, Mitford, Horsley, Widdrington, Davidson, Lisle, Delaval.
North Tynedale: Charlton, Robson, Milburn, Dodds, Stapleton, Hunter, Yarrow, Thompson, Corbett, Stokoe, Errington.
Redesdale: Hall, Potts, Hedley, Reed, Dunn, Shaftoe, Redhead, Wanless, Clennell, Snowdon, Coxson, Anderson, Wilkinson, Forster.
South Tynedale: Ridley.

Scottish Middle March
Liddesdale: Armstrong, Elliot, Scott, Douglas, Beattie, Henderson, Nixon, Laidlaw, Oliver, Crosier.
West Teviotdale: Scott, Rutherford, Oliver, Douglas, Elliot, Laidlaw, Turnbull, Chrichton, Crosier, Telfer, Pile, Turner, Foster.
East Teviotdale: Kerr, Young, Burn, Pringle, Tait, Mow, Frissell (Fraser), Aynsley, Davison, Hall, Robson, Dalgleish, Gilchrist.

English East March
Forster, Grey, Cuthbert, Watson, Selby, Heron, Storey, Carr, Chamberlain, Collingwood, Dunn, Strowther, Swinhoe, Mustian, Johnson, Vardy, Ord, Wallace, Fluke, Wilkinson, Brewhouse.

Scottish East March
Hume, Trotter, Dixon, Cockburn, Redpath, Swinton, Edgar, Gordon, Archbold, Craw, Cranston, Bromfield.

*

The word reiver comes from the verb reif and noun stouthreif used in the contemporary records to refer to the crime of theft using force or violence which may have its origins in the Old Norse word rifa, to tear. The Danes certainly had a hand in creating the conditions that led to the reiving culture and Halfdan Ragnarsson's Great Heathen Army conquered and divided up the kingdom of Northumbria in 875. The first Viking raids on Britain in 793 had landed on the Northumberland coastline at Lindisfarne, also called Holy Island, and continued for decades.

The families at the time certainly weren't referring to each other as reivers and they are variously described as clans, gangs, crews and riding surnames by officials. The modern term mafia has been applied in this book as the Border families operated in a similar way to the Sicilian *Cosa Nostra* 'Our Thing' long before organised crime on a hierarchical basis had been recognised by the Law.

Those parallels were again drawn in January 2018 as the Italian authorities launched a major clampdown on the Families of the Calabrian 'Ndrangheta by arresting 169 people involved in a number of rural enterprises such as the harvesting and distribution of food and wine as well as more urban criminal activities including taking over municipal services, restaurants and such like. The 'Ndrangheta are reported to run on close blood family ties resembling those of the Anglo-Scottish riders in the Sixteenth century and the mass arrests were in a similar vein to the assizes held at Jedburgh and Hawick at the time when the Borders were putting an end to the criminal reign of the cattle thieves with a number of family members all being tried together.

The families were running many raids together over many years; Huey Douglas of Swineside hit Mark Ogle of Kirkley with Thomas Douglas for two oxen in 1580 and in 1584 he was complained on again for targeting dozens of sheep from the widow Jackson of Sturtongrange with Edward Douglas. John Douglas, the son of Rinian of the Dike, rode with George Douglas of Caphope, Peter Hall, George Davison and Robert Henderson to steal 92 sheep from Prendwick common in 1582 and was with John Oliver of the Linehouse to steal an ox from Lindhope off George Murray of Rill in 1584, to give a couple of small examples.

Francis Armstrong, the son of Whitehaugh, was raiding as early as 1585 when he took 28 oxen from Lionel Ogle of Edington and his criminal career continued for at least 20 years, while in the West March the Bells, Carlyles and Kirkpatricks, with others numbering 100, rode into England and burnt along the Esk while taking 100 nolt, 40 nags and a great haul of booty in 1586 and this wasn't a one-off.

When Hector Armstrong of Twedden was killed by a garrison of horsemen and footmen under the command of Captain Reed and Constable Ord in Liddesdale during the Pacification in 1603, the action was justified by Sir William Hutton as 'the best service that was done for the border of England these twenty years, for he (Armstrong) was a principal murderer, a great and common thief, a spoiler and a leader of the rest.' The Scottish commissioners were demanding Thomas Hetherington of Holeshiels to answer for the murder some two years later, and Hutton noted that 'the poor man Holeshiels (was) marvellously frightened with fear to enter into Scotland.' Hutton was puzzled, and questioned: 'If the Commissioners of Scotland shall so earnestly seek for redress of such a notorious thief, what good shall we expect of them?'

The implication of the March officials in allowing the conditions for the crime gangs to flourish can't be underestimated; a mafia can only exist with the collusion and collaboration of people in positions of power. Without the turning of a blind eye by the authorities, or their active participation for profit, a criminal organisation on a hierarchical basis cannot prosper. This was displayed at Morpeth in the early 16th Century when Cokes Charlton, a border reiver of some repute from North Tynedale, was broken out of prison at the castle. While it seems a straight-forward daring jailbreak by the 'hard and heather-bred lads' to free Charlton, who was famously guilty and 'indicted of many and diverse felonies and is the most notable thief in these parts,' the law-abiding folk of Northumberland felt that his gang had been given more than a little help from high places.

It isn't recorded who bust Cokes and a number of other Tynedale prisoners out of Morpeth in the summer of 1523. However, a contemporary note states that William Swinburne of Capheaton took Henry Yarrow, of Tynedale, at the breaking of Morpeth Castle, so it doesn't take a great deal of detective work to start pointing the finger at the criminal families of the North Tyne valley. A number of those that were freed were recaptured and executed, but Cokes was gone back into the barren hillsides.

On Good Friday in 1525, Hector Charlton, Henry 'Pluck' Dodd and Nicholas Charlton stole the sacrament, a firkin of wine and 800 loafs of bread from the sepulchre at Bellingham church and took them back to Tarsett Hall. They returned the sacrament the following day and got a Scottish friar to hand it out to 'a number of evil-disposed people.' Hector wasn't without a sense of humour and told the priest Sir Edward Todd that he kept company with his brother Gerard 'Topping' and other felons of Tynedale to 'espy bowrdes (watch birds) that he may cause the lord Dacre to laugh when he comes home,' according to a letter sent by Sir William Eure from Rothbury.

Thomas Dacre, Second Baron Dacre of Gilsland, had been a War hero at Flodden and described himself as 'the most hated Englishman alive' since he had found the mangled body of the King of Scots on the battlefield some ten years earlier. As a Cumbrian, Dacre held most of his land in Cumberland and the family seat was at Naworth, but he also had some 20,000 acres in Northumberland including Morpeth Castle and the barony of Morpeth. Dacre rose to the position of Warden of the East and Middle Marches of England, making him ultimately responsible for justice from both the Scottish and English reivers who were riding hard and plundering far and wide at the time.

A number of complaints were levelled at him by the disgruntled folk of Northumberland, including letting the Redesdale reivers commit 'murders, robberies, felonies and other heinous offences' without punishment, and allowing themselves to be 'enforced to pay yearly unto the said thieves and their adherents tributes and so to live under their protection.'

He was accused of allowing the Armstrongs and their followers, 'to the number of 300 men, great thieves and murderers and traitors to both realms' to find redress without punishment and giving license to those same Armstrongs 'being traitors and most common thieves of England or Scotland' to turn up weekly at Carlisle market and 'thereby to sell all things necessary for their living and sustenance.'

It was felt that he'd made appointments with English thieves and conspired with them in their robberies and he was blamed for a lack of justice that had made Northumberland 'almost desolate and barren of inhabitants.' They said that he'd allowed Scottish offenders to 'go home again at their liberty' without redress, though he had permitted the Tynedale crime lord Hector Charlton to ransom some for 20 nobles, which was paid 'with goods stolen from the King's true subjects.'

When it came to Cokes Charlton, the complainants felt that Dacre wouldn't allow him to be arraigned nor face justice for his offences but allowed him to be reprieved to his castle at Morpeth 'from which the thief afterward escaped and since that time has done abominable theft and other offences in Northumberland.'

Dacre denied all the charges; he said that 'many of the Redesdale men were thieves, and so they were before he ever had any rule there'. He had an answer for them all. Dacre was dead two years later aged just 40, killed in a fall from his horse, so just how implicated he was with the Border Crime Families will never be really be known.

His son and heir, William Dacre, sent a list of prisoners to the Earl of Northumberland in 1528 and the names of those being held captive are all too familiar.

Prisoners at Carlisle Castle: Dand Nixon, Clement's brother; John Nixon, of the Maynes; Cristoll Routledge, Lyon's son; James Routledge; George Routledge, Donned Rolland's son; Matthew Little, called Gutterholes; Peter Whithead; Davy Crowe; Cristoll Noble; Jock Nixon, called Deaf Jock.

Prisoners at Hexham: Thomas Errington, called Pepe; John Errington, called Angel; Gib Errington, of Greenridge; Edward Charlton, pledge for all his band; George Horde; Christopher Lyddall; Wallace of the Kirkhouse.

Prisoners and pledges at Morpeth: Henry Robson, of the Falstone; Sandy Yarrow, Henry Yarrow's brother; Clement and Ralph Charlton, sons to Thomas Charlton of Carroteith; Dumb Davy Milburne; a son of Eddie Dodds; Will Charlton, brother of Gib of the Bought Hill.

Sir Robert Bowes reported in 1550 that if someone had been raided by one of the North Tyne or Redesdale families, then they'd be better off taking a part of the goods back in compensation rather than pursuing them through the Law as 'if the thief be of any great surname or kindred and be lawfully executed by order of Justice, the rest of his kin or surname bear as much malice, which they call deadly feud, against such as follow the law against their cousin the thief as though he had unlawfully killed him with a sword. And will by all means they can seek revenge there upon.'

The Reivers stubbornly stuck to their land and family. More than 400 years later, they're still there. Everyone in Northumberland at least knows somebody off a Riding surname or has the blood of the families in their veins. Bowes again noted in his *State of the Frontiers and Marches between England and Scotland* that the people 'inhabit in some places three or four households so that they cannot, on such small farms, without any other crafts, live truly but either by stealing in England or Scotland. And the people of that country (especially the men) be loath to depart forth of the same but would rather live poorly there as thieves than more wealthily in another country.'

The gentlemen that surrounded the March officials were also instrumental in enabling the thriving reiver culture. The Fenwicks were an important Northumbrian family that had obtained lands around Hartburn as early as 1412, so when Richard Fenwick of Stanton talked to the Border Commissioners in September 1597 his words had some brevity and were damaging to the old crook Sir John Forster. Fenwick didn't hold back in his scathing judgement of Forster, who had been removed from the Middle March Wardenry for a second time in October 1595, the first being in September 1586. Fenwick claimed that there had been 16 murders, all 'protected and overseen' by Forster, in the previous 20 years and he gave a few examples, including Thomas Fenwick of Stanton being murdered by his nephew Roger Fenwick of Rodley, and Ralph Hinemores of Whelpington being killed by Roger Fenwick of Harterton and Cuthbert Rochester of Cambo. He also claimed that the felonies overlooked by Forster while warden 'would fill a large book.'

In the previous 10 years, while he had been justice of peace, Fenwick had seen 30 great Scottish thieves taken while robbing in England, he himself capturing seven of them, and while he wanted the goods restored to their owners and the thieve's 'heads stricken off by the ancient Border Law,' Forster and his kinsman William Fenwick of Wallington refused and had 'hot words' with him before setting the offenders free. He claimed that six or seven were caught stealing again 20 days later and were again set free, so he was somewhat pleased when he was relieved of his justice position soon after.

Fenwick claimed that Sir John had beheaded Roger Hall of Shilmoor for a small offence and that since the execution there were only two or three shepherds of Forster's living there with 2-3,000 sheep of his, alongside around the same amount of sheep belonging to John Rutherford, the laird of Hunthill, and William Rutherford, 'great Scottish thieves, who these 12 years have resetted in their houses 10 or 12 banished English thieves. And these Rutherford's friends and banished thieves, have often murdered and robbed hundreds of the Queen's subjects: and no man's sheep durst go there but Sir John's.' However, he did go on to praise Forster's replacement Lord Eure very highly, so one has to be suspect if he was looking to gain favour with the new Warden or had been leaned on to do so. Fenwick said that since Eure had taken office greater justice was being done and that previously he had seen 'four or five score thieves and March traitors - many of them gentlemen and great thieves - at a gaol delivery and a warden court, arraigned at the bar, and Henry Widdrington, William Fenwick of Wallington, and the best gentlemen in the Middle March on the said thieve's trial, yet none condemned but poor friendless thieves: and all the Scottish thieves that came to the said Lord Eure's hands since he was lord warden, are beheaded; which was not done in the twenty years before.'

The William Fenwick of Wallington that he was implicating was an interesting character and was almost the first man killed at the Raid of the Reidswire in 1575 as it was an arrow fired at him by Martin Crosier that kicked everything off. Two other Fenwicks and Robert Shaftoe were killed soon after and although the Scottish Warden, the Laird of Carmichael, went to settle things down and promised to 'hang a hundred on a hill for that day's work,' he suddenly changed tune and charged three miles into English ground with his whole force, slaying Sir George Heron and others, and taking many more prisoners for ransom, including Forster.

Fenwick of Wallington had office as the keeper of Tynedale and in

1595 the notorious outlaw Davie 'Bangtail' Armstrong very publicly threatened to kill him after he'd been apprehended and brought to trial at Durham assizes. Fenwick gave up his position suddenly in July 1596 after falling out with Eure over 'his ceasing kindness with Cessford, now opposite warden, without his (Eure's) privity.'

The following year, William Fenwick was accused of riding in the company of the likes of a notorious thief and murderer called Nicholas Weldon of Weldon and William 'Black Will' Ridley, a fugitive that had taken up a dwelling in Tynedale under Fenwick's protection. Eure claimed that Weldon had been outlawed during Sir John Forster's time in charge and despised him for beheading his uncle Christopher Weldon for March treason. Nicholas had, he claimed, attempted to bring in 100 Scots to burn his house and break his stable, but they'd been rumbled by his night watch. Weldon was in a gang with the likes of William Shaftoe, a deputy bailiff of Forster's, and William Lawson, who were broken out of Hexham gaol in 1596. Their crimes included felony charges of theft, burglary and taking Englishmen prisoners into Scotland and ransoming them. The gang had also spoiled the town of Ivestone.

The talk did little to damage Fenwick of Wallington's reputation and he was one of the riders, alongside Lord Eure, Sir William Bowes (now the Tynedale Keeper), Mr. Ralph Gray and his family, Francis Ratcliffe, Robert Clavering and others of the gentry that attended the transfer of pledges at the West Ford meetings in 1597. Fenwick died in 1613 aged around 63 years, involved in the action to the very end. His former boss, and father-in-law, Sir John Forster had died in his bed at Bamburgh castle aged around 82 in January 1602. The East Teviotdale riders had tried to assassinate the old rogue in his seaside fortress in 1597 when 30 of them arrived on horseback and were on their way up the stairs when his wife saw them and managed to get the bedroom door bolted shut.

Forster had spent a lifetime double-dealing and protecting his own interests. He knew it was all a up for grabs; the sheep and cattle theft, the robberies, the collection of protection money, the taking of hostages and the honour murders were all a means to an end – to accumulate land and wealth. Perhaps the methods would be considered crude and uncomplicated by today's standards, but the

Families of the loosely affiliated 'Ndrangheta – such as the Grecos, Alvaros, Pelles and Belloccos, who are also noted for the scale of violence in their feuds – would recognise the territorial gangs of the Border in an instant.

Just as the Reivers were venerated and romanticised by Ballads and songs, so the Calabrian mafia's exploits have been recorded in music, celebrating the familiar themes of vengeance, betrayal, tough justice and imprisonment in the album of Italian folk songs released by Francesco Sbano in 2000. Denunciations by the church have also been a feature of both gangs with the Pope telling the Italian crime syndicates to repent and change their ways as recently as 2013, while the borderers were the subject of several proclamations including the Archbishop of Glasgow Gavin Dunbar's infamous 1525 'motion of cursing' that features on a polished chunk of granite in a Carlisle underpass today.

Not everyone that bore the surnames was an active member of the Border mafia and similarly many family gangs contained people of other surnames riding under the umbrella and protection of that unit, as shown in many examples throughout this book.

But the names have become synonymous with the earliest British organised crime and just as the authorities had to resort to extreme measures to destroy the powerful hold that the families long held over the area, so the southern Italian lawmakers had to resort to extreme measures in their efforts to defeat the 'Ndrangheta.

The *New York Times* reported in 2017 that the children of mob-connected families in Calabria were to be taken away from their parents and removed to other parts of Italy in an attempt to break the family-centric nature of their crews. It drew haunting parralels to the purges that had taken place some four hundred years earlier in the hills of home.

***

BIBLIOGRAPHY

Books
Calendar of Border Papers Vol 1 & 2.
Pitcairn's Criminal Trials in Scotland Vol 1 & 2.
Accounts of the Treasurer of Scotland, various volumes.
The Manuscripts of the Earl of Westmorland, Captain Stewart and others.
The history and antiquities of the counties of Westmorland and Cumberland.
A survey of the Lakes of Cumberland, Westmorland and Lancashire.
The Register of the Privy Council of Scotland, various volumes.
Calendar of State Papers relating to Ireland.
Calendar of the Manuscripts of the Most Honourable Marquess of Salisbury, preserved at Hatfield House, Hertfordshire.
The Border Exploits.
The Hamilton Papers.
A History of Northumberland: The Topography and local antiquities.
State Papers, Correspondence relative to Scotland and the Borders.
A Last Elizabethan Journal.
History of Newcastle-Upon-Tyne, MacKenzie and Dent, 1827.

Websites
British History Online
Northumberland Assize Records at Northumberland Archives, The National Archive.
https://www.nytimes.com/2017/02/10/world/europe/breaking-up-the-family-as-a-way-to-break-up-the-mob.html
http://www.abc.net.au/news/2018-01-10/italian-mafia-group-ndrangheta-targeted-in-mass-arrests/9316420
www.convictrecords.com.au

Jon Tait was born in Ashington, Northumberland in 1972 and now lives in Carlisle with his family. He has a degree in Journalism and is the author of a best-selling walks book, *Northumberland: 40 Coast and Country Walks* (Pocket Mountains, 2013).

*